Conversations with Ted Kooser

Literary Conversations Series
Monika Gehlawat
General Editor

Conversations with Ted Kooser

Edited by John Cusatis

University Press of Mississippi / Jackson

The University Press of Mississippi is the scholarly publishing agency of
the Mississippi Institutions of Higher Learning: Alcorn State University,
Delta State University, Jackson State University, Mississippi State University,
Mississippi University for Women, Mississippi Valley State University,
University of Mississippi, and University of Southern Mississippi.

www.upress.state.ms.us

The University Press of Mississippi is a member
of the Association of University Presses.

Library of Congress Cataloging-in-Publication Data

Names: Kooser, Ted, interviewee. | Cusatis, John, editor.
Title: Conversations with Ted Kooser / edited by John Cusatis.
Description: Jackson : University Press of Mississippi, 2025. |
    Series: Literary conversations series | Includes bibliographical references and index.
Identifiers: LCCN 2024038183 (print) | LCCN 2024038184 (ebook) |
    ISBN 9781496855558 (hardback) | ISBN 9781496855565 (trade paperback) |
    ISBN 9781496855572 (epub) | ISBN 9781496855589 (epub) |
    ISBN 9781496855596 (pdf) | ISBN 9781496855602 (pdf)
Subjects: LCSH: Kooser, Ted—Interviews. | Poets, American—20th century—Interviews. |
    Poets, American—21st century—Interviews.
Classification: LCC PS3561.O6 Z46 2025 (print) |
    LCC PS3561.O6 (ebook) | DDC 811/.54 [B]—dc23/eng/20240924
LC record available at https://lccn.loc.gov/2024038183
LC ebook record available at https://lccn.loc.gov/2024038184

British Library Cataloging-in-Publication Data available

Books by Ted Kooser

Poetry

Official Entry Blank. Lincoln: University of Nebraska Press, 1969.
A Local Habitation & a Name. San Luis Obispo, CA: Solo, 1974.
Not Coming to Be Barked At. Milwaukee: Pentagram, 1976.
Sure Signs: New and Selected Poems. Pittsburgh: University of Pittsburgh Press, 1980.
One World at a Time. Pittsburgh: University of Pittsburgh Press, 1985.
The Blizzard Voices. Minneapolis: Bieler, 1986; Lincoln: University of Nebraska Press, 2006.
Weather Central. Pittsburgh: University of Pittsburgh Press, 1994.
Winter Morning Walks: 100 Postcards to Jim Harrison. Pittsburgh: Carnegie Mellon University Press, 2000.
Braided Creek: A Conversation in Poetry, with Jim Harrison. Port Townsend, WA: Copper Canyon, 2003.
Delights & Shadows. Port Townsend, WA: Copper Canyon, 2004.
Flying at Night: Poems 1965–1985. Pittsburgh: University of Pittsburgh Press, 2005.
Valentines. Lincoln: University of Nebraska Press, 2008.
Splitting an Order. Port Townsend, WA: Copper Canyon, 2014.
Kindest Regards: New and Selected Poems. Port Townsend, WA: Copper Canyon, 2018.
Red Stilts. Port Townsend, WA: Copper Canyon, 2020.
Cotton Candy: Poems Dipped out of the Air. Lincoln: University of Nebraska Press, 2022.
Raft. Port Townsend, WA: Copper Canyon, 2024.

Nonfiction

Local Wonders: Seasons in the Bohemian Alps. Lincoln: University of Nebraska Press, 2002.
Lights on a Ground of Darkness: An Evocation of a Place and Time. Lincoln: University of Nebraska Press, 2005.
The Poetry Home Repair Manual: Practical Advice for Beginning Poets. Lincoln: University of Nebraska Press, 2005.
Writing Brave and Free: Encouraging Words for People Who Want to Start Writing, with Steve Cox. Lincoln: University of Nebraska Press, 2006.
The Wheeling Year: A Poet's Field Book. Lincoln: University of Nebraska Press, 2014.

Children's Books

Bag in the Wind. Somerville, MA: Candlewick, 2010.

House Held Up by Trees. Somerville, MA: Candlewick, 2012.

The Bell in the Bridge. Somerville, MA: Candlewick, 2016.

Mr. Posey's New Glasses. Somerville, MA: Candlewick, 2019.

Marshmallow Clouds: Two Poets at Play among Figures of Speech, with Connie Wanek. Somerville, MA: Candlewick, 2022.

Chapbooks and Special Editions

Grass County. Lincoln, NE: Windflower, 1971.

Twenty Poems. Crete, NE: Best Cellar, 1973.

Shooting a Farmhouse / So This Is Nebraska. Denver: Ally, 1975.

Voyages to the Inland Sea, Volume VI: Essays and Poems by Harley Elliott and Ted Kooser, edited by John Judson. La Crosse: Center for Contemporary Poetry, Murphy Library, University of Wisconsin-La Crosse, 1976.

Old Marriage and New. Austin, TX: Cold Mountain, 1978.

Hatcher. Lincoln, NE: Windflower, 1978.

Cottonwood County: Poems, with William Kloefkorn. Lincoln, NE: Windflower, 1979.

On Common Ground: William Kloefkorn, Ted Kooser, Greg Kuzma, and Don Welch, edited by Mark Sanders and J. V. Brummels. Ord, NE: Sandhills, 1983.

Etudes. Cleveland, OH: Bits, 1992.

A Book of Things. Lincoln, NE: Lyra, 1995.

A Decade of Ted Kooser Valentines, 1987–1996. Omaha, NE: Penumbra/Abattoir Editions, 1996.

Journeying to a Place of Work: A Poet in the World of Business. Fargo: North Dakota Institute of Regional Studies, 1998.

Riding with Colonel Carter: An Essay and Two Poems. Grand Island, NE: Sandhills, 1999.

A Conversation, with Jim Harrison. West Chester, PA: Aralia, 2002.

Ferrying Light: Three Poems. New York: Goldfinch, 2004.

Out of the Moment: Twenty-One Years of Valentines, 1986–2006. Waldron Island, WA: Brooding Heron, 2006.

After Years. Eugene, OR: Long Goose, 2007.

Two Years in the Catbird Seat: My Experience as US Poet Laureate. Emory, VA: Emory and Henry College, 2008.

Together: New Poems. Waldron Island, WA: Brooding Heron Press & Bindery, 2012.

Pursuing Blackhawk. Mason City, IA: Cedar Creek, 2013.

At Home. Syracuse, NY: Comstock Review, 2017.

Cora. Anamosa, IA: Route 3, 2019.
A Suite of Moons. Omaha, NE: Gibraltar Editions, 2021.
A Man with a Rake. Seattle, WA: Pulley, 2022.
Crown Car Wash. Garland, NE: Self-Published, 2023.

Edited Collections

The Poets Guide to the Birds, with Judith Kitchen. Tallahassee, FL: Anhinga, 2009.
The Windflower Home Almanac of Poetry. Lincoln, NE: Windflower, 1980; Lincoln: University of Nebraska Press, 2024.

Ted Kooser Contemporary Poetry, Series Editor

Carter, Jared. *Darkened Rooms of Summer: New and Selected Poems.* Lincoln: University of Nebraska Press. 2014.
Wanek, Connie. *Rival Gardens: New and Selected Poems.* Lincoln: University of Nebraska Press, 2016.
Brown, Fleda. *The Woods Are on Fire: New and Selected Poems.* Lincoln: University of Nebraska Press, 2017.
Costanzo, Gerald. *Regular Haunts: New and Previous Poems.* Lincoln: University of Nebraska Press, 2018.
Sutphen, Joyce. *Carrying Water to the Field: New and Selected Poems.* Lincoln: University of Nebraska Press, 2019.
Saiser, Marjorie. *The Track the Whales Make: New and Selected Poems.* Lincoln: University of Nebraska Press, 2021.
Scheele, Roy. *Produce Wagon: New and Selected Poems.* Lincoln: University of Nebraska Press, 2022.

Contents

Introduction   xiii

Chronology   xxiii

An Interview with Ted Kooser   3
  Arnold Hatcher / 1976

"A Moment of Order in a Chaos of Language":
An Interview with Ted Kooser   14
  David M. Cicotello and William A. Heffernan / 1982

An Interview with Ted Kooser   24
  Mark Sanders / 1983

A Way to Start:
A Conversation with Ted Kooser   33
  Peter Whalen and Chris Fink / 1999

Winter Morning Walks:
A Conversation with Ted Kooser   40
  Jay Meek / 2000

Interview with Ted Kooser   57
  Mary K. Stillwell / 2003

"American Life" from Its Poet Laureate   65
  Terry Gross / 2005

The American Grain of Ted Kooser   82
  Grace Cavalieri / 2005

An Interview with Ted Kooser   100
    Stephen Meats / 2005

On the Outside Looking In:
An Interview with Ted Kooser   109
    Harbour Winn, Elaine Smokewood, and John McBride / 2006

The Crossing Over:
The US Poet Laureate on the Aesthetic of the Simple Poem   119
    Andrew Varnon / 2006

Something Just Happens:
A Conversation with Ted Kooser   125
    David Baker / 2008

The First Order of Wonders:
An Interview with Ted Kooser   140
    William Barillas / 2008

"Simple, Clear, Direct":
Ted Kooser Talks Poetry with AP Literature Students   150
    Charleston School of the Arts / 2010

An Interview with Ted Kooser   163
    Judith Harris / 2010

Starving for Order:
A Conversation with Ted Kooser   175
    Daniel Simon / 2017

Interview with a Poet:
Ted Kooser   187
    Tyler Robert Sheldon / 2020

Renowned Poet and Nebraska Resident Ted Kooser
Is Still Hitting His Stride   191
    Chris Christen / 2021

A Conversation with Ted Kooser:
In Dialogue with Judith Harris   194
   Judith Harris / 2023

July 2023:
A Conversation with Ted Kooser   204
   Mary K. Stillwell / 2023

A Poem Is "A Hand-Drawn Treasure Map":
Ted Kooser in Conversation with John Cusatis   210
   John Cusatis / 2024

Index   229

Introduction

During his conversation with North Dakota poet Jay Meek in 2000, Ted Kooser brings up the idea of "consciousness," that "unique human" quality that "sets us apart from the natural world" and "lets us write poems":

> I was out walking this morning and got to thinking about how human consciousness, awareness might be a better word, sets us apart from the natural world. Makes us alien, to use your term. Not until we die and our ashes are dispersed or buried, or our bodies finally decay despite embalming, do we become a true part of the world that our awareness as living, conscious humans separated us from. Of course, it is this unique human awareness of nature, of the other world, that lets us write poems. So in a sense, each poem testifies to our awareness of our separateness. My two old dogs are going to die before long, but they don't know that. If they knew it, they'd be writing poems, it seems to me. Consciousness may have been an evolutionary fluke, and perhaps when our species is gone, it will never arise again.

Robinson Jeffers, a kindred spirit in many ways, and an early influence on Kooser, also marveled at the enigmatic fact of human consciousness in one of his lesser-known early poems, a triptych of sonnets simply titled "Consciousness" (1926). Jeffers inquires, "What is this unreasonable excess, / Our needless quality, this unrequired / Exception in the world, this consciousness?" In his memoir *Memories, Dreams, Reflections* (1961), the psychologist Carl Jung, whom Jeffers read and admired, extolled human consciousness as the source of the world's "objective existence," referring to mankind as "the second creator of the world":

> Man is indispensable for the completion of creation. . . . [H]e himself is the second creator of the world, who alone has given to the world its objective existence—without which, unheard, unseen, silently eating, giving birth, dying, heads nodding through hundreds of millions of years, it would have gone on in the profoundest night of non-being down to its unknown end. Human consciousness

created objective existence and meaning, and man found his indispensable place in the great process of being.

One can take this hierarchy a step further: for those who read his poems, Ted Kooser is the *third* creator of the world. For Kooser's readers, the wonder of creation does not go "unheard" or "unseen." "I try to pay attention to people and things," Kooser tells the poet Grace Cavalieri. Yet Kooser does not merely open our eyes and ears to the presence of an unseen screech owl. He offers us "each reedy whinny / from a bird no bigger than a heart" whose call "flies out of a tall black pine / and in a breath is taken away / by the stars." Yet "with small hope / from the center of darkness / it calls out again and again." Nor does he simply provide a glimpse of an ice skater dexterously traversing a distant winter lake. We hear her as she steps, "click-clack, onto the frozen top of the world" and "with a clatter of blades" we watch her begin "to braid a loose path that broadened / into a meadow of curls," before she leaps "in the air the way a crane leaps," and after a "snappy half-turn," lands, arms out, "skating backward right out of that moment, smiling back / at the woman she'd been just a moment before."

Kooser's lucid yet alluring language revitalizes the everyday world and transforms it, evoking not only its beauty, but its wonder, its promise, and its unity. An owl becomes the human heart persisting in the seemingly abysmal dark, and a skater conjures a sandhill crane in a gravity-defying dance, who was "just a moment before" an ordinary woman. Whether in poetry, prose, or children's books, Kooser invigorates his subject through rich, highly original figurative language, in a manner that Cavalieri, along with many others, calls "magic." He aims to unveil plain marvels with his words, not to skillfully shroud complex ideas. "The poem is its own idea," he tells David Cicotello, and its purpose is not to conceal, but to reveal. He elaborates in his 2010 conversation with the poet and critic Judith Harris:

> To show my readers something remarkable about an ordinary, ubiquitous thing is part of my calling as a writer. The most meaningful compliment I've ever received came from a reader, years ago, who told me that after reading a poem I published about mice moving their nests out of a freshly plowed field, she would never look at a plowed field in the spring in quite the same way. "Yes!" I said to myself, "that is what I want to do with my life: to serve others in that way, to be of service."

As Kooser's comment reveals, his poems act more like a *lamp* than a *mirror*, to borrow the Romantic critic M. H. Abrams's distinction. The abiding critical standard, Abrams notes in *The Mirror and the Lamp* (1953), at least until the Renaissance, was "mimesis," or as Shakespeare's Hamlet famously sets down for the First Player, the "end" of art is "to hold . . . the mirror up to nature." Abrams explains that, beginning with the Romantics, the "higher" goal of poetry was to be "expressive." The poet's impression of the world—after being filtered through his imagination—became more important than the actual world he was representing. Abrams explains, "The subsequent and higher act of re-creation, among its other functions, by projecting its own passion and life, transforms the cold inanimate world into a warm world united with the life of man, and by the same act, converts matter-of-fact into matter-of-poetry." The Romantic poet William Wordsworth embraces, illuminates, and "transforms" the objective world, for example, when his "heart with pleasure fills, / and dances with the daffodils." Kooser builds on the Romantic tradition, and he seems to draw his highly original, often controlling metaphors, from an inexhaustible wellspring. As William Barillas writes in *The Midwestern Pastoral: Place and Landscape in Literature of the American Heartland* (2006), "Kooser has elevated unassuming subjects, both people and places, usually by means of startling metaphors that heighten the sensual and associative power of his images." Barillas points to a typical example in the opening lines of one of Kooser's early poems, "So This Is Nebraska," which "effortlessly transforms a highway into a horse and the plumage of birds into combustible flashes of color." Kooser writes in the first stanza, "The gravel road rides with a slow gallop / over the fields . . . / . . . its billow of dust / full of the sparks of redwing blackbirds."

"I like to look at the ordinary until the extraordinary begins to show through its skin, like a candle burning in a paper sack," he tells Jay Meek. Kooser gives the ordinary world a voice, distills its personality. Awakens *it* and awakens *us*. As Ralph Waldo Emerson, another kindred spirit, pointed out in his essay "The Poet": "Most of mankind senses the natural world speaking to them, but many cannot translate its meaning." The consummate poet, Emerson writes, "puts eyes, and a tongue, into every dumb and inanimate object." Kooser is in conversation with nature, whether insentient, sentient, or human, and he eloquently translates that conversation through his distinctively deft handling of language, whether figurative or literal.

The epigraphs that introduce Kooser's two latest major collections reinforce his understanding of his role as a chronicler and proclaimer of the world's wonders. "As a writing man, or secretary," he quotes E. B. White at the opening of *Cotton Candy: Poems Dipped out of the Air* (2022), "I have always felt charged with the safekeeping of all unexpected items of worldly or unworldly enchantment, as though I might be held personally responsible if even a small one were to be lost." And Kooser's *Raft* (2024) begins with a quote from Romans 12:6–8: "Having gifts that differ according to the grace given to us, let us use them." In his prose volume *The Wheeling Year: A Poet's Field Book* (2014), he writes: "[A] person can lean on the warm hoe handle of a poem, dreaming, making a little more out of the world than was there just a moment before. I'm just the guy who gets it started."

Ted Kooser has been getting "it started" for more than six decades. Born in Ames, Iowa, in 1939, he entered Iowa State College in 1958 as an architecture major, following the advice of a school counselor who recognized Kooser's gift for drawing. Frustrated with the complex mathematical word problems, Kooser left class one day, walked to Lake Laverne on the Iowa State Campus, hurled his slide rule out into the lake, and switched his major to distributive studies, which allowed him to pursue a secondary English degree. Soon, Kooser met his first writing mentor, Will Jumper, and began publishing poems in the student literary journal *Sketch*. He graduated in 1962. Following a year of teaching high school, he and his newly married wife, Diana, moved to Lincoln, Nebraska. After a year of graduate school English, in which he befriended his new mentor, Pulitzer Prize–winning poet Karl Shapiro, he took a job as an insurance underwriter with Bankers Life Nebraska, finishing his degree by attending night classes. He sustained his literary life, developing the habit of waking up before dawn to write, and publishing his first full-length book, *Official Entry Blank*, in 1969, while his poems were appearing in dozens of national literary journals.

Two more major collections followed during the 1970s, and in 1980, University of Pittsburgh Press collected nearly eighty poems from Kooser's earlier books and a dozen new ones and published *Sure Signs: New and Selected Poems*. The book caught the attention of Dana Gioia, who proclaimed in the *Hudson Review* that Kooser was "a master of the short poem." For Gioia, Kooser's poems were irresistible: "I found it impossible to put *Sure Signs* down until I had finished the entire book," he wrote. "It was like sitting next to a box of chocolates before dinner. I kept intending to put the book down to finish later, but kept sneaking one more poem until there were none left." Three years later, Gioia celebrated Kooser's impressive, if still regionally defined, artistic success in an essay titled "Explaining Ted Kooser," published in the critical study of four Nebraska poets, *On Common Ground: William Kloefkorn, Ted Kooser, Greg Kuzma, and Don Welch* (1983), edited by Mark Sanders and J. V. Brummels. Gioia renamed the article "The Anonymity of the Regional Poet" when he reprinted a slightly revised version in his essay collection *Can Poetry Matter* (1991). Like Sanders, Gioia recognized that calling Kooser a "Poet of the Great Plains" belied the universality of his work. In a literary world where critics "have been trained to celebrate complexity," Kooser's clarity, colloquial diction, and everyday subject matter—the traits that had garnered him an increasingly wide readership—caused many critics and academics to ignore him. Gioia writes, "There are no problems to solve, no ambiguities to unravel, no dizzying bravado passages to master for the dexterous critic eager to earn an extra curtain call."

And this is how Kooser preferred it. Dismissing the critical yardstick of complexity (and distancing himself specifically from the modernist poetics epitomized in T. S. Eliot's *The Waste Land*), Kooser told Barillas in 2007, "For me writing a poem involves making use of available materials in the locality where I am. I'll make the poem out of whatever I can grab up. I'm not going to go to the library and check out *The Golden Bough* when I can make a poem out of available things." Gioia wrote that Kooser's poetic achievement required an assessment based not on "current critical standards," but on "four simple criteria": quality, originality, scope, and integrity. While the American literary establishment of the early 1980s may not have recognized Kooser as a major poet, Gioia predicted, "he will be an enduring one." Kooser, he said, writes "poetry concerned with themes of permanent value, written flawlessly in an original and distinctive way." Judged by his four criteria, Gioia went on, "Kooser surpasses some of his more highly praised contemporaries." More than twenty years before Kooser's rise to international acclaim, Gioia proclaimed: "Kooser has written more perfect poems than any poet of his generation. In a quiet way, he is also one of its most original poets."

Preferring an even quieter way of leading his writing life, Kooser left Lincoln in 1984. After he and Diana divorced, Kooser married Kathleen Rutledge, a journalist (and later editor) at the *Lincoln Journal Star*, and with the help of Kooser's second National Endowment for the Arts Fellowship, the couple bought sixty-two acres outside rural Garland, Nebraska. Kooser was showing sure signs of securing a national audience by this time. Just months after Gioia's essay was published in *On Common Ground*, Kooser's poems appeared in the *New Yorker* and *Poetry*. Pittsburgh Press published his next two highly acclaimed books, *One World at a Time* (1985) and *Weather Central* (1994). The latter begins with the poem "Etude," set off from the others as a sort of prologue. Kooser's biographer, Mary K. Stillwell, calls the poem "an exquisite illustration of the poet's mature facility with the metaphor," devoting nearly five pages of incisive critical analysis to this richly textured fifteen-line poem. "Etude" begins with the narrator "watching a Great Blue

Heron / fish in the cattails." But soon the bird is transformed into a blue-suited office worker stealthily composing a love letter, who quickly replaces the heron as the subject of the poem. As so many of Kooser's metaphors do, it artfully takes over, never quite forgetting the subject it replaced:

... His pencil is poised
in the air like the beak of a bird,
He would speak the whole world if he could,
toss it and swallow it live.

Kooser retired as vice president of Lincoln Benefit Life in 1999, six months after being diagnosed with head and neck cancer. His spirits naturally diminished by his diagnosis, he had difficulty continuing the morning writing regimen he had begun decades before. He began taking predawn walks instead, advised by his doctor to stay out of the sun as he recovered from his treatment. During these two-mile journeys, he was, as always, inspired by the landscape and began writing again, gathering his new poems and mailing them on postcards to his friend Jim Harrison, the poet and novelist. Kooser collected the best of the poems he penned between November 9, 1998, and March 20, 1999, into his first full-length book in six years: *Winter Morning Walks: 100 Postcards to Jim Harrison.* Kooser had not only physically, but artistically, hit his stride during these walks, many critics agreeing he had written his strongest book yet.

One poem from this collection, which, like "Etude," serves as the prefatory piece for the book, is sufficient to illustrate the quality, originality, scope, and integrity of the colossal body of work Kooser would deliver in the twenty-first century:

The quarry road tumbles toward me
out of the early morning darkness,
lustrous with frost, an unrolled bolt
of softly glowing fabric, interwoven
with tiny glass beads on silver thread,
the cloth spilled out and then lovingly
smoothed by my father's hand
as he stands behind his wooden counter
(dark as these fields) at Tilden's Store
so many years ago. "Here," he says smiling,
"you can make something special with this."

The untitled poem demonstrates Kooser's skill to neatly integrate various aspects and observations of his daily and past life into a unified whole, drawing attention to the connectedness of seemingly disparate items through the use of fresh metaphors and weaving it together cohesively with a consistent rhythm and his deft handling of alliteration, consonance, assonance, and internal rhyme.

The poem begins with a haunting Dantean allusion, as the narrator (as always, Kooser) enters a dark road leading to a menacing chasm, whose lustrous frost becomes less threatening, as the road transforms before the poet's eyes into "an unrolled bolt / of softly glowing fabric." It is not the Roman poet Virgil who arrives to assist Kooser, but his long-deceased father, a textile salesman at The Tilden Store in Ames, Iowa, during the poet's childhood. The "soft glowing" fabric takes on a numinous presence as it is, "lovingly/ smoothed by my father's hand / as he stands behind his wooden counter." The fabric, unrolled like the welcoming words of a poem, becomes the controlling metaphor and calls the poet to his task to "make something special with this." The poem resonates with universal significance, as the traveler on the dark, cold, uncertain road to the future is called on to create order through his art from the "material" all around him.

Kooser's father's word *make* recalls the origin of the word *poet*, which comes from the Greek *poiētēs*, meaning "maker." In addition, the word *textile* is cognate with *text*, which originates from the Latin verb *texere*, "to weave." Kooser, whose texts, whether in verse or prose, celebrate the unity and order in the natural world and the solace of human connection—as illustrated by his father's arrival on the dark road—make use of words such as *weave, braid, knit, tie*, and *sew* to underscore the pervasive thread he sees uniting everything and everyone. For example, the epigraph from a recent poem about human connectedness, "It Doesn't Take Much," collected in *Raft* (2024), is lifted from Whitman's "Song of Myself": "And of these one and all I weave the song of myself." And Kooser titled the book that followed *Winter Morning Walks*, which he cowrote with Harrison, *Braided Creek*, to signify the seamless weaving of the two poets' words.

On January 26, 2006, Kooser, now a Pulitzer Prize winner in his second term as United States poet laureate, delivered a speech at the University of Nebraska Medical Center on healing through poetry, in which he expressed his gratitude to Dr. William Lydiatt and the team at the Medical Center for saving his life. After reading the poem above from *Winter Morning Walks*, he commented: "Every day, I tried to make something special from that gravel road." Reflecting on the same poem with the poet Jay Meek, Kooser recognizes that the fabric/road is not only a metaphor for the materials from which to draw poetry but also to shape his life: "And so I have been given this road, if not literally by my father, then figuratively, have had it opened before me by my illness, and his admonition to me is to take what is before me, to take what life I have, and to make something special with it." He continues: "There's a passage in Ecclesiastes that I have kept close at hand for many years: 'Whatsoever thy hand findest to do, do it with thy might, for there is no work, nor devise, nor knowledge, nor wisdom in the grave whither thou goest.'"

Kooser embodies this biblical edict to this day. After retiring from a highly successful career as an insurance executive, the humble, self-proclaimed introvert, who lives twenty miles from the nearest city in rural Nebraska, was elevated to international fame, and at sixty-five he resolved to put all his energy into his national laureateship. "I was at first terrified," he tells the poet David Baker, "but I decided that if the Library of Congress was willing to take a chance on a poet from the Great Plains, I'd better do the best job I could. So I threw myself into it and pressed forward." Always dedicated to bringing engaging poetry to the maximum number of readers, Kooser started a syndicated column, "American Life in Poetry," which he continued more than a decade after his two-year tenure, reaching more than four million readers.

In the twenty-five years since his retirement, Kooser has published ten major books of poetry, five nonfiction books, and five children's books, aside from more than a dozen chapbooks and special editions, earning popular and critical recognition and winning major awards in all three genres. In addition, he has edited nine other books, eight of them as part of the Ted Kooser Contemporary Poetry series, which has brought the work of lesser-known poets to an expansive audience. In 2022 alone, Kooser published a full-length book of new poems, *Cotton Candy: Poems Dipped Out of the Sky*; a chapbook, *A Man with a Rake*; and a children's book, *Marshmallow Clouds: Two Poets at Play among Figures of Speech*, coauthored with poet Connie Wanek and illustrated by Richard Jones. The last of these was awarded England's prestigious CLiPPa Award in 2023, which, according to the Centre for Literacy in Primary Education, "encourages and celebrates outstanding poetry published for children."

Yet Kooser still considers the highest artistic success to be "the appreciation of someone who lets me know that what I've written has been meaningful." After two hectic years in Washington, DC, and the endless readings and interviews his laureateship and Pulitzer brought about, he relishes his day-to-day life back in Garland. He explained in our recent interview: "I'm done with that public stuff and am happy to just slide my poems out under the door, hoping that someone passing by will like them." And he has been doing just that, sliding his poems under the door of his large and appreciative Facebook following. He tells the poet Mary K. Stillwell, "As you know, with traditional print journal publishing, we poets submit five or six poems to one journal or another and wait six or eight months before getting a rejection. If a poem gets accepted, there's another six or eight months' wait before we get our two free contributor's copies." He adds, "But with Facebook there's an immediate response, and a lot to be learned from the number of 'likes' and what's said in the 'comments.'"

Kooser's most recent Facebook submissions continue to chronicle his daily observations and recall treasured memories. Whether he is watching a bird frolic in the snow or delivering newspapers in a blizzard seventy years ago with his father, he manages to distill the wonder out of the seemingly ordinary in measured language worthy of that wonder. Though Kooser remains peerlessly prolific in his mideighties, his poems evoke the calm and patient demeanor of the poet himself and quietly beckon his reader to slow down. Just as his mother taught him, Kooser teaches us "to look at the world, to see the life at play in everything."

In his poem "A Man with a Rake," from his latest collection, *Raft*, Kooser observes a man who has paused while raking leaves, the end of the rake handle "locked in a knot in his fingers." The rake is gradually transformed into the hand of a ticking clock.

> Before this he had been watching the rake
> tick around clockwise, minute to minute,
> a fine afternoon passing forever away
> but he's figured out now how to slow it
> all down, both hands clasped on the end
> of the second hand, holding it back.

While his poems encourage readers to slow down, the poet himself shows no signs of doing so. He continues his predawn writing regimen, aiming to compose a new poem each morning. Tributes to Kooser's growing legacy abound. At least two journals have devoted entire volumes to his achievement. Poet and critic Mark Sanders published a hefty follow-up to 1983's prescient *On Common Ground*, titled *The Weight of the Weather: Regarding the Poetry of Ted Kooser* (2017), in which he notes that "Kooser's poetics" are "unparalleled among his contemporaries." More recent homage is paid to Kooser in a children's picture book titled *Ted Kooser: More Than a Local Wonder*, written by Carla Ketner, published in November 2023. Each of these books, like this latest, *Conversations with Ted Kooser*, aims to supplement the legacy of Ted Kooser, the generous individual and genuine poet, who has not just awakened, edified, and entertained his readers over the fifty years (and more) that these interviews cover, but who has inspired and consoled them, made them feel good about the world, despite the shadows that offset the delights.

In another recent tribute, *More in Time*, named for the phrase Kooser frequently uses to close his emails, sixty-six writers, composing in verse or in prose, offer accounts of how Kooser has changed their lives. Many point to his allowing them to see the world in a fresh, new way, like his picture book character Mr. Posey, who just needed to clean his glasses. Kooser acknowledges this is a service he is grateful to provide. In one poem, titled "Ted Kooser Is My President," Naomi Shihab Nye remarks simply, "His deep assurance comforts me." Kooser is thankful to be able to offer this service, too, happy to snap on a "yard light" in the deepening darkness, as his farmer does in "Flying at Night," "drawing his sheds and barn / back into the little system of his care."

JC

Chronology

1939   Theodore John Kooser is born on April 25 in Ames, Iowa, to
        Theodore Briggs Kooser, a department store manager, and Vera
        Moser Kooser, a homemaker.

1942   Ted's sister, Judith, his only sibling, is born.

1945   Begins school at Beardshear Elementary. As a fourth grader, he
        is given a copy of Robert McCloskey's illustrated children's book
        Lentil, which becomes a profound, abiding influence.

1957   Graduates from Ames High School. Enrolls in Iowa State
        College of Agriculture and Mechanical Arts (now Iowa State
        University) as an architecture major. Enjoying the drawing
        but not the math, he switches his major to English education
        and joins the Writers Round Table, where he meets Dr. Will C.
        Jumper, the group's advisor and Kooser's first writing mentor,
        to whom he dedicates his first book. While at Iowa State, he
        contributes pen-and-ink illustrations and poems to the student
        literary magazine, *Sketch*. One of these poems, "Cold Pastoral,"
        is included in *Official Entry Blank*.

1962   Earns BS in English Education from Iowa State. On November 17,
        marries Diana Tressler, an educator, whom he met at Iowa State.
        Teaches high school English for one year in Madrid, Iowa.

1963   Leaves Iowa for Lincoln, Nebraska, to study English at the Uni-
        versity of Nebraska with Karl Shapiro, winner of the 1945 Pulitzer
        Prize for Poetry.

1964   When his graduate assistantship is not renewed for a second
        year, he begins working for the insurance company Bankers Life
        Nebraska as an underwriter.

1967   Founds Windflower Press and the literary journal *Salt Creek
        Reader*. His son, Jeffrey Charles Kooser, is born on July 17.

1968   Earns an MA in English from the University of Nebraska.

1969   University of Nebraska Press publishes Kooser's first book of
        poems, *Official Entry Blank*.

1970   Begins teaching part time at the University of Nebraska. He and
        Diana divorce.

1971   Windflower Press publishes *Grass County*, eight new poems by
        Kooser accompanied by his pen-and-ink drawings.

1973   Publishes his second chapbook, *Twenty Poems*, with the Best
        Celler Press, Crete, Nebraska.

1974   Solo Press publishes his second major collection, *A Local Habita-
        tion & a Name*, which includes an introduction by Karl Shapiro.

1976   Pentagram Press publishes *Not Coming to Be Barked At*, his third
        major collection. Granted a fellowship from the National Endow-
        ment for the Arts. Wins the *Prairie Schooner* Prize in Poetry.

1977   Marries Kathleen Rutledge, a journalist, who becomes managing
        editor of the *Lincoln Journal Star*.

1978   Publishes the limited special editions *Old Marriage and New*
        and *Hatcher*. Wins the *Prairie Schooner* Prize in Poetry for the
        second time.

1979   Windflower Press publishes *Cottonwood County*, featuring twenty-
        four poems by William Kloefkorn and twenty-eight by Kooser.
        Theodore Briggs Kooser, the poet's father, dies on New Year's Eve.

1980   In June, University of Pittsburgh Press publishes *Sure Signs: New
        and Selected Poems*, drawing from Kooser's first three major col-
        lections and the chapbook *Cottonwood County* while adding a
        dozen new poems. Dana Gioia, writing in the *Hudson Review*,
        calls it "a first-rate collection." *Sure Signs* wins the Society of
        Midland Authors Poetry Award. Kooser edits and publishes the
        Windflower Home Almanac of Poetry. Publishes first issue of his
        new literary journal *Blue Hotel*.

1981   Publishes second and final issue of *Blue Hotel*, a double issue
        titled *Seventeen Danish Poets in Translation*.

1983   On January 1, Sandhills Press publishes *On Common Ground*, a
        critical study of Kooser and three other Nebraska poets, edited
        by Mark Sanders and J. V. Brummels. "The Fan in the Window"
        appears in the September 19 issue of the *New Yorker*, and the
        November issue of *Poetry* includes "The Birthday Card," "The
        Mouse," "The Sigh," "The Urine Specimen," and "The Witness," all
        of which are later collected by University of Pittsburgh Press in
        One World at a Time and *Flying at Night*.

1984   Earns second National Endowment for the Arts Fellowship.
        Wins Columbia University's Stanley Kunitz Poetry Prize as well

as the first of many Pushcart Prizes. Purchases sixty-two-acre property outside of Garland, Nebraska, where he and his wife continue to reside.

1985   University of Pittsburgh Press publishes *One World at a Time*.

1986   The Bieler Press of Minneapolis publishes a limited edition of *The Blizzard Voices*, a poetic recollection of the blizzard that devastated the Great Plains in January 1888, which had been produced as a play by Nebraska's Lincoln Community Playhouse in the early 1980s. Illustrations are provided by Michigan artist Tom Pohrt.

1988   The Nebraska Arts Council awards Kooser the Governor's Arts Award.

1989   Windflower Press publishes *As Far as I Can See: Contemporary Writing of the Middle Plains*, edited by Charles L. Woodard and illustrated by Robert L. Hanna.

1994   University of Pittsburgh Press publishes *Weather Central*. Awarded the annual Richard Hugo Prize from the journal *Poetry Northwest*.

1995   Lyra Press publishes the limited-edition chapbook *A Book of Things*.

1996   Penumbra Press follows with *A Decade of Ted Kooser Valentines*.

1997   First grandchild, Margaret Emily Kooser, is born on December 15.

1998   Vera Moser Kooser, Ted's mother, dies on March 23, 1998, at the age of eighty-nine. Later that year, Kooser dedicates "Lights on a Ground of Darkness" to her, which appears as an essay in *Great River Review* and begins with the elegy "Mother," collected in *Delights & Shadows*. Kooser is diagnosed with cancer in June and begins treatment. Finding it difficult to write for several months, Kooser begins taking two-mile walks in the predawn hours in the fall and finds the inspiration to return to writing poems, which he sends to his friend, writer Jim Harrison, on postcards. He later chooses one hundred of these poems to make up his 2000 collection, *Winter Morning Walks: One Hundred Post Cards to Jim Harrison*.

1999   Sandhills Press publishes *Riding with Colonel Carter: An Essay and Two Poems*. The journal *Shenandoah* awards Kooser the James Boatwright III Award for the best poem or poems submitted that year. Kooser retires from Lincoln Benefit Life.

2000   Carnegie-Mellon Press publishes *Winter Morning Walks: One Hundred Post Cards to Jim Harrison*. The book earns the Marie Sandoz Award from the Nebraska Library Association and the Nebraska Arts Council Merit Award in Poetry that year.

2001 *Winter Morning Walks* receives the Nebraska Book Award for Poetry. Rutledge is named editor of the *Lincoln Star Journal*.

2002 University of Nebraska Press publishes Kooser's prose volume *Local Wonders: Seasons in the Bohemian Alps*.

2003 *Local Wonders* wins the Nebraska Book Award for nonfiction and is chosen as a finalist for Barnes & Noble's Discover Great New Writers Award for nonfiction. The book also wins the Friends of American Writers Literature Award, is awarded gold-medal recognition for autobiographical writing from *ForeWord Magazine*, and receives Honorable Mention from the Society of Midland Authors. Copper Canyon Press publishes *Braided Creek: A Conversation in Poetry*, a collection of haiku-like verse cowritten with Jim Harrison. "The House of Bones" is selected by guest editor Yusef Komunyakaa for *Best American Poetry 2003*.

2004 Copper Canyon Press publishes *Delights & Shadows* in May. Kooser is appointed poet laureate of the United States in August. Founds "American Life in Poetry," a syndicated column featuring a poem a week from a contemporary American poet, which he edits for fifteen years and ultimately attracts more than 4 million readers a week. The project is cosponsored by the University of Nebraska–Lincoln, the Library of Congress, and the Poetry Foundation, publishers of *Poetry* magazine. Kooser, along with coauthor Jim Harrison, wins his second Society of Midland Authors Poetry Award. Granted an honorary doctorate from the University of Nebraska.

2005 University of Nebraska Press publishes Kooser's memoir of his maternal grandparents, *Lights on a Ground of Darkness* in January, and *The Poetry Home Repair Manual: Practical Advice for Beginning Poets* in February. In March, Kooser invites legendary American singer-songwriter John Prine to the Library of Congress to discuss songwriting, among other topics, before a live audience. University of Pittsburgh Press issues *Flying at Night: Selected Poems*, which collects the poems from Kooser's first two books with Pittsburgh, *Sure Signs* (1980) and *One World at a Time* (1985). Kooser wins the Pulitzer Prize for Poetry for *Delights & Shadows* in April. Begins his second term as poet laureate in August. In October, his essay "Small Rooms in Time," which first appeared in *River Teeth* in spring 2004, is published in *Best American Essays 2005* in October. Kooser later includes the essay in his collection *Splitting an Order* (2014). South Dakota State University grants Kooser an honorary doctorate. The State University of New York at Binghamton awards Kooser the annual Milt Kessler Poetry Book Award for *Delights & Shadows*. The collection also earns Kooser his third Society of Midland Authors Poetry Award, an American Library Association Notable Book Citation, and the Midwest Booksellers Association Poetry Award. Wins a Pushcart Prize.

2006   In January, Kooser is invited to the University of Nebraska Medical Center where he delivers a speech on healing through poetry as part of the medical center's effort to more fully educate its students by integrating art into their medical training. In March, University of Nebraska Press publishes *Writing Brave & Free*, Kooser's second handbook for beginning writers, cowritten with Steve Cox. Awarded a Presidential Professorship from the University of Nebraska, a title he maintains. Serves as one of the three jurors for the Pulitzer Prize in poetry selection.

2007   Named a Distinguished Alumnus of Iowa State University and honored with the Alumni Achievement Award from the University of Nebraska. Wins the Midwest Bookseller Association Poetry Award.

2008   University of Nebraska Press publishes *Valentines*, collecting verse that Kooser pasted on postcards and sent to female recipients each Valentine's Day, which by 2007 numbered more than twenty-six hundred. He began the ritual in 1986, and the collection includes twenty-three poems with illustrations by Robert Hanna. Granted an honorary doctorate from University of New York at Binghamton. Wins the Midwest Booksellers Poetry Award as well as the Word Sender Award from the John G. Neihardt Foundation.

2009   In February, Anhinga Press publishes *The Poets Guide to the Birds*, coedited with Judith Kitchen, an anthology of 160 contemporary poems about birds, including ten from *Winter Morning Walks*. Kooser's second grandchild, Penelope Helen, is born in April. Lincoln Public Schools opens Kooser Elementary School in Lincoln, Nebraska, in the fall with a formal dedication ceremony. Candlewick Press, Kooser's children's book publisher, donates 160 books to the new school. Kooser wins a Pushcart Prize. Wins the annual Mildred Bennett Award from the Nebraska Center for the Book.

2010   Candlewick Press publishes Kooser's children's book *Bag in the Wind*, illustrated by Barry Root, in February. Kooser donates

	$25,000 to his namesake elementary school to start an endowment fund. Kooser is the inaugural winner of the annual Hall-Kenyon Prize in American Poetry, named in honor of the poets Donald Hall and Jane Kenyon.
2011	The Nebraska Center for the Book selects *Local Wonders* as the One Book, One Nebraska title for 2011. Kooser again chosen as a member of the three-person Pulitzer Prize for Poetry jury.
2012	In March, Candlewick Press publishes Kooser's second children's book, *House Held up by Trees*, illustrated by Jon Klassen. It is named a Best Illustrated Children's Book by the *New York Times* and a Best of 2012 Picture Book by the International Literacy Association. Kooser wins a Pushcart Prize.
2013	University of Nebraska Press publishes *The Life & Poetry of Ted Kooser*, a full-length critical biography written by poet and scholar Mary K. Stillwell, who studied under Kooser at the University of Nebraska. *House Held Up by Trees* wins the Nebraska Book Award for children's books. It is also named Best Children's Book of the Year by the Children's Book Committee and the National Council of Teachers of English Children's Literature Assembly named it a Notable Children's Book in Language Arts. Kooser wins the Mark Twain Award from the Society for the Study of Midwestern Literature.
2014	Kooser turns seventy-five in April. University of Nebraska Press publishes his prose volume *The Wheeling Year: A Poet's Field Book* in September, and Copper Canyon Press publishes *Splitting an Order*, his first full-length collection of new poems since 2004's *Delights & Shadows*, in October.
2015	*The Wheeling Year* earns the Nebraska Book Award and the Independent Publisher Gold Medal Award. *Splitting an Order* wins the Midwest Booksellers Association Poetry Award and is named one of three finalists for the High Plains Book Award in poetry.
2016	Candlewick Press publishes Kooser's third children's book, *The Bell in the Bridge*, illustrated by Barry Root, in May. Kooser wins the Comstock Writers Group Chapbook Award for *At Home*. Honored by the South Dakota Humanities Commission for Distinguished Achievement in the Humanities.
2017	Stephen F. Austin State University Press publishes *The Weight of the Weather: Regarding the Poetry of Ted Kooser*, a collection

of interviews, memoirs, commentary, and criticism, edited by Mark Sanders.

2018   Copper Canyon Press publishes *Kindest Regards: New and Selected Poems* in May, collecting poems from each of Kooser's major collections—excluding the coauthored *Braided Creek*—and the chapbook *At Home*.

2019   Candlewick Press publishes Kooser's fourth children's book, *Mr. Posey's New Glasses*, illustrated by Daniel Duncan, in April. The Ted Kooser Health Humanities Center is dedicated at the University of Nebraska–Omaha.

2020   Copper Canyon Press publishes *Red Stilts* in September. *Mr. Posey's New Glasses* is awarded the distinction of "Honor" as a finalist for the Children's Choice Book Award. Kooser wins a Pushcart Prize.

2021   University of Nebraska Press publishes *More in Time: A Tribute to Ted Kooser*, a collection of poetry and prose tributes from sixty-six writers, edited by Jessica Poli, Marco Abel, and Timothy Schaffert.

2022   In March, Pulley Press publishes eighteen new poems by Kooser, *A Man with a Rake*. Five of these appear two years later in *Raft*. The same day Candlewick Press publishes Kooser's fifth children's book, *Marshmallow Clouds: Two Poets at Play among Figures of Speech*, cowritten with poet Connie Wanek and illustrated by Richard Jones. In September, University of Nebraska Press publishes *Cotton Candy: Poems Dipped out of the Air*.

2023   *Marshmallow Clouds* is named the winner of England's prestigious CLiPPA award by the Centre for Literacy in Primary Education, which "celebrates outstanding poetry published for children." In November, University of Nebraska Press publishes the children's picture book *Ted Kooser: More than a Local Wonder*, written by Carla Ketner and illustrated by Paula Wallace.

2024   In September, Copper Canyon Press publishes Kooser's seventeenth major poetry collection, *Raft*. University of Nebraska Press reprints Kooser's 1980 anthology the *Windflower Home Almanac of Poetry* in December.

Conversations with Ted Kooser

An Interview with Ted Kooser

Arnold Hatcher / 1976

This interview was first published in *Voyages to the Inland Sea VI: Essays and Poems by Harley Elliot and Ted Kooser*, edited by the poet and scholar John Judson (1930–2019) (La Crosse: Center for Contemporary Poetry, Murphy Library, University of Wisconsin–La Crosse, 1976). It is reprinted with permission of the editor's son, Gary Judson.

Arnold Hatcher: Don't be offended, Ted, but there are undoubtedly some people who will be reading this interview who've never heard of you. Would you mind saying some things about yourself by way of an introduction?

Ted Kooser: Well, let's see. . . . I'm thirty-six years old, divorced, have one son, Jeff, age eight, I make my living as an underwriter, which is sort of a lay medical clerk in an insurance company. When you apply for health insurance, and the agents ask you all of those "Have you ever had this; have you ever had that?" questions, I'm the one who gets to read the answers and who decides if you get the policy. I've been doing this work since I dropped out of graduate school in 1964. And I also write, and paint, and edit Windflower Press, and once in a while I teach a night course in poetry writing for the University of Nebraska.

Hatcher: What happened with you and graduate school?

Kooser: When I came to Lincoln, in the fall of 1963, I had a "readership," which is a sort of scholarship that you are awarded but that you actually earn by grading papers for someone in the department It paid a little, and my wife was teaching school near here, so we had enough money to live. I fully intended to pursue graduate studies all the way through the PhD at the time. But what happened was this: Karl Shapiro was teaching here then, and I took several courses from him, six hours of creative writing and three more in a seminar he taught on William Carlos Williams. These courses were spread over two semesters of that year. When I got to the end of the second semester, my advisor told me that he wasn't going to recommend me for any more money because I hadn't been playing the academic game. He thought that I should've taken Bibliography, Old English, and so on and not Karl's classes! You see, Karl was someone that the department respected but who they really didn't trust with their graduate students. At least my advisor felt that way. So I threw up my hands and dropped out.

I didn't have any idea what I was going to do with my life after this happened. I thought that maybe I could make my own way through school, living on Diana's salary and whatever I could pick up working part time painting signs and so on. I spent about half of the summer just sitting in a daze, wondering what I would do, and then I decided that I had to start making a little money. I saw an ad for a job as a "management trainee" at one of the local insurance companies, and I thought I'd see if I could stand it for a couple of months until school started. In short, I got the job, and I began to like it, and I never went back to graduate school, except to take enough night classes to finish my MA.

Hatcher: Would you say that you are happy the way things worked out?

Kooser: Oh, yes. It took me a long time to get over my need to identify with the teaching profession, though. I somehow felt that doing what I was doing was not respectable. I really wanted to teach, you see, but my opportunity had been spoiled for me by my own interest in taking classes from Karl and by the rigidity of the system. The chairman of the department, one of the finest men I know, felt sorry for me I think, and he let me teach one section of creative writing each semester, at night. It helped me a great deal to be regarded by him as a fit instructor. He was succeeded by another chairman who had also been extremely kind to me. I have not taught for the past couple of years, for various reasons, and I think I've outgrown the need to be thought of as a teacher.

I guess all this sounds as if the teaching was for *me*, and not for my students; actually, I think I did a good job at it!

Hatcher: So now you're following in Wallace Stevens's footsteps, working for an insurance company. . . . What's it like there?

Kooser: I'm hardly following Stevens. He was an executive, you know. Vice president. I'm more or less a clerk, like Bartleby. What's it like? . . . Well, it's an eight-to-five, actually four thirty, job, five days a week. When I go home at four thirty, I leave it behind me. I don't have to correct papers into the wee hours or try to work up a paper for the PMLA. I like to work, and I enjoy the people that I work with, for the most part.

Hatcher: I'm sure that your job has had some effects on your poetry, hasn't it?

Kooser: Definitely. I think that the biggest effect is in the level of language I use. You see, all day long I have to talk to and communicate with people who for the most part don't know anything about literature. There's no lofty discourse on the arts over coffee in an insurance company! What I think has happened is that my level of discourse in my poetry has been brought down to a more basic level by working with these people. Those poets who are working within the academy often write poetry which complements their academic life, poems full of literary sensibility, in-jokes, and so on. I have come to the point where I am trying to communicate with people who aren't knowledgeable about poetry or who may never have read any poetry at all. I show my poems to the people who I work with from time to time, just to see if I'm getting through to them, and I'm delighted when I am!

I had a wonderful compliment from Denise Levertov in the *American Poetry Review* recently. She was discussing a poem of mine, "Old Soldiers' Home," and she said that a person wouldn't have needed to graduate from high school to understand it. I don't think I've ever heard anyone say anything about my work that pleased me more than that.

You know, Karl Shapiro told me once long ago that if I wanted to be a good poet, I ought to get out of school. I can see now what he was saying. You write poems toward your community; it's only natural that you would. If you write poems toward your community as a teacher, you are likely to limit your communication to teachers. They will support and sustain you, and perhaps that's all you really want. If so, fine. But I, personally, would rather write poems that people on the street can understand and enjoy. Not poems, of course, that don't cause them to stretch a *little* to understand them. Not [Rod] McKuen poems. Poems that present new things to them in ways that they can appreciate and understand. Poems *about* things, and other people . . . poems with good stories behind them. Too much of the poetry today is about nothing, or next to nothing. I call it "the Poetry of the Ingrown Toenail." Poems about little whiny problems. It's no wonder so many people are turned off by contemporary poetry. So much of it is about minor complaints.

Hatcher: You are identified with regionalism and sense of place. Do you have any feelings one way or the other about this?

Kooser: That identification bothers me only when I suspect that someone is saying that I am posing as a regionalist to capitalize on the current interest in regionalism. Bret Harte, as you'll recall, went west to capitalize on the available folklore of the Old West, writing stories and, for that matter, twisting stories around just for the money in it. Twain hated him for his phoniness. Well, I'd hate to be thought of as a sort of Bret Harte of poetry.

I think it's important to remember that I've lived in Iowa and Nebraska all of my life. I have nowhere else to write about. I certainly have not set out to be a Midwestern poet, but I am one, by geography alone.

Lately, we've seen in the little magazine and literary quarterlies more and more talk about Midwestern poetry, sense of place, regionalism, and so on. It is interesting to note that the magazines involved in this are all being published in the Midwest; you won't find *Paris Review* or *Partisan Review* or *Hudson Review* discussing these things. You see, many writers and editors in the Midwest are defensive about their lives out here. They are constantly confronted by the truth that the big money in writing and publishing goes east. The biggest grants go to magazines in the east, like *Paris Review,* and from what I've read, these magazines really have other ways to get money, patrons about them, and so on. The magazines out here have to struggle along with little money and little support. All this leads to a resentment of what is called the Eastern Literary Establishment.

So, over a period of time, editors, critics, and writers of all kinds who live on the plains have tried to publish the idea that we too have an important culture, worthy of attention. I agree with that; we *do* have such a culture, a rich one, but I'm not sure that the argument doesn't go unheard everywhere but out here. We are all sympathizing with each other but nobody outside is listening.

The whole argument is a little pathetic. We will never succeed in getting a poet living in Kansas onto the front page of the *New York Review of Books.* Nothing we can say in our articles and interviews and editorials will do that. *If,* however, he is a *very* good poet, he may get there on his own. It will be infinitely harder for him to get their attention than it would if he were living in Manhattan, but it can be done.

In defense of the eastern literary community, I'd have to say that, after all, they are inundated by their own art. They really don't have a lot of time to be noticing what's going on out here.

The poet who will make it on the front page of the *New York Review* will also make it into all of the literary magazines in the Midwest and West. He will be a poet who is writing well and beautifully and truthfully. It won't be a poet who is trying to climb the literary ladder, at least I hope not. We desperately need a poetry that is true to the heart, not a poetry that is true to this or that school or this or that fashion. The minute you start to think about what you *ought* to be writing, you begin to write illustrations of theory, not poems. I wish that everyone would just try to write as well as they know how, and to write truthfully. The little magazines are absolutely *full* of poetry of second intensity, third intensity. A lot of it has to do with the fact that poets feel obliged to publish lots of poems in lots of magazines; after all, teaching jobs are often based on the number of publications, and teaching is about the only thing that can support a poet. It's a real mess, I think. The minute poets get the idea that poetry can be a vacation, I think they lose their perspective. The arts have always been a secondary activity. The work of society goes first. Oh, it may be that there have been societies which had full-time artists and respected them, but they were always artists who were making art that had utility to those societies . . . potters, silversmiths, painters on commission, doing celebratory portraiture, and the like.

Modern poetry has no utility to society. Oh, I guess it has a *little* utility, but for the most part, all of the poets in the country could suddenly disappear, and no one but their spouses and children would notice. And their students, of course. It would take their students at least a week to get over it.

No, I think that poets and writers must realize that they cannot be true to their art if they are making it for money. The poet must accept his lot; he will always be alone within our society, and unless he is independently wealthy, he will always have to work for a living, doing something that has utility for the society: digging ditches, roofing buildings, selling aluminum siding, teaching school.

Hatcher: . . . working for an insurance company . . .

Kooser: Ah, yes, even that!

I'd like to back up a minute. I think that I've left the impression somehow that to appear on the front page of the *New York Review of Books* is to make it. It *is*, under present standards. We still look to New York for our judgments. I wonder if this is altogether necessary. Why can't we declare our independence of New York? Or, to avoid the *we*, which implies a group position, why can't an artist living in the Midwest or in the Southwest or in the Northwest simply declare himself free? Artists in the hinterlands have proven that it is possible to subsist there without a lot of money, and it's money that keeps us looking East. Who needs New York? Who wants to be Updike or Roth or Bellow? And, I think that to want to be rich is to be willing to be corrupted.

I'm sorry that I'm rambling about like this. I hope that I'm getting across. To summarize this hodgepodge, let me say that I believe that what is wrong with American writing today is that writers are being true to things other than their hearts. So rarely do we see a poem in one of the little magazines that is honest that we want to tear it out and make a thousand copies of it and strew them from a plane.

Hatcher: Do you think your own work fulfills your personal standards?

Kooser: Yes, sometimes. I write a lot of poems that are undoubtedly influenced by what is in fashion. It's very difficult to avoid this. But, over the past few years I've read less and less that interested me, and so I've stopped reading most of the magazines. You can't be influenced by what you don't see, and, after all, my struggle with language is between my brain and its articulation, not between my articulation and literature. I can carry on my own struggle to write well and honestly without help from the outside.

Hatcher: Surely, though, you continue to read poetry!

Kooser: Yes, but looking for it in the magazines seems to be an awful waste of time. I prefer to read the collections of poets who have already shown me their honesty, like Dick Hugo. And I read poems of dead poets whose work I love . . . Ransom, Jarrell . . . I think a great deal of Denise Levertov's poetry, Gwendolyn Brooks's, Linda Pastan's, Nancy Willard's. These are all women whose work transcends the polemics of writing women's poetry.

Women, who have certainly been oppressed, and other oppressed groups, minorities, often write poetry filled with social outrage—poems of political intent. What I think they overlook is that poetry is a terrible means of political expression. Look who reads it! How many registered voters read poetry magazines? And the people who read poetry magazines are already converts. Most of them already believe in equality for women, for blacks, for Chicanos. They don't need convincing. These groups need to get to the voter, and they're not going to do it with poems.

Hatcher: But don't you think that there is a place in poetry for poems of social protest?

Kooser: Oh, yes, but let me put it this way: I object to the use of a poem or may I say something that is shaped like a poem as a vehicle for public address. These pieces are speeches, not poems. They just don't hold up on the page.

To completely avoid the state of society is also unhealthy, of course. I am asking for a poetry which knows its place. There are, for example, women who can write poems which clearly reflect the oppression of women without puffing them out with polemics. These women are writing truthfully of their own experience, are writing with an *I* and not a *we*. Marge Piercy is such a poet; so is Louise Glück; so is Adrienne Rich.

Hatcher: There seems to be a great interest in surrealism again. I guess it would be called *neo*surrealism this time around. How do you feel about this sort of writing?

Kooser: I think that many young poets, sensing the popular resurgence of surrealism, have begun to fabricate dreams and fantasies as source material for their poems because their lives and the dreams which they actually have do not provide them with enough genuine experiences to fulfill their desire to write hundreds and hundreds of poems. A life, waking or dreaming, does not ordinarily provide a poet with an experience worth writing about every day, or at least I think that is true of most people. But since many of our younger poets want to publish a great deal, in order to fill out their curriculum vitae, they use surrealism as an excuse to write about nothing, lots of poems about nothing. Another way to do this, to have lots of production, is to write lots of poems about writing poems, about language, everything turning in upon itself. Most of these poems will serve their purpose, filling out the lists of publications, and then vanish. There are poets writing today who will not have a single poem in print in twenty years, poets who are relying on surrealism as their primary emphasis now. I guess I should say that I mean none of their poems written *now* will be in print in twenty years. They may be able to write more durable poetry after they become a little more secure.

Hatcher: Another subject now . . . you seldom read your poems in public. Why is that?

Kooser: Nor do I usually enjoy watching other poets read *their* poems in public. I am nearly always embarrassed for the poetry; which takes a terrible beating at the hands if its own maker, often being compromised and twisted by the delivery. It is of some interest to see how a poet reads his work, I'll have to admit, but I really believe that a poem belongs on a page and not in an auditorium.

I am not only embarrassed for the poem but for the poet as well. He too is compromised by the theater of the reading. A poetry reading is a means of using a poet for something other than a maker of poems; it is a means of making him an entertainer. If the audience of poetry readings had their way, there would be no more books of poems; instead, there would be poets on every corner, wearing interesting costumes and entertaining people, like organ grinders, or for that matter, the *monkeys* of the organ grinders. Whenever *I* read to a group, I feel like Jack Benny.

I've thought lately of getting a ventriloquist's dummy and taking it with me to my readings. I could then have the dummy say my poems. The audience would surely *love* that!

But seriously, Arnold, I believe that most poets compose as I do, in solitude, committing the language to the manuscript in silence and with reverence for the gifts of association that the solitude delivers to them. Somehow, I feel that if the communication is to be complete, the reader should share in the solitude. I would like to think of my readers as being alone with my poems. I would not think of entering a room and distracting them with a poor reading voice and a bright necktie.

I might be criticized for neglecting to honor the tradition of oral poetry, in which the poet, or the storyteller, recites to a group of illiterate people by the fire. It presents a pleasant picture. But those things happened long ago, and under different circumstances. There were no books; there were few people who could have read them anyway. If a person wanted to hear a story like this, he had to walk miles cross-country under all sorts of terrible conditions to hear it, and, for that reason, few could attend. Printing was devised out of the need for more accessible stories, particularly religious stories, and although printing cost society the intimacy and drama of the fireside reading, it did widen the audience of literature.

Our present society exhibits a nostalgia for simpler times, and I suspect that the poetry reading may be part of this. Now, though, a person doesn't have to walk ten miles across a frozen moor to get to the fireside; he can park right out front!

I will say, though, in conclusion, that the arguments I have against readings may have been invented in self-defense. I am quite uncomfortable in front of groups and get terribly nervous when I have to give a reading. Part of the anxiety probably comes from shyness, and part from the idea that my poetry has somehow turned against me, making me do something that I don't want to do.

For the poet who needs money, the poetry reading is a good thing, too. Teaching and readings are two means of support that many poets engage in . . . also poetry in the schools.

Hatcher: Now, about your writing habits . . . people are usually interested in writing habits . . .

Kooser: I write a poem that I think is good enough to keep about every week or ten days. I write when I feel like it, and I seldom try to write when I don't feel right about it. Although every writer is different, I find that I write best when I wait for the right moment. I can usually feel it coming on, and I then must sit down by myself and let it work itself out.

I used to try to write every day, but I feel as if there is only so much emotional weight available to me at a particular time, and that if I write daily, the poems are diluted. If I wait between poems, I am much more likely to have something of importance to bring to them.

But, as I said, every writer works differently. It has taken me a long time to figure out what was best for me, and everyone must do this for themselves.

Based on what I've said, it sounds as if I should be able to put together forty or fifty poems that I like each year. Actually, that isn't so. After a few weeks, many of the poems that I thought were worthwhile have lost their interest. At the end of the year, I may have fifteen or twenty poems that I'd like to carry forward toward a book.

Hatcher: Do you submit most of your poems to magazines as you write them?

Kooser: I usually wait for a week or two. If the poem still looks good to me, I'll send it out to an editor whose judgment I respect, like, say, E. V. Griffith of *Poetry NOW*, or Jerry Costanzo of *Three Rivers Poetry Journal*, Hilda Gregory and Bernice Slote here in Lincoln at *Prairie Schooner*. I consider very carefully rejections from these people, and I question the advisability of sending out a poem any more after a couple of good editors have turned it down. Fortunately for me, all of the poems that I've written during the past couple of years, or all but a few of them, have been accepted for publication, which surely must say something for my method of writing, waiting for the poem rather than trying to force it out.

I should say that I don't believe that it should be the editor's sole responsibility to decide the value of a poet's work. The poet should be doing it too—should be editing his *own* work. All poets should be able to tell the difference between their best work and their third-rate work. They may not be able to tell their best from the second-best, but they can tell their best from third-rate and fourth-rate stuff. Some poets send out everything. It's extremely risky, I think.

Take this, for example: let's say that a poet sends out a batch of poems which includes first-rate work as well as fourth-rate work, and the submission goes to an editor who is either incompetent or malicious. That editor might well accept ten of the worst poems and publish them as a representative selection. It could do a great deal of damage to that poet.

All in all, I think that a poet must choose his magazines carefully and choose his work carefully. As is evident to me, there isn't enough care of this sort given in many instances. Without naming her, I know of one young woman who sends out everything she does, or it looks like it. When I was editing the *New Salt Creek Reader*, I'd get fifty poems in a batch from her that I was supposed to sort through. Sometimes there would be half a dozen versions of the same poem! It occurred to me that these poems were being offered to me without restraint; I could print any of them that I wanted to.

What if I'd printed five different versions of the same poem? I could have called the section of the magazine *A Selection of Poems by So-and-So*!

Hatcher: But you didn't do it. . . .

Kooser: No, I couldn't. But someday, someone will. All of this is more of the same stuff . . . the emphasis on publication, getting lots of stuff in print. Perhaps if someone respected in the academic community would make a stand for quality in publication and not quantity, it might help. If they could suggest to the people in charge of hiring writers to teach in universities that it's the quality of the writing that matters, not the number of publications, perhaps things would get better. Unfortunately, I don't know if too many hiring committees want to try to judge quality. They don't have the time.

You see, everybody can get published somewhere if they persist in sending out work. Some ignorant editor at *Sweep Up Quarterly* or *Last Ditch Review* is going to accept it. When this poet gets enough of these publications, he can approach the hiring chairman and say, "Well, I've been published in a *number* of little magazines, including *Sweep Up Quarterly* or *Last Ditch Review*," and unless the hiring chairman does his homework, he'll never look at these magazines to learn how really awful the work may be. I'm not sure that these people doing the hiring realize that there are quite a few *Sweep Up Quarterlies* in this country, all of them desirous of filling up fifty pages every quarter. It's literary pollution.

Hatcher: But if these magazines are so terrible, how do they survive?

Kooser: Most of them don't, fortunately. They may last for a couple of issues, but they still have provided space in those two issues for a hundred poems, a hundred additions to the curriculum vitae. Offset printing is not awfully expensive, and it isn't too hard to get out a couple of issues of a magazine. It's easy to get plenty of poems to publish. You just mention that you're looking for work, and the poems come flying from everywhere, many of them on English Department stationery, by the way; poems from people who are tired of teaching freshman English and who want to work toward a cushy six-hour job teaching creative writing. When I was editing, I don't think I was ever pleasantly surprised by poems that came in a department envelope. Another disastrous mistake that you can make in starting a magazine, by the way, is to get listed in *The Writer* or *Writers Digest*! Jesus! You can't imagine the stuff that comes in! The presence of these writers' magazines on the stands encourages a lot of miserable people to write and submit and then to be heartbroken by rejection. It's sad. I have seen submissions by people who were so neurotic that they wrote me threatening letters when I turned their work down. But they all want to be rich, rich writers so that they can get on the *Johnny Carson Show* and gossip with Truman Capote and Burt Reynolds. The writer's dream.

Hatcher: Perhaps we should close now. Do you have anything that you'd like to say in conclusion?

Kooser: Let me put it this way; here's an original thought I had the other night; see how you like it: *Money is the root of all evil.* Has a nice ring, doesn't it?

"A Moment of Order in a Chaos of Language": An Interview with Ted Kooser

David M. Cicotello and William A. Heffernan / 1982

This interview was originally published in *Pendragon* 3, no. 1 (1984). It is reprinted with the permission of David M. Cicotello. Recently retired from teaching, Cicotello is at work on *Six Days on the Ledge*, a memoir about his life-changing survival, rescue, and recovery experience.

"I think of myself as a poet who resides in a region and writes about it. I do not write for it. A regionalist writes *for* his or her region," says Ted Kooser.

Further, Kooser points out, "I can tell you a little bit about what my poems should do, but I don't think I can tell you what the poems of other people should do. Or, rather, I can tell you what I try to do.

"Any time a writer compiles a list of details, a mood shows through. In that way, a list of details like *dead leaves, gray sky, thin air* suggests a mood. I like to write this way. It's quite satisfactory for me to merely suggest something or other. I studiously avoid making pronouncements of any kind. I like to think that I have deluded the reader into thinking he or she has made up his or her mind about the experience I have presented in concrete details, but I'm *really* in charge, having limited the selection to those touches that correspond to my feelings."

In the following interview, Kooser offers additional observations about his activities of composing in language. We wish to thank the National Endowment for the Humanities for fellowships in residence at the University of Nebraska–Lincoln, where this interview was conducted during the spring of 1982. Our thanks also to Ted Kooser, who volunteered his good will, his poetry, and his thoughtful responses.

David M. Cicatello: Please begin by describing the starting point in your writing. What motivates you? How do you begin taking up a subject?

Ted Kooser: My poems seem to be of two different kinds. First, there are those which arise from an idea, a complete argument like *It's sad the way progress can be so destructive.* The task of the poet is to dress up the idea in such a manner that a reader will be compelled to pay attention to it. I might choose as a subject the demolition of an old building, for example. And I would express my idea without ever phrasing it.

It is then the reader's job to unravel the poem and find the idea. We're taught this type of detection in the public schools. The answer which wins the prize is *It's sad the way progress can be so destructive.*

It all seems rather pointless, doesn't it? But the poet knows that nobody is going to listen to him if he comes right out and says *It's sad the way progress can be so destructive.* That's too ho-hum. So what he does is to try to make his idea attractive and compelling. And the reader shares in the excitement because he or she feels a part of the discovery.

I don't have very good luck with poems which start with ideas, and I don't like to write them. There is very little of the spontaneous about them and not much excitement for the poet. The poem is often dead in the water, from the very first line forward.

The second kind of poem arises from a different level of consciousness, it seems to me. The first kind requires a complete thought, and in my example, you can see that I have a complete sentence. The second kind surfaces like a couple of pieces of flotsam from a sunken wreck. Two words, three words, maybe, that are tied to something still within the unconscious mind. These words are often the very first verbal abstractions of nonverbal feelings. Let me give you an example.

I like to take drives in the country at the end of winter, and among the sights I enjoy most are the old snowdrifts which are dying back, covered with road dust, stubbornly trying to hoard their coldness against the spring. Until I began to write about these drifts, I had only a feeling for them. I liked them; that's all.

Then, just the other day, I was out driving and looking at these old drifts, and suddenly, two words surfaced: *white shadows.* The drifts were lying in the shadows of other things, outlining those shadows perfectly, and were, in effect, white shadows. Those two words started the following poem, which I finished that day [Originally published in *On Common Ground* in 1983. Kooser dropped the first line when the poem appeared in *One World at a Time* in 1985]:

"A Fencerow in Early March"

Its shadow is white;
the last snowdrifts
have drawn themselves up
out of the light,
clinging to winter.
Beyond them,
a muddy stubble field
has sponged up
all the darkness:
the February nights,
the iron stoves,
the ink of every letter
written in longing.
And the fencerow
goes on, up and over
the next low rise
and the next, casting
its cold, white shadow,
its gate still closed
on spring.

This kind of poem is delightful to write. It's all play, whereas the other kind is all hard work. In the idea poems, one has to work at his task as if he were writing a thesis, fitting all the parts in around the center.

In this snowdrift poem, the poem goes off on its own flight of fancy, springing outward from *white shadows* and going wherever it wishes to go. Is there an idea behind it? I don't know, and I care less. I had great fun writing the poem, and I like it because it makes a record of that fun.

I've talked to people about this before who have asked me if I didn't feel frustrated as a writer because I was not truly expressing my ideas in poems like this. They were people, like most of us, who grew up believing that a writer's mission is to communicate his or her ideas. That's true of essayists, of course, and journalists. But poets? Nope. I like to think that the poet is free to play. And the fiction writer, too.

If one is concerned about communicating ideas, one may of course do so in poems. Lots of poets have, and there are lots of good poems written with ideas at their core and as their motivation. Poems like Gray's "Elegy" ["Elegy

Written in a Country Churchyard," Thomas Gray, 1751]. But I don't think that I'm ever going to be that kind of poet. It's just not any fun.

And if I were ever to become concerned about showing myself for who I am, I think I can do so with poems like the snowdrift poem. They show me being a person who enjoys writing, who enjoys flights of fancy.

Poems like mine are difficult, though, for teachers. It's hard to get a pin through the thorax of a poem like mine and show the students where the idea lies hidden. The poem is its own idea, its own dream.

Cicotello: Does keeping a journal help you retrieve information you wish to consider when writing a poem?

Kooser: Oh, yes. But I don't keep a journal in the true sense of the word, as a record of the day's events. I do keep workbooks full of ideas and fragments. In the example above, it would be likely that I might have written *white shadows* in one of my notebooks, hoping to pick it up at another time, that is, hoping to make something out of those words.

Heffernan: Aging, decay, and mortality seem to be dominant themes in your poetry. Can you explain how you've come to be preoccupied with death as a subject?

Kooser: Other people have asked me about this, and I always feel a little uneasy, as if I were being considered for commitment to an institution.

I don't think I'm any more preoccupied with death than other people, but I may be wrong. They don't write their thoughts down, remember, and I do.

Death is, after all, what defines life. It's the other side. The Spanish, or some of them anyway, would say that a great feast gets its savor from having death standing in the shadows of the dining hall. I believe in that. According to Lorca, the flamenco dancer knows all about this as he or she dances closer and closer to complete exhaustion and death. A lot of joggers are doing the same thing. It's exhilarating to flirt with death and survive. I suspect that those people who try to put death out of their minds are only half alive.

I should add, though, that I often turn to my poetry when I am in a melancholy mood. I do this because writing a poem is often my salvation from a depression. Naturally, some of the melancholy rubs off on these poems.

I rarely write when I am feeling really good. I don't need to. This may explain what you're seeing in my poems. Believe me, I'm not a morbid person. I'm happy, and I'm lucky. The world lets poets play, you see, and thanks them for it.

Heffernan: As part of the theme of transience, you seem to be interested in the transitions between seasons and the effects on nature. You seem especially caught by the change into winter and severe weather. Is this part of the theme of mortality, or do you intend your description of winter to be seen in a different way?

Kooser: People who live on the Great Plains pay more attention to the weather than do people who live in stable climates. Many of us were brought up by farmers and ranchers who spent a good part of their time looking over their shoulders to see what the weather was going to do.

I don't see so much weather in the poems of people living in Arizona, say, or California, and I suspect that it's because the weather just isn't a power in their lives.

I enjoy the dramatic seasonal changes we have in Nebraska, and there's no doubt but that each new season carries a person closer to his or her death. I always feel exhilarated with the coming of winter, but that's not because winter is a symbol of death, but because I have had enough summer and fall and want to move on. Winter for me is a time of reading and isolation, and I enjoy it for those reasons.

I often include the weather in my poems because it locates them in time and place. It personalizes them in this way. And it also sets man against the enormity of his environment, in the way that the Japanese painters place those tiny human figures in their big landscapes.

I think that it's wonderfully amusing that we have come to a time in which man can destroy every form of life on earth with a flick of a switch, and yet a good blizzard can have everyone cowering in their houses like the meekest creatures.

Heffernan: You also seem fond of dogs since they appear in a fairly large number of your poems, and even by implication in the title of one volume, *Not Coming to Be Barked At.* Is this just a coincidence?

Kooser: I guess I've never noticed that dogs play any important role in my writing, but I do find it interesting that the question comes up just as I have finished a short story about a man imprisoned by dogs. I think dogs are interesting because they seem to tread a line between civilization and savagery. My story is about that, and, I suppose, that may come out in whichever poems include dogs. The only one that I can think of at the moment is "First Snow," a poem that I'm fond of, but not because of the fact that there's a dog in it.

Heffernan: While you could hardly be called a confessional poet, you do devote several poems to your divorce from your former wife and your relationship with your son. Do you think autobiography, particularly painful and personal autobiographical experiences—as in Snodgrass's, Lowell's, or Sexton's work—can be successfully made into poems?

Kooser: Of course it can. Snodgrass's "Heart's Needle" is a good example. But it is a poem with a good deal of restraint. Lowell too often lost restraint and seemed to feel that he could get away with just about everything once he had the floor. I don't like Sexton's work all, but that's because I don't feel comfortable with the person I sense to be behind the poems.

Of course, all writing is autobiographical, since a writer can't write about things he doesn't know. This knowledge may in some instances extend no further than knowing the name of the thing, but in knowing its name, the writer makes it a part of his life.

As to writing about painful personal experiences, I believe that there isn't anything in this life that can't be made into poetry. I have been able to write a few poems about some of the painful things that have happened to me, but there are many experiences that I've had that I haven't been able to write about. I haven't as yet found the way to transform these feelings into poems.

The important thing for me is to be able to develop some detachment so that I can stand back and look coolly upon what has happened to me. Deciding what one can do in a poem requires some dispassionate analysis. My divorce and the separation of my son from me happened a dozen years ago, and it has only been within the past few years that I have had the detachment to write well about these things.

Cicotello: Describe the role of audience in your writing. What assumptions or considerations of audience operate when you compose a poem?

Kooser: I want to be understood. That's very important to me. For that reason, I try to avoid language which may exclude readers. Naturally, you begin with the exclusion of everyone who doesn't read poetry. That leaves you with a large body of poetry readers, many of whom will be fairly comfortable with figurative language, metaphor, and so on. I don't like to include things in my poems which call for the reader to go to the dictionary or encyclopedia. That simply disturbs the moment of communication, I think. I always try to write in complete sentences, with proper punctuation, and no special effects like the use of the lowercase *i* or the ampersand. These things seem to be merely clever to me and call too much attention to the poet, away from the poem. I believe in a style of writing that leaves the language somewhat transparent so that the writer's style is not the first consideration. I want the reader to go directly into the poetry, without pausing to consider the punctuation, the capitalization, and so on. Style is something that the reader should notice after the fact.

I am interested in an honest, straightforward communication with my reader, and I want him to know that I give him some consideration.

Communication is a serious and important business, and I'm not going to play games with my audience or make fun of them.

All of these things go into my thoughts about my reader.

And, by the way, I expect the same of the poets I read. If a poet is not interested in communicating with me, I have no time for him or her.

Heffernan: Karl Shapiro has compared your poems to Edward Hopper's paintings, and perhaps he meant that the starkness of the images reminded him of Hopper's settings. Why have you chosen to present your world in such bare outlines? Is this how you see the world? Is it, perhaps, an effect of the region you describe?

Kooser: I live in a landscape that is flat and in which one can see many miles. Most of the sensory stimulation in such a landscape is visual. Things are too far away to feel or smell or taste or even hear. Using a lot of visual imagery, which I do, is not, I think, so much a choice as a response to the landscape. People have said that they sense space in my poems, and I suspect that this concentration of visual imagery is what causes this sensation. I also draw and paint, and I am a very visual person. That's at play, too.

One thing that I think my poems have in common with Hopper's paintings is that I am not a participant in whatever is going on. Oh, sometimes, of course, but in many of my poems I am looking on from seclusion. The great Hopper paintings of people sitting in cafes at midnight, of people seen through the windows of their houses—I look on people in the same way, as a distant observer.

Heffernan: Again, like Hopper's paintings, many of your poems are about lonely or deserted people. In fact, in one poem, "West Window," you observe that "we grow / to be alone." Does this describe the human condition as you see it?

Kooser: Yes. I think that we are all alone. In the poem you describe, I was speaking of watching older people and how they so seldom have a spouse or even a good friend at the end. My grandfather, for example, outlived his wife, one of his daughters, and one of his great-grandchildren. If one lives long enough, there's no one left.

Someone, May Sarton I think, has said that the greatest sadness in life, one of the great sadnesses, rather, is to live to an age at which there is no one who can remember what you were like as a child.

I don't know that I've ever read anything more moving than that.

Heffernan: There seem to be several influences on your work; for example, the stanza forms, line lengths and language suggest another Midwest poet, Robert Bly. Would you comment on other poets who have influenced you?

Kooser: That's interesting. I do like Bly's poems, very much. But I don't think I've ever paid any attention to their structure, at least not on any conscious level. It's his wonderful, freewheeling imagination that I like so much—how he goes bounding along over the ground of the poem like a jackrabbit or an antelope. Have you ever heard of a jackalope? It's a mythical beast, a cross between a jackrabbit and an antelope. You see their heads mounted in country taverns all over Nebraska—jackrabbit heads with antelope horns. They're a sort of trick on the tourists. Anyway, a jackalope is very cunning, very fast, and very daring. They share a lot of characteristics with Coyote, or Trickster, of the American Indian mythology. They're playful, too. Bly is like Jackalope—very intelligent, very wise, very playful—and his imagination can run like the wind, leaping and bounding this way and that. It's a thrill to read him. But, believe me, he's no trick on the tourists. He's very, very real. And serious.

His translations of the poems of Thomas Tranströmer have been as inspiring to me as any poetry I've ever read. I can go back to them again and again and be refreshed. And, of course, Bly's own poems have had a great deal of influence on me, both as a person and as a writer.

You asked about other poets, though; let's see. The poets I was reading when I started getting serious about writing poetry of my own were Ransom, Robinson, Frost, Jarrell, Jeffers. They remain favorites of mine. Ransom's poem "Dead Boy" has never paled for me, after nearly twenty-five years. I was a college student then, and I did my duty and read Pound and Eliot, too. Pound's notions about imagery had their influence on me, and this interest carried me forward to Williams, another favorite, although I don't like his longer poems.

In graduate school, I came to know Karl Shapiro and his poetry, and I think he is probably the finest craftsman of his generation as well as being a very wise and human poet.

Today, I suppose I'm a little bit influenced by many poets—some influence here, some there. At the moment, my favorite collection of poems is Donald Hall's *Kicking the Leaves*, which came out several years ago. I also follow William Stafford's poems very closely, and those of Leonard Nathan, a fine poet and a good friend. His book from Princeton, *Returning Your Call*, was nominated for a National Book Award, and the Pitt Poetry Series has since done two of his books.

I'm very fond of the poems of the late Elizabeth Bishop, too. Her ability to write descriptive verse has taught me a lot. I am also quite fond of Denise Levertov's poems, those of Maxine Kumin and Linda Pastan, too.

But there are hundreds of poets writing today who occasionally write a poem that I am moved by. All in all, their work may not interest me very much, and then, whammo!, up pops a really wonderful poem. One has to do a lot of reading, though, to find them.

Cicotello: Describe the process of revision in your writing. Do you revise extensively or barely at all?

Kooser: Extensively. I may go through a dozen sheets of paper before I get close to the version I'm looking for. But I do not like to do this within a concentrated period of time. I seldom go back and make revisions if a couple of days have elapsed. A particular poem takes a certain set to the mind, a certain pitch, and that seems to fade away after a day or two.

Cicotello: Recently, *Kansas Quarterly* published your short story "A Drowning." Do you plan to continue writing fiction? And does one form—poetry or fiction—provide you with a greater artistic satisfaction?

Kooser: I would really like to write stories, and I'll surely continue to try. There are things you can do in a story that you can't do in a poem, and vice versa. I find it difficult to switch back and forth, though, with any facility. Have you ever noticed the way that a robin listens for worms? She cocks her head to one side. I think that when I write poems, I have my head cocked to one side, and when I write fiction I have it cocked to the other. They are completely different languages in many ways. Poetry is often static in time, and fiction is forward-moving, linear. Something is happening in a story, and something has already happened in a poem.

As to my satisfaction with what I write, I'm equally satisfied to have written what I consider to be a good story as to have written what I consider to be a good poem. During the process of writing, though, I think that there are more highs in working on a poem. You know, when a particular figure of speech just pops into your head from somewhere, or when you suddenly discover an association between two very dissimilar things, a metaphor. It's like having the gods on your side. You feel like jumping up and down for pure joy. Maybe this happens to fiction writers. I don't know.

Cicotello: As an accomplished writer and as the editor and publisher of Windflower Press, what advice do you have for beginning writers anxious to break into print?

Kooser: It's very hard to convince young writers to wait. I was once a young writer, and I know how important publication seems to be. I'm embarrassed by the poetry that I was writing in my twenties, and I wish that it weren't in print. But I suppose that one day I'll also be embarrassed by the poetry that I'm writing in my forties. I do think that perhaps a younger writer can't be hurt too much by publishing in the little magazines, where the work can be buried forever if need be. But the drive to get out a book of poems early is not a worthy or wise decision.

And there is this to consider: one's first book may be the only book that will receive any critical attention. It's better to wait until the first book is really a good one. I know of several instances in which young poets got out a book early, which was badly reviewed, and from then on, no one would pay any attention to the poetry of those writers.

Cicatello: Finally, Robert Frost once defined a poem as "a momentary stay against confusion." How might you define a poem?

Kooser: My definition would paraphrase Frost's, I guess. I'd say that a poem is a moment of order in a chaos of language.

An Interview with Ted Kooser

Mark Sanders / 1983

The following interview was first published in *On Common Ground: The Poetry of William Kloefkorn, Ted Kooser, Greg Kuzma, and Don Welch*, edited by Sanders and J. V. Brummels (Ord, NE: Sandhills, 1983). It is reprinted with the permission of Mark Sanders.

Mark Sanders: You wrote an essay entitled "The Two Poets" for the Spring 1983 issue of the *Nebraska Humanist*. In the essay, you make a distinction between two types of poets: the public poet, and the poet who writes poetry. Your advice to beginning poets was they should write and not try to be a poet. That's a pretty sound suggestion. But how much should this advice pertain to poets who have become successful?

Ted Kooser: I believe wholeheartedly that poets, and artists in general, should avoid becoming embraced by the popular culture. Artists need detachment, and it's hard gaining that detachment and protecting it when you're participating in the popular culture by sitting between two pretty starlets on *The Tonight Show*. It's probably better that poets be kept under the front porch with the dogs.

Sanders: You are one of the more successful poets residing in Nebraska. If success affects art negatively, how do you keep from producing poor poetry or, as Judson Jerome calls it, "proetry"?

Kooser: I'm not comfortable with the word *success* when it's applied to me. I was brought up by people who equated success with money, and I don't think that they were unusual in that thinking. It could be said that I am a moderately successful businessman—I make a good salary at my job at the insurance company—but I am not a successful poet. In twenty-five years of writing and publishing poetry, I'd guess that I've received less than $2,000 for the sale of poems. I've made additional money doing readings, but that's not being a successful poet; that's being a successful performer of poetry. I don't know any poets who are successes as poets, nor do I care to. When money gets mixed into art, the art begins to decay. Once an artist discovers that he or she can make money by creating a certain kind of work, his or her work rarely progresses beyond that point. If every poet in this country were to be given a million dollars, it would mean the end of poetry. Not that poets and artists should suffer. I don't believe that anyone should have to suffer, but I mean that the arts should be kept apart as much as possible from financial considerations. Money stinks. A friend of mine is a nationally recognized landscape painter. Several years ago, he began attracting large sums of money for his paintings—$2,000, $3,000 apiece. He began painting more and more of these successful paintings, and he's made a lot of money, but his painting is arrested. He's doing the same thing over and over. I've felt the temptation myself. Several months ago, I sold a poem to the *New Yorker*. It was the first time I'd been paid for a poem in years, and I got a little over $100 for it. Gosh, I caught myself saying, if I could write like that more often, I could make a lot of money! But what I was really saying was, if I could write the kind of poems that Howard Moss likes, I could make a lot of money. But who wants to spend his life writing poems for the poetry editor of the *New Yorker*? No, I want to write poems for me. There's another kind of success, I guess, and that's in getting published, even though there's not much money involved. Surely you know poets who have perfected a particular kind of poem that is easy for them to get published. It would be unfair of me to point a finger at a particular poet as an example, when there are thousands, but you know what I mean. Those poets are going to keep on writing the same damned poem over and over again all their lives, just because it's been successful for them. That's why I think highly of a poet like Greg Kuzma, who keeps experimenting, keeps exploring. Artists who undertake such explorations make mistakes. It isn't always safe. But they also open new territory. Art is all about this sort of pushing the frontiers out, pushing the horizons out. Faulkner once said, "To try something you can't do . . . then try it again. That to me is success." Of the four poets presented in your book [*On Common Ground: The Poetry of William Kloefkorn, Ted Kooser, Greg Kuzma, and Don Welch*], Greg is probably the most serious artist in this sense. He is tireless in his trying of new things. Don Welch is probably next in line. I see his work changing, expanding its range. Bill and I are a little safer, I think. We are more likely to write the Kloefkorn poem, the Ted Kooser poem, though both of us seem to be worried about it, and if you look at the overall range of what we've done over the years, you can see both of us changing to some degree.

Sanders: In the last few years, there has been a big hoopla over writers in Nebraska. A search for a new poet laureate was started, and finally, after many writers dropped out of the running, including yourself, Bill Kloefkorn was awarded the honorary title of Nebraska State Poet. What was your attitude toward all the proceedings? Where did good come from it, and where was the bad in it?

Kooser: The controversy over the appointment of an official state poet is all in the past now, and there's not much to be gained raking over the coals. Those of us who opposed it had good reasons to do so, and we all had our reasons. For me, I was sure that naming a state poet would bring a lot of attention to one particular poet and no attention to other poets, many of whom could use some recognition. In a sense, my suspicions have been borne out. Bill Kloefkorn has been asked to do poetry readings from one end of the state to the other, and the sales of his books, at least from my own press, have increased tenfold. But I guess we need to keep it in mind that before all of this happened, nobody was getting much attention. The question remains: Is it best for nobody to get any attention or for one person to get a lot of it? I do want to say that Bill was as good a choice as could have been made. He likes people, likes reading to them, and is a terrific performer of his own work. Lots of people go to poetry readings to be entertained, and Bill is a great entertainer. He's also a poet who knows poetry, and some of that sensibility and love of poetry is bound to run off on his audiences, which is good. All in all, I wish that this state poet business had never come up. It led to a lot of hard feelings among the writers and toward the Nebraska Committee for the Humanities, a worthwhile organization whose misfortune it was to get involved in such a sensitive issue. They really waded in blindly and got in high water before they knew what happened. I was one of the ones, if not the ringleader of those, who stood on the bank and tried to raise the water level by pissing in it.

Sanders: In the interview printed in *Voyages to the Inland Sea*, you told Arnold Hatcher that modem poetry had little utility to society. When Bill was given his distinction, John Ciardi remarked in his address, borrowing from Auden, that poetry made nothing happen. Did you mean the same thing, and do you agree with that philosophy?

Kooser: I was there, but I can't remember what Ciardi said. And that *Voyages* interview goes back a long time. But I do believe that poetry has little practical value. We all know that, don't we? You can't carry water in it. You can't drive it to the grocery. One of the wonderful things about art is that it's worthless.

Sanders: How do you compare yourself to your contemporaries in this state? Do you all serve the same function as "poet," or do you see your work as exclusive yet complementary to theirs?

Kooser: There are a lot of poets in Nebraska, and most of them have matured to the point that they are doing their own work, in their own manner, and are not under the influence of anyone else. Naturally, some of the younger poets have imitated the work of older poets, but they'll get over that. I can see Don Welch's influence on his former students, Bill's influence on his former students, and so on. But the really mature poets are doing their own thing. You'd have a hard time finding much common between the poems of Don and Bill and Greg and me and Roy Scheele and the other poets who are getting their work out and establishing national reputations. I wonder if any of us are really reading each other very carefully. I doubt it. I mean, studying each other. I may be alone in this, but I'm really not very interested in anyone's work but my own.

Sanders: When you consider that such writers as John G. Neihardt, Weldon Kees, Willa Cather, Mari Sandoz, and Wright Morris have shaped Nebraska's literary culture, do you find what is being done currently to have the same importance as their contributions?

Kooser: I'd rather not get into comparisons, Mark. We're really talking apples and oranges here. Cather and Sandoz and Morris are prose writers, and Neihardt was really a nineteenth-century poet. Kees's work is more like what Don and Bill and Greg and I are doing, but that's mainly because he was a twentieth-century poet writing in his tradition, and so are we. I have faith that some of the poets living and working in Nebraska today have written, and will write, strong and enduring poems and that these may become a part of the literary culture you're talking about. But those same poets will also write a lot of bad poems, a lot of failures, just as did Neihardt and Kees. Ninety-nine percent of all poems are failures. Winfield Townly Scott said that, and he's right. It's a good thing to keep in mind.

Sanders: If you could do something to influence the contemporary literary climate of the state, or even the Midwest, what course would you suggest other than what is currently happening?

Kooser: I don't really want to influence the contemporary literary climate. I think it ought to be left alone.

Sanders: You once told me you thought "regionalism" was getting more attention than it deserves. Can you explain that feeling and what would you rather have attention given to?

Kooser: Most of the talk about regionalism and sense of place is little more than boosterism. The people doing all the talking are trying to defend their own writing and that of their friends. The defense is usually a lot better than the writing. There's nothing new about any of this. Writers have always been their own best cheerleaders. It seems to me like a tremendous waste of time. If writers spent more of their time writing, and less time patting themselves on the back, we'd all be better off.

The idea behind most of the sense-of-place talk is that there is some magical unifying theme pervading the writing of certain writers. This is complete nonsense as far as I can see. What writers on the Great Plains share is the Great Plains. They live there, and they share the same summers and winters. Some of this commonality of experience is bound to get into the poetry, and it does. People have known for years that the best way to involve a reader in what he's reading is to introduce concrete imagery, and when you live in a place, you draw your imagery from what's around you. You can't draw from experiences you haven't had. Bill Kloefkorn and Don Welch and I have all lived nearly all of our lives in Nebraska, Kansas, and Iowa, so when we go to our experiences, we have nothing else to draw from. Greg Kuzma has lived here, but he's also lived in the East, and he draws from both regions. He has a book called *Adirondacks*, for example.

What's important to me is whether the poetry that gets written is any good. Where it got written doesn't make much difference. Oh, I like to see the work of Great Plains poets getting published in national magazines, getting good reviews, but that's because I know and like these people, not because we're in the same Kiwanis Club, or better, the same fraternity, with a secret handshake.

Sanders: You've been writing for nearly twenty years—writing and publishing. Out of all that time, out of everything you have done as a poet, what is your greatest success, what has been most gratifying?

Kooser: Twenty-five years, actually. . . . A number of things have happened which have pleased me—the publication of my first poem, the publication of my first book, my first appearance in an anthology, my first critical notice in a national magazine. All of the firsts were very happy occasions. I've also greatly enjoyed meeting and corresponding with writers whose work I admire. Today, I am particularly happy to receive letters from distant strangers who have come across my poems and liked them. I especially like letters from school children. Several of my poems have been included in textbooks, and that's made me happy. I've always wanted to reach an audience of people who are not poets or poetry followers, and those textbook publications seem to confirm my ability to reach a broad audience with my work.

Sanders: You are now a second vice president for an insurance company. Has this been beneficial to your poetry? Do you ever feel any desire to get back to the classroom? What has working at the company done for your sense of audience awareness?

Kooser: I don't think that my job has been particularly helpful, but it has not interfered either. Teaching might have interfered. Teachers have to give of themselves more than I am willing to. When I taught night classes, I found myself giving away good ideas, and particularly good metaphors, which are hard to come by. I'm not interested in letting students take my metaphors and misuse them.

Sometimes I think it would be fun to teach again, and I may someday, but there are other considerations, including money. I'd have to take a 50 percent cut in income to go back to teaching. As to the last question, I think that the fact that I work all day long with people who are not literary has helped to keep the language of my poems from becoming literary. I often try out my poems on my coworkers, some of whom would never read a poem without my imposition, and I watch carefully to see if they understand what I've written. It's a good test.

Sanders: You were an editor for a number of years. First, it was the *New Salt Creek Reader* and then the *Blue Hotel*. Both of these were pretty little magazines. What was your motivation for starting these, and what happened to them?

Kooser: I started my *Salt Creek Reader* because I wanted to be in on what was going on in the literary world. I wanted the community of correspondence and publication. Eventually, after I'd begun to publish my own work in magazines and had struck up correspondences with other poets, like my friend Steven Osterlund, I felt that I could keep my place in the literary community without all the work and expense of publishing a magazine. So I discontinued my magazine. Later, I started up another, the *Blue Hotel*, thinking that I missed the activity, but I soon discovered that I wasn't all that interested in it. I got out one very good issue on the poetry of Brewster Ghiselin and a double issue, which is an anthology of contemporary Danish poetry, and then I let it go. The money was always a problem, too. It's expensive, as you know, Mark, to publish magazines and books. There are government programs which give out grants of support, but frankly—and this is odd since I'm on the state arts council—I'm not sure that the government should be backing literary magazines. I've given up asking for grants for my Windflower Press because I think that it, like any other little mom-and-pop grocery, ought to be able to survive on its own merit, *if* I'm putting out a product that has any utility for people. Too much of what the government has supported in its literary programs has been a complete waste of money because the product that was produced was of no value to anybody. I don't feel the same way about direct fellowships to artists, though. That seems to make more sense to me. But every artist and publisher who goes to the government for money must ask himself or herself, "Does my acceptance of support from this government stand as an endorsement of what this government is doing in the world?" In some sense, the artist is going in business with the government to produce art, and should we be going in business with a government that behaves as it does in its support of repressive countries like South Africa? You can go to jail for refusing to pay your income taxes, but you can't go to jail for refusing to accept government support.

Sanders: Since you have been an editor, and since you are a critical reader, what do you find wrong with contemporary poetry?

Kooser: We probably ought to avoid distinctions like *right* and *wrong*. Poetry, like all art, is by its nature right. It's an affirmation. . . . But I'm taking advantage of your question. As a reader, I can only attest to what I like and what I don't like. There is a lot of poetry being written and receiving high praise that I don't like at all. But somebody must like it. Louise Glück, whose poems I admire, recently selected Michael Ryan's *In Winter* for the National Poetry Series. Ryan's book is dreadful, I think, but it's obvious that my opinion is in the minority. Here's what I like to see in poetry: First, I like poems that move me. I am moved by poems in which strong feelings are present but are held or controlled by language which is slightly detached and restrained. I detest poems of self-pity, though, and poems of self-absorption. I love poems which celebrate things—telephones, pigs, rocks, you name it. I also like poems that are well made. I find myself moved by those skills, too. I can't stand sloppiness. To go back to your question, I'd have to say that if I were to pass judgment on my contemporaries, and it looks as if I'm about to, I'd venture that the *me*-ism of the sixties, the focus of attention upon the individual and not the community, has been too amply reflected in our poetry. I said that I didn't want to get into right or wrong, but I do think that it is morally wrong for people, all people, including poets, to spend so much time and energy in self-absorption. On a bigger scale, this is what nationalism is all about, and it's nationalism, I think, that places the whole world in great danger. But poets can't do much about that, I don't think. Artists merely reflect the world that they live in. It's the world that we live in that I'm unhappy with, I suppose. And the poets are more to blame for the state of the world than are the rest of the people.

Sanders: You occasionally write book reviews. Does this help you to keep focus on your own writing?

Kooser: I do enjoy writing book reviews, but I find myself saying the same things in all of them, and perhaps I should stop. I have a few axes to grind, a few statements about poetry that I like to make, and I've said these things again and again. The publication of these ideas is getting redundant.

Sanders: *Hatcher* and—from what I understand, because I haven't seen it yet—*Blizzard Voices* are departures from your poetic voice. Why the departure? Did it allow you to examine other voices, such as Bly in his translations?

Kooser: I did *Hatcher* for fun, and while *Blizzard Voices* is a little flatter than most of my lyrics, it's still mine. A poetic voice is a hard thing to define, although I can recognize the poetic voice of other poets. I like to think of myself as a writer, not just a poet, and I believe that writers should write all sorts of things—plays, novels, essays, poems, book reviews, etcetera. I don't want to confine myself to poetry. I want to keep trying new things.

Sanders: When *Sure Signs* first came out, I read a review of it in an East Coast magazine that wasn't exactly kind. How did you view that, and how did you come to terms with the review?

Kooser: *Sure Signs* got a nasty review in the *New York Times Book Review*. The reviewer, somebody named Molesworth, took on six or seven new books, mine among them. The whole review was sneering in nature. He was as hard on Charles Simic and Louise Glück and the others as he was on me, so I was getting kicked in good company. The more your work gets around, the more likely it is that it will find its way to somebody who hates it. It hurts to get a bad review, but I've had lots of good ones, too, and they've more than offset this one bad one. Some reviewers are helpful. Mary Kinzie wrote about *Sure Signs* in the *American Poetry Review*, and I learned some things about my work from what she said. Dana Gioia, whom I understand is writing something for this book, is my most devoted critic, and he's taught me a lot. A lot of writers won't read their reviews, but I do.

Sanders: A couple more questions: what do you think about the concept of this book, despite its slow progress? Where, do you think, should I go from here?

Kooser: I wouldn't object to any book that paid attention to me and my work. I like the attention. I don't know what you intend to say in your introduction, Mark, but I hope that you won't try to define a "school" of Nebraska poetry or to insist upon a commonality between the four of us, because I don't think it's there. Besides, we all are independent and should be viewed as individuals. I'm very pleased that you've gone to all of this work on our behalf, and I thank you for including me. I don't know what you should think of doing next. If I were you, I'd hole up and devote my energies to my own poems for a good long while.

Sanders: What's next for you?

Kooser: I don't have any definite plans, but I would like to spend more time on my short fiction. Short stories are very challenging, and I'd give anything to be good at writing them. I'll keep writing poems, too, of course.

A Way to Start:
A Conversation with Ted Kooser

Peter Whalen and Chris Fink / 1999

This interview originally appeared in *Cream City Review* 24, no. 2 (Fall 2000). It is reprinted with permission of *Cream City Review*.

Ted Kooser enjoys a long-standing relationship with Cream City Review. *In the autumn of 1985, Kooser appeared in our pages for the first time. He has published several poems in* CCR *since then. Fourteen years later, on November 13, 1999, Kooser gave his first public reading since cancer treatment and recovery, traveling from Garland, Nebraska, to Woodland Pattern Book Center in Milwaukee. Earlier that day,* Cream City Review *editors Chris Fink and Peter Whalen sat down with him at Ma Fischer's restaurant on Milwaukee's Lower East Side.*

Peter Whalen: You've stuck exclusively to the short poem. Why?

Ted Kooser: If you write a poem that is a conceit, in effect, an Elizabethan conceit, where you're working with one metaphor, there's only so far you can inflate it before it blows up in your face. There's only so much you can put in. I would give anything to be able to write a poem as good as Robert Frost's sonnet "The Silken Tent." It's the description of a woman as a silk tent in the wind, and it's a marvelous conceit. But it couldn't have been any longer. By the end of the fourteenth line, he had done everything he could possibly do with the poem.

Whalen: Your poems are often one or two sentences, and the phrasing seems so natural. How do you accomplish that?

Kooser: I'd like to have the poems be like good watercolor paintings. A good watercolor painting looks like the guy just picked up the brush and went swish, and that to me is the ultimate objective, to have something that looks, in effect, effortless and free. But it's damned hard to do. You really have to work at it to pull it off.

From front to end. I'm also going for an overall rhythm that is not a pro-sodic rhythm as we think of it. There is a certain kind of rhetorical rhythm that you hear in persuasive conversations that I try to build into a poem without thinking about it. The poem should sound like a declaration. I won-der how many versions [William Carlos] Williams went through to write "The Red Wheelbarrow." That is not a poem that would've fallen right out of his head. It is perfect. It is perfect in every way. And he must have had to really juggle this and that to get it right.

Fink: Richard Hugo says that a poem has a triggering subject and a gen-erated subject. Does that paradigm work for you?

Kooser: I think Hugo is right about that. When a poet sets out to write a poem about an idea, it's too big a chore. I have a little poem about nuclear holocaust, about a barn swallow finding its nest, and how it's taken hun-dreds of thousands of years for this swallow to learn this one thing, how to find its nest in the dark, and all that learning would be destroyed in nuclear holocaust. If I had started off writing that poem thinking that I'm going to write about the damages of nuclear holocaust, I wouldn't have known where to start. But what happened is, I had been watching a swallow, and as I was trying to describe the swallow, the idea of nuclear holocaust emerged as part of that process. That's the way it works best for me. I would guess it works best in most incidences, because your own ideas on the big issues are going to come out whether you want them to or not.

I like Hugo's work a lot. Hugo was willing to take the big chance of being regarded as too sentimental, and sometimes the poems do get a little too sentimental by my personal standards. (There are only personal standards when assessing sentimentality). But you don't go back into a safe place to do these poems. If you're not willing to take some risk out there on the edge of sentimentality, you're not going to have any effect at all. You know that a cold, emotionless poem is safe, but it doesn't do anything.

I wrote to Hugo about that late in his life. I told him that I was reminded of an old Charlie Chaplin movie where Chaplin is skating along the edge of a mezzanine in a department store. It's under construction, and the railing has been removed. The tension in the scene, seeing Chaplin come along the edge on one leg, and coming back, reminded me where Hugo's poems are. They're out there on the edge, and some of them fall into the downstairs underwear department. But back against the wall where it was safe to skate, they wouldn't have done anything at all.

Whalen: Besides Williams, who else influenced you? I know you're a painter; does some of that come into your poetry?

Kooser: My work is very visual. What we all learn from Williams is his attention to what's right under our nose. That poem of his about eating the plums ["This Is Just to Say"], people would dismiss it as being simplistic in many ways, but it changed the whole course of things. People began to think that it's all right to write a poem about something in their icebox. That was his genius. But I don't think *Patterson* works very well because it is such a big, ambitious poem. It's the little poems of Williams's that really changed the way we look at things.

Here's a digression, a story I want to get in. When Karl Shapiro was in Nebraska in the fifties, he had, as his graduate assistant, a woman named Glenna Luschei. One day, the first edition of *Howl*, from City Lights, came in the mail. Karl sat in his chair in his office, and Glenna was in the office with him, and he read that book cover to cover. Then he turned to Glenna and said, "Glenna, our lives will never be the same." Isn't that wonderful? To have that kind of prescience to understand that this poem was an important poem. He didn't like it particularly, but he had the notion that this book was going to change everything, and it did.

Fink: Beginning creative writers—they all have a notion about what poetry is supposed to be, and it seems like it's usually the wrong notion. I think your poetry is a good introduction to one way that poetry can be done really well. It seems that each poem shows you a way to pay attention—how to look closely at things and people, under rocks or in old houses and things like that. So I was wondering, what advice might you give a beginning poet in their first creative-writing class? Or what assignment might you give?

Kooser: Williams was a big influence on me, in showing me the art of observation. That poem of mine "Abandoned Farmhouse" has been in dozens of anthologies. People have told me that it's teachable because it teaches people to look at things, to see if they can see some sort of truth behind this piece of what's left behind.

When I was teaching beginning creative writing, one of the first things would be to have an exercise in description, looking at what you're picking up on, just looking at something and trying to describe it. One good way of doing that is to get a little form into the thing, to write thirty lines of description in iambic pentameter or something like that. I want people to be looking at things for the specifics, to be looking very closely.

Fink: Williams said that people are dying miserably every day because of a lack of poetry. Do you agree?

Kooser: He's dead right about that. If we could engage people in this art, their lives would be enriched by it, but I don't know that any of us ought to make a mission of setting out to engage them. I'm interested in writing poems as objects and making poems. I'm not trying to champion a cause. That would be futile, really. Absolutely, I'd like certain things to happen, but I have enough problems writing a poem inside the poem. You know, the kind of choices you have to make, and things like that, and trying to get it to really work. That's plenty of work for any of us.

Fink: Who do you see as your ideal reader? In the poem "Selecting a Reader," there's a wonderful image of this woman walking around the bookstore with her dirty raincoat on. She picks up your book initially then puts it back on the bookshelf after she's done with it. She will not buy the book. Are you trying to change that? And whom do you see as your audience?

Kooser: I'm writing for a person who has a middle range education and is not sophisticated literarily, who may read some poems, but is not necessarily professionally dedicated to them in any way. If you can show a person a poem they like, perhaps that'll generate an interest in poetry, and then they'll let you go beyond that. So I guess we're talking beginning level poetry readers in a way.

As far as the woman in "Selecting a Reader," she's got more important things to do with her money. We have to be realistic about the world. People don't give a shit about poetry. Most people don't care about buying books of poetry. Why would they pay $12.95 for a paperback of poetry if they'd rather go out to lunch and spend it?

Fink: I've used your poems to teach middle-school kids and college students, and I always have a lot of success with them. Students really respond well, and I think that writers of all levels can learn a lot from your poems.

Kooser: You know, I love the notion that I've got an audience of middle-school kids—people who aren't such sophisticates. That's wonderful. I sort of have a middle-school mind myself. I mean, I don't think of myself as being very learned, as this interview will show.

Whalen: You've said that accessibility is a choice. Obviously, some poets choose not to be so readily accessible. Why, then, do you choose to communicate that way?

Kooser: We all have a human need to be liked. So if you're in an English department, and that's your community, and they like irony and symbolism and obfuscation and deconstruction and so on, you're likely to write to please them. That's unfortunate because it so limits your audience to that community. Think of all the poets who are really big hitters in contemporary poetry, and think of how really very small their audiences are because they're limited to that very erudite, sophisticated poetry community. As a fiction writer, look at a lot of the short stories written by people with teaching positions, and you'll find a kind of uniformity of experience. For a while, ten or fifteen years ago, there were all kinds of short stories about teachers jogging with each other, and there'd be affairs, interdepartmental affairs. It's a paucity of experience. There's just not that much to write about.

Whalen: Related to that, and back to your work as an insurance man— sometimes I wonder if the academy is the right place for a poet. It seems that having a job outside academia allows you to be more accessible because you're out there working with nonliterary people speaking a nonliterary language.

Kooser: It's just your words. Your choice of words helps you that way. You're a poet. That's a passion of yours. You're going to write the poems no matter what you do. Poetry as a vocation is pretty tough because it's filled with awful rejection; even English departments will reject a lot of what you do. Fred Chappell's got a wonderful essay in which he describes a young poet making it in the department, getting a book out, and sending it to a bunch of people in the department, then getting back one copy torn in pieces, and another one with a sympathy card and all this kind of stuff. That book is called *A Way of Happening*, and it's a marvelous book. I can't be down on poets who choose the academic life because it's something that they want to do. If they find it fulfilling and so on, that's fine, but not all of us are going to do that. My advice would be to find something that feels like it has social worth to you. And teaching can be that.

Whalen: How did writing poetry come about for you? What was the initial spark?

Kooser: Frankly, I think it had to do with girls. You know, I wasn't any good at anything else. I wasn't much of an athlete, and all of a sudden, I would see pictures of rangy old John Berryman in *Life* magazine with young women hanging all over him, and I thought, "Well, maybe that's the ticket."

Also, my family was very conventional with very conventional values. My father managed a department store, and my mother was a traditional homemaker. All my life I really wanted to be different from other people. Writing poetry was a way of setting myself apart. Being on the outside, fighting to be on the outside, rather than on the inside.

Fink: Do you have people you rely on to help you edit your poems?

Kooser: For thirty years, I've exchanged work with Leonard Nathan, who's a poet at Berkeley. I look at a lot of his work, and he looks at mine, and that's been pretty helpful. You have to be careful in choosing the person you do that with. You really want to be sure that you admire what they're doing with their poems.

Whalen: What are your feelings about the workshop environment?

Kooser: There's a kind of common denominator in there. Oftentimes a workshop lessens the original poem considerably. By the time you please everybody, well, it's like being a politician. By the time you get to the top political position in the country, you've made so many compromises that, you know, there's nothing left of you.

I studied English at Nebraska. I went there because Karl Shapiro was there, and he and I became very good friends. I spent a lot of time with him, and I learned how the poet lives his life, which is, I think, one of the really nice things about universities. You may learn some things in the workshop class, but it's seeing a writer who's living the writer's life that makes the real difference. Warren Fine, who taught here once, wasn't good about getting to his classes. He met his students in his house, in the bars. But they learned about how one writer was living his life.

Whalen: Could you describe your revision process?

Kooser: I do a lot of revision, usually within the first couple of days. Then later on, I let it cool down a little to see if it makes any sense at all. My revision is toward clarity and brevity rather than away from it. I try to look at the poem and say, "Could I say this more clearly without losing some of the effect?" and "Can I change the phrasing of this so the grammar is less awkward?" A lot of my poems are these long, periodic sentences. If you don't get the phrases to line up right, they don't work; the references suffer a screw up, so a lot of my revision is in changing those things around to make the poem work better. That's the kind of thing you can notice in twenty-four to forty-eight hours. Most of my short poems went through a number of changes. You could say they go through thirty or forty versions.

Whalen: Besides being creative in your poems, you have to be creative with your time. That's as much of it as anything.

Kooser: You have to be selfish with your time, particularly in a domestic situation. A lot of times the family has to sacrifice, and it's really too bad, but it happens.

Whalen: What sacrifices did your family have to make?

Kooser: The poet is going to say, "Leave me alone. I'm going into this room, and I'm shutting the door. I'll take care of your problems at another time." One of the great stories about compromise relates to William Stafford, who used to get up early every morning to write. His daughter, who was a little girl at the time, discovered that if she got up an hour earlier, she could have an hour with Bill by herself. So Stafford began getting up an hour earlier than that. That's the kind of guy he was, but most poets wouldn't do that.

Whalen: I love that. Do you do most of your writing early in the morning?

Kooser: Very early. Anywhere from four thirty on, depending on when I wake up. Now that I'm retired, I'm usually done by eight thirty or nine with writing for the day, although I might do some revisions or something like that. I keep a workbook, and I start writing as if I were simply writing a journal entry. What's the weather like and so on. Every once in a while, some little thing will trip me, and I'll go off in that direction.

Whalen: It sounds like there are definitely things you still want to accomplish as a poet, to keep writing poems and not waste time.

Kooser: Writing poems is what I can do. There's a kind of poem that I can write that nobody else can write, and I want to keep doing that. Writing poetry is the thing that I am best at, and that's what I want to do with what time I've got. I don't waste time now. I've always been pretty organized, but I waste a lot less time now than I did.

Whalen: You've submitted some prose poems, and that seems like something new.

Kooser: It is really. I think it's the first time I've sent any prose poems out. I always paid attention to prose poems, and I had some things that I felt were naturally leaning in that direction.

Fink: There's a line in your prose poem "Wild Asparagus" in which the poet is thinking about making the asparagus stalk into a flute, except he doesn't know how to do it correctly. He laments that "you have to have plenty of time to do everything."

Kooser: Absolutely. I like to paint, and I've always painted a little. Before I got sick, my idea of retirement was that I was going to do a lot more painting. I figured if I lived twenty years, I could be a lot better painter at the end of twenty years, and that was going to be a part of my life. Now I'm not sure that I want to give time to being an amateur painter when I could be giving time to writing poems that might mean something to somebody. I don't want it to sound like I'm in imminent danger or anything like that because actually my prognosis is pretty good. But when these things happen; you start looking over your shoulder and you never stop.

Winter Morning Walks:
A Conversation with Ted Kooser

Jay Meek / 2000

This interview first appeared in *North Dakota Quarterly* 68, no. 1 (Winter 2001). Jay Meek (1937–2007), a poet and novelist, had previously served as poetry editor for the journal. Permission to reprint the interview was granted by his wife, Martha George Meek.

When I learned that Ted Kooser's eighth book of poems, *Winter Morning Walks*, would be published by Carnegie Mellon University Press and that it consisted of a hundred postcard poems, I was delighted. For Carnegie Mellon would also soon issue my first novel, *The Memphis Letters*, and it was clear there were resemblances between our two books. My novel was made up of fictional letters sent to a person whose name had been selected out of the Memphis telephone book. Ted's poems had in fact been mailed, and both of our works invited parallels between the letter writer and poet, the reader and the recipient of news. We agreed to begin our own exchange, about our interests in language, our pleasure in imagining, and the lives we each had given in goodly part to poems.

Ted is a man of easy bearing and wit. If it is true that Dr. Samuel Johnson could make up a pun upon any subject, even the king of England—whom he declared was no subject—Ted Kooser can make up a poem at sight of a common object, a bolt of cloth, or frost on a dark road, and make the familiar shine with a strange loveliness. *Winter Morning Walks*, which he began in 1998 after he was diagnosed with cancer, is a selection of one hundred short poems from a sequence he mailed to Jim Harrison.

Ted asked that our dialogue be a conversation, rather than an interview, and we held it for the most part on electronic mail. Our correspondence ran from November 2 to December 26, 1999, and, while I lived in Norway, during February through March 2000. In June, after I returned, we resumed our talks, until they felt complete, on September 15, 2000. We let time pass between us rather than open a line of immediate exchange, and sometimes our interludes created for us the slow expectations that pass between writers of posted letters. Although the exchanges were to be conversations, one can hear how different the discourse is for each of us and how near our voices are to the voices of our poems.

Jay Meek: Your new book, *Winter Morning Walks*, is made up of poems attached to the backs of postal cards and mailed to Jim Harrison, across the space of five months. Would you talk about how the sequence got started and what literally went into making a poem, from drafting it to sending it in the mail?

Ted Kooser: In June of 1998, I was diagnosed with cancer of the tongue and had surgery, followed by six weeks of radiation. From June through October, I was pretty sick and miserable, and I wrote only one poem, a little haiku-like piece that speaks from the center of my dismay: "Coal in my tongue / how long had you lain there / waiting to burn me alive?"

Then, on the ninth of November, following my regular two-mile morning walk (I walked before sunrise because I'd been warned of skin sensitivity following radiation), I sat down and wrote a short poem, the one that begins the dated sequence in the book. Jim Harrison and I had been exchanging haiku for a couple of years, and I pasted this first effort on a postcard and sent it to him. I felt encouraged to have written anything at all, and the second morning, I wrote another poem and did the same, mailing it to Jim. Soon it became a regular routine with me: the walk before dawn, then time in my favorite chair composing the morning's poem. I was recovering!

I wrote the draft in longhand in my notebook or on a block of watercolor paper that had a rich texture I liked. Then I set the poem up in type on the computer, pasted the poem on a postcard, and off it would go. I sent some of the watercolor-paper drafts to other writer friends, making big postcards out of the worksheets, showing the poem developing toward its final draft. I'm not exaggerating when I say that, for a while, my morning writing exercise was the only thing that kept me feeling that I still had some life left in me.

Meek: How did Jim Harrison respond, in what way?

Kooser: If I remember correctly, Jim responded after receiving the first few poems by enthusiastically remarking in a letter that it looked to him as if I'd opened a whole new vein of creativity. As the months passed and the poems accumulated, he would from time to time mention one or another of the poems, but he didn't offer suggestions for revisions. Our letters have never moved toward the kind of "workshop" correspondence that I've had with, say, the poet Leonard Nathan, who has been a dear friend for nearly thirty years.

Meek: Do you think of the one hundred cards as being a hundred poems, or one poem?

Kooser: Because the separate "entries" were written on different days, in different moods, while I was writing them, I thought of each as a poem complete in itself. But once I'd compiled and culled the manuscript, I began to see them as parts of a whole. They are all united by the overshadowing experience of cancer and recovery and, in that sense, seem to be stanzas.

Meek: Ted, tell me how many books came before *Winter Morning Walks*, and which of them is most like this collection.

Kooser: Let's see. . . . Seven that could be considered full-sized collections, and none of them is much like this collection. Each of the earlier books was a compilation of poems published in magazines over a period of between five and ten years, and this book was written in five months. There are a number of "postcard poems" in *A Local Habitation & a Name*. And I suppose these new poems are like most of my earlier ones in that they are brief and imagistic. I rarely write a poem of more than, say, thirty lines.

Meek: For years, at Valentine's Day, you've sent friends a postcard with a poem on the side reserved for address. For you, is there a relation between a poet and reader that's at all similar to the one between a letter writer and correspondent?

Kooser: Absolutely. When I write a poem, I always have an imaginary reader in mind. This person has varied in nature over the years but generally is a person of average intelligence who is charmed and delighted by interesting arrangements of words. I often think of my late mother, a bright, receptive woman who was by no means a literary sophisticate. I ask myself, "Would Mother be able to understand what I'm saying?" If I think not, I revise toward a clarity that might help her through the poem. Many of my efforts that I have come to regard as failures are poems that, because of my own silliness or cleverness or "putting on airs," went over the head of my mother.

Meek: I try to write for the part in me that's both skeptical and willing to listen. I know when I write that the reader always exists in the future for me, just as I will exist in the past, whether I'm sending a letter or sending off a poem. And, as a reader, when I identify the hand on an envelope, or find a new book by a poet I know, even before I open it, I feel a momentary gasp at such news it'll bring of illness or health and of my own responses to another's fortunes.

Kooser: I too thrill to the mail. By the way, I've noticed that several of the people with whom I correspond have turned away from writing computer-printed letters and have gone back to their good stationery and fountain pens. I suspect this is because when you get a computer- printed letter you have an inkling (so to speak) that the same letter might be on its way to a number of people. But a handwritten letter is unique, and it is a great honor to receive one. Not only is the experience intimate; it is *indelibly* intimate. Every time you unfold the letter to look at it again, the intimacy is still there. No conversation between two people can match it because conversation is ephemeral. So perhaps a poem, like a handwritten letter, is an indelible intimacy. What do you think?

Meek: Indelible, yes, but always in need of saving. One of the first things I did when we knew the Red River flood of 1997 was going to sweep over us was to save boxes of letters, carrying them from my study to the second floor. And in need of sustaining. Every letter from a friend feels as intimate as a poem, as urgent and intrusive—in speaking the most blessed things, or most familiar—as it breaks upon the day. I believe all mail should arrive in the morning.

Would you like to talk about the presence of human dailiness in your poems, the new ones or earlier, how the "familiar species" and the rare or imagined come together in them? Or in another writer's work?

Kooser: Many of my poems do look closely at or into the ordinary. I was recently asked to choose an American painting and write a poem about it for a book that's being compiled. I chose a George Ault painting called *August Night at Russell's Corners.* You may have seen it, or one of its three "sister paintings." Ault went at his subject on four different canvasses. The one I chose is in the permanent collection at the Joslyn Art Museum in Omaha. It shows a rural intersection at night. One overhead lamp illuminates the sides of two red buildings. The road between them vanishes into the darkness. The subject is ordinary, the effect enchanting, or haunting. My poem goes:

If you can awaken
inside the familiar
and discover it strange
you need never
leave home.

I believe that. There is plenty right under my nose to keep me engaged. I think if I had time, I could happily go back into some corner of our property with a ball of string and four sticks and pick out a square yard of earth and spend months looking at all the variety there.

Meek: The writers who've rendered Dickinson letters and Thoreau journal entries into poems don't seem to understand that the excerpts are embedded in the common verbal experiences of the days they record and so simply by their acts of extraction appear to argue that the passages should have been and still should be poems. What for you is the relation between the journal entry and poem?

Kooser: For me, journal entries often lead to poems. In fact, my journals and my workbooks are the same. I start writing a journal entry, get caught up by some word or phrase, and veer off into trying a poem. The poems in *Winter Morning Walks* are very much that way, titled like journal entries, giving the date and the weather, then going on into an observation. The experiments you mention in turning prose journals (or letters) into verse are misguided. They suggest that verse is superior to prose and that we ought to try to pry as many poems out of the language as we can. It's really a way of getting out yet another book, isn't it? We ought to be able to enjoy Thoreau's journals as journals. If we want to edit them into selections, fine. But to try to line them out as verse seems a little excessive to me. Though I will say that Robert Bly's extractions from Thoreau made an engaging little book.

I want to throw in something about postcards, Jay. About thirty years ago, I began to collect old postcards for their quaint and colorful lithographic art. Then I began to notice the handwritten messages, which had a kind of literary form imposed by the limited space one had to use. The feelings expressed were both restrained and economical, just as I think poems should be. Using the raw material of these old cards, I tinkered around with turning a few of them into poems, and some of these were in my book *A Local Habitation & a Name*.

In view of what I just said about robbing Thoreau's journals to make poems, this practice may sound contradictory, but the postcard messages were undiscovered, unlike a journal with tens of thousands of copies in print. I wanted to show people things they were never to see otherwise. Ordinary things, too. These messages come out of the most ordinary of lives. They are about the weather, the crops, sickness, and small triumphs. Somebody dies; somebody graduates from business college in Milford, Nebraska, third in his class!

Meek: In *Great River Review*, you published a lovely recollection about visits you made to your maternal grandparents in Guttenberg, Iowa. It's called "Lights on a Ground of Darkness: An Evocation of a Place and Time." Isn't that the town you've also painted in acrylics and written poems about?

Kooser: Oh, yes, I've written many poems about that place and about the people I knew when I was a boy visiting there. And I've included details from their lives in my paintings. That place is at the heart of everything I am, and I want to have my ashes sprinkled in the river there, near the abandoned pearl-button factory where I fished with my uncle when I was little. Like everything, Guttenberg has changed dramatically since I was small, but the high, wooded bluffs and the broad Mississippi are much the same. And many of the people who live there still have a little trace of German in their voices and much of the immigrant past in their hearts, or so I imagine.

Jay, I want to tell you about something that happened yesterday that I think would be a wonderful lesson for any writer. A little bit of good comes out of just about everything. The day before, I dropped a heavy one-piece garage door on my head while I was pounding on a stuck roller, and it knocked me flat when the pin in the roller sheared off. It cut up my head a little but would have really done some serious damage if it hadn't been for an old highbacked lawyer's desk that was sitting beneath it that took most of the weight (a desk I've been wanting to get out of the garage but hadn't yet got around to finding another place for).

Yesterday, I went to the Earl Carter Lumber in Lincoln, having been told that they stocked rollers for doors like mine. The person who helped me was a big, helpful man in his late fifties and, making conversation while he looked for the parts, he mentioned how good our weather has been. "We'll be pitching horseshoes on Thanksgiving," he said. "They'll be bringing the shoes and the stakes." I told him that I had had an uncle who had cerebral palsy and who couldn't talk well or walk well but could pitch horseshoes with the best. "Isn't that great!" he said. "You know, I had an uncle who was tristate horseshoe champion three years running. I asked him one time how I could get as good at it as he was and he said, 'Son, you got to pitch a hundred shoes a day.'"

That's the good that came out of dropping a two-hundred-pound door on my head, that one line. Anybody who wants to be a writer, or to get good at anything, ought to be committed to that kind of steady practice, don't you agree?

Meek: I'm sorry for your injury, whatever the moral of the door. I caught my fingers in our garage door several years ago and went around for a week with metal splints on them as if I were Klaatu. I rather liked it. But I didn't get any words from it, and maybe for me poems begin with "cloud capped towers" and silences and insubstantial things.

I like looking into things. I've tried to sharpen my seeing and the ways one can see, and as much as music always reminds me of the motion that belongs to poems, so photographs and painting tell me each time that poems are as much a spatial art as they are—like music—beautifully linear. A poem always moves against itself, somehow across itself, tracking, like a ball finding its way by rolling down a Rube Goldberg contraption.

Kooser: I like this last analogy, a little more complex than Frost's idea of the poem as an ice cube riding on its own melting ["The Figure a Poem Makes"]. Do you see or sense rhythms in your poems that are not defined by standard prosody? What I mean is, in many of my poems, I feel a rhetorical structure that is rhythmic rather than it is syntactical, as if the entire poem is a sentence (and often I do write poems in a single sentence) that is composed on a rhythmical arc or wavelength of some kind. Prosodists can talk about measure, line by line, but this is something that underlies the whole poem. This would be the Rube Goldberg contraption, the ramp down which the ball rattles. Does this make any sense?

Meek: Here's how I see it. Syntax for me is a way of divvying up cadence, of pacing lines, and of keeping everything from going off at once. By syntax, I want to suggest the tenuous relations among the things that are named, and I want my phrasing to modulate the ways in which they're held. But it's no less important that syntax express the nature of the poem, as a form, by enclosing instances of its built-in resistance to itself—in the tension of line—and that from it might come the important centeredness of the poem. Line stacked upon line. The poem lifting off the page at least as much as it weighs down. More than one conductor, as my daughter has told me, tells the violinists, "Play the rests." Even the silences need to be shaped and sounded.

It was music for me, concert music, that was my love in college, and I longed to become a conductor, even after I'd graduated. I know other poets who've wanted to conduct. Of course, it seems—we're encouraged to believe—the music comes right out of that stick. Years later, I discovered that when I'm writing well, words come out of my hands, my fingers. Revisions, out of the head.

Kooser: I very much like what you've said about syntax. And I love that business about "playing the rests."

Meek: Let me mention another kind of "syntax" I'm on the lookout for in my poems and prose poems. When I open Eudora Welty's "A Memory" from her first book, *A Curtain of Green*, I feel so astonished that there is a point beyond which I can't read further, and I have to put the story down. Such attention, such duty, and mindfulness, as we find in her narrator: "To

watch everything about me I regarded grimly and possessively as a need."
So that's important to me, how things are held in the weave. And that's
the rhetoric I aim for, I'd guess, to suggest by the way a sentence moves—
by tone and indirection and long phrasing—its bent of mind, its care, its
attenuations. As if the syntax of the sentences stood for the complex relationships among the things named and summoned up. But I confess I'm at
a loss when it comes to that most basic sense of rhetoric, in having what
Aristotle felt essential for a poet—"an eye for resemblances"—except, as I
mean to suggest, other and similar kinships by how syntax gathers them in
its keep, extending and looping back.

It's clear to me that your acts of perception, your tropes, if they are at all
rhetorical, are considerably more than embellishments. In *Winter Morning
Walks*, they're so much at the heart that they become both the agency of
thought and the process of thought. Does that make sense? Your poems
aren't acts of seeing, alone but of recognizing precision and outline in the
things around us, and the value we find in perception and cognition. I wonder if you'd like to select one of the poems from the book where that seems
to be true and talk about it.

Kooser: By chance, I am just now looking at the galleys, which came
yesterday. Here's one of the pieces, picked at random ["december 24"]:

> All night I heard tapping,
> like a teacher at a blackboard:
> a bad bearing, I guessed,
> in the furnace fan.
> But early this morning,
> passing the kitchen window,
> I discovered the fancy
> football plays of frost
> chalked onto the cold black glass.

The original association here, and the actual impetus for the poem, is the
sound of tapping and its resemblance to the sound of chalk on a blackboard.
These associations arise spontaneously, usually at a time when I have prepared myself to receive them by quietly sitting with my notebook, maybe
jotting down random words and thoughts, however nonsensical. That the
tapping sounds like chalk on a blackboard is a kind of non sequitur, you
might say. It flies in out of nowhere, meaning little on the surface. But I have
learned to trust in these little revelations, for the lack of a better word. So

I take the association and turn it in my mind until I begin to understand how it extends into something broader. Who uses a blackboard? Teachers, coaches. There is frost on the window, and it is dark beyond; how can that be tied into the association?

Of course, I say, the window against the darkness is a blackboard, and the marks of frost are the chalk marks. Then I labor to remove any detail that does not work toward the enhancement of the original association. There are certainly things about windows covered with frost that are not at all like blackboards, and if these come to mind, I dismiss them as I revise. A metaphorical poem like this one can go weak and flabby if there are details that work only on the tenor or the vehicle side and not on both.

I have at times told student writers that they need to remember that every word they put in a poem inspires a lot of associations in the readers' minds and that once that word is in the poem, you have to honor it not only in the phrase in which it appears but all the way to the end. For example, if the word *chicken* appears in line 1, the reader will have a chicken in his or her head that is likely to stick there throughout the poem. That chicken, and the associations we can expect the reader to have about its "feathers, eggs, clucking," has to fit into the overall structure. If the poem is about playing badminton, that chicken is still sitting there on the side of the court. Eventually, of course, if the poem is long enough, the chicken will fade. But before it fades, it will have an afterimage of associations that lasts for quite a few lines, or so I have come to believe from my own reading. A poem gifted with good possibilities, some unique association, may fail because the whole poem is not carefully tuned to the single note of that one metaphor. And that accounts for the brevity of so many of my poems. Those metaphors can only be inflated and extended so far. Frost's poem "The Silken Tent" is a masterpiece of this kind, filling a whole sonnet with a single, beautiful, consistent conceit.

At the risk of sounding like a mystic, Jay, I believe that when I show you that the tapping is like chalk marks on a blackboard, at some level you say to yourself, well, if the tapping of a furnace fan is like chalk taps on a blackboard, then maybe this thing over here is like that thing over there, and suddenly you get a little rush because it comes to you that all things may be related to each other. It's like touching Emerson's Oversoul. Good metaphor, handled deftly, can give you that kind of a rush. When Tranströmer says that a light bulb just shut off, and fading into darkness is like "a tablet of light dissolving in a glass of darkness," most of us feel a terrific thrill. I think it's because we briefly sense this relatedness of all things.

Meek: That's exactly right. It's the entry for December 24, "Well below freezing and still." And there's a lot here, in the fine balance of the fifth line, or the lean you give to fancy, as if to suggest the fanciful. And I can't help notice that in the image of chalk on the board, and frost against a black field, there's a figure similar to one you call on in your essay "Lights on a Ground of Darkness." Can we see these early morning walks as taken against such a dark ground, where lights, gems, shine through?

Kooser: Yes, indeed, a very dark ground, considering the problems with my health that I was facing. I do want the light, though, to spark from ordinary things. I like to look at the ordinary until the extraordinary begins to show through its skin, like a candle burning in a paper sack. I'm thinking of calling my next collection "Local Wonders" which would suggest some of the wonder in the ordinary.

Meek: Isn't there also in poems such as this one a correspondence that comes from a world we are alien to? We find deer tracks and featherings, and "on a barb there's a little scrap of hide / like a piece of cornshuck." Traces of things, often quite stunning and elegant. I'm thinking of the smoke that comes from farmers burning thousands of sandhill cranes "killed in a sudden spring blizzard." Their smoke appears "indecisive, standing on thin legs / leaning one way and then another."

Kooser: I was out walking this morning and got to thinking about how human consciousness, awareness might be a better word, sets us apart from the natural world. Makes us alien, to use your term. Not until we die and our ashes are dispersed or buried or our bodies finally decay despite embalming, do we become a true part of the world that our awareness as living, conscious humans separated us from. But, of course, it is this unique human awareness of nature, of the other world, that lets us write poems. So in a sense each poem testifies to our awareness of our separateness. My two old dogs are going to die before long, but they don't know that. If they knew it, they'd be writing poems, it seems to me. Consciousness may have been an evolutionary fluke, and perhaps when our species is gone, it will never arise again. The allegory of Adam and Eve and the Tree of Knowledge is about the separateness brought about through attaining consciousness, isn't it?

Meek: That's what we learn from Goodman Brown's compulsive flight back to the primal woods, isn't it? That we know we are naked, and, what seems as true for us as for Brown, we know that we know. And among the blessings of our outcast hurt are those acts of a deliberate awareness we know as letters and poems.

One quality I admire in your new poems is their keen pulse of repetition, by which the observer in making his rounds is so clearly connected to life in other instances, reading its signs as a watcher of the morning. I have in mind your poem of December 12, a day noted as being "Sunny, still and cold."

Found, on the gravel road I walked this morning,
one beer can, part full of frozen tobacco juice
that when I shook it came apart like chunks of amber,
and a quarter-sized piece from a fluted china plate,
with a soft pink rose the size of a pencil eraser
and a curl of flying, pale blue ribbon. In a nearby tree,
five noisy crows who had seen me stooping there
were busy creating a plausible story.

The notations on a morning's weather that you provide as headings to these poems have the effect of immediately grounding a reader. After we've decided that much, we can then go on, walker and crows alike, to construct in different ways the same "plausible story." Your speaker makes me think of Thoreau in his morning duties, waking another day to a correspondence from other than human nations.

Kooser: I do like to set poems into the context of a specific day, a specific set of physical circumstances, because like most of us I respond to my surroundings. The metaphors that are given to me on a cold and rainy Tuesday are to me an important part of that specific day. The same figures would not likely arrive on the sunny next day.

Meek: I admire in your poems, new and old, the hard core that lets a narrative go unsaid, beyond first mention. Like your acrylics, they use all their space—"variously inhabit it"—and I've wondered if you don't actually envision in poems the space to be filled.

Kooser: I don't know, Jay, about the last. I don't think I envision the space as you suggest, or at least it doesn't quite feel that way. I think it's more a matter of pacing and timing, as in the oral delivery of an anecdote or story. There comes a moment when I know it's time to pull that magic string that brings all the little knots up into the one big one.

Meek: *Winter Morning Walks* begins with an introductory poem in which the "quarry road" you walk unfolds in the "morning darkness" like a "bolt / of softly glowing fabric . . . spilled out and then lovingly / smoothed by my father's hand." Did your father own a dry goods store? As you remember him spooling out the cloth, you have him say to a customer, "Here, . . .

you can make something special with this." That seems to say something very particular about the nature of imagination for you, your imagination, especially since it's clear that this trope starts off the book for a reader. And doesn't the father serve as the weaver-in-absentia, the discloser who casts out the bolt that unfolds the fresh cloth, and—as I seem to remember from my boyhood—releases its rich scent?

How much the final lines of the introductory poem resonate for me, without claiming anything like "meaning," but certainly not disclaiming such connections as one might have made in the language, of the father who has made the poet, who casts and casts out, whose words after all these years stay with the son. Those lines are like a spell cast over the hundred poems.

Kooser: That poem was written about halfway through the sequence, and the minute I wrote it, I knew that it should be moved to the front to introduce the others. After all, it is the road (and walking it and taking advantage of its wonders) that is the common element in all the poems. Here is my father, holding the open road before me and saying, "You can make something special with this." That is, out of regular morning walks along a common gravel road a person can make something special. Earlier in this conversation, I mentioned my short poem, or statement:

If you can awaken
inside the familiar
and discover it strange
you need never
leave home.

That applies here. My father was a retail store manager in a small town. The store in which he worked was probably about the same size as the dime store in your family. He had started out in business right out of high school as the drapery salesman. In that role, he appears in this poem, rolling out a bolt of fabric and saying, as a good fabric salesman might say to a customer, "You can make something special with this." And so I have been given this road, if not literally by my father, then figuratively, have had it opened before me by my illness, and his admonition to me is to take what is before me, to take what life I have, and to make something special with it. There's a passage in Ecclesiastes that I have kept close at hand for many years: "Whatsoever thy hand findeth to do, do it with thy might, for there is no work, nor devise, nor knowledge, nor wisdom in the grave whither thou goest." It is the only biblical passage I can quote without wondering if I got it correctly.

If I owe my literary interests to anyone in the family, I owe much to my father, who was a marvelous small-town fabulist and raconteur. I remember one of his friends saying, "I'd rather hear your father describe somebody than see the person myself." He was not a literary man, though. We had only a few books in the house, a set of the novels of John Fox Jr., a collected stories of Balzac, a Shakespeare. Remember V. K. Ratliff, Faulkner's itinerant sewing-machine salesman? The people in the little towns await his arrival to hear him deliver the news. Dad was that kind of man. He could have had a successful career in the theater, but of course there was no avenue in that direction in Ames, Iowa, in the 1930s. He'd been in high-school plays and talked about that experience with great pleasure all his life. He and Mother belonged to a play-reading group when I was a boy, and the members sometimes met at our house. Iowa State University was nearby, and my parents had friends on the faculty who were a part of this group. I remember them reading from Noel Coward once or twice, but my memories are pretty dim as to the specifics of those evenings. I only remember how enchanted I was by them.

Meek: Of course, it's striking how much either of our fathers must have relied on communal experiences to place what for them was art, to define it. However differently they made it, they had to take part in it for the unadorned life was in some way insufficient. I believe that to be true for my own father. And yet I think how much he must have mistrusted, I want to say—although it's not that, but rather "reserved a special place for"—metaphor. Except in hymns. How can anyone be supported by imaginings that exceed their agents, or by any vehicle that makes its tenor loopy? Or by music, which unnerved even such a transformative poet as Rilke? Maybe that's why I can't easily give myself to figurative language or associational thought. But I do love to read poets who swing on birches and don't care to come down.

I wonder if what I have in mind isn't the dubious tendency of some metaphors to trash what they transform. An aesthetic of newness and consumption. I see a quite different aesthetic in these morning poems of yours where old things linger, where familiar objects stand in for familiar objects, and strangeness is the act of a mind extending itself across what it knows. Maybe it's less an act of discovery than of confirmation. In a barbershop quartet, dissonances among harmonic voices.

Kooser: I am very interested in your ideas in the last paragraph. Could we say that metaphor can't be used to get at the truth? That it might be used to make the truth a little sharper, clearer, perhaps more engaging but that it holds no inherent truth in itself?

Meek: Of course, some metaphors form their own truths. But I see your poems as transparencies in which objects are held to one another, as if in brotherhood, while reverberations pass strangely between them.

I believe there are metaphors that have their own kind of dispensation, like prayer or music, and that they reach beyond conventional forms of reference and response. I suppose I'm thinking mostly of compensatory metaphors as figures that cannot transform us—or our place or our condition—but rather ensure that what we want to free ourselves from will continue and continue to imprison us.

The reader might feel transported by the language, as we do in arriving at the grand last paragraph in Katherine Anne Porter's "Flowering Judas." In it, the intensity of language and the evocative reference of language effect in the reader a release from the terrible closeness that Laura has to live through: no past, no future, everything caught in the narrative present. But when she wakes in the morning, her life will be unchanged; she'll still have to negotiate among dubious figures, quite literally powerless to leave on her own. We get to feel exhilaration, and transport, but at her expense.

One more thing for today. When I consider the importance of having an "eye for resemblances" and a delight in play. I think of a poem in your *A Book of Things*:

> The nest of some tiny bird,
> each blade of dead grass
> seemingly spun into its place
> on the potter's wheel
> of her busy movements,
> preparing a vessel for song.

I love the comparison of the nest to a cup or bowl, and, secondarily, as something shaped by either the bird's turning body or human hand. These are two things you keep true to one another, each with function, each rather homely and dear. Both terms of the metaphor remain distinct, the nest as vessel and the unspoken cup or bowl as vessel. And what helps keep them separate is that as vessels they're from the same set of things, which holds them in balance, in their own literal company.

I understand *A Book of Things* as a preface to *Winter Morning Walks*. It's pleasing to see your new book of poems as a summoning up of family and neighbors, of your dogs, of places and things you've known and cared for. They're rich in the celebration of living of recurrent sightings and of returning to the words one chooses to live with, as if they too had become old friends. And like so many of your poems, they're remarkably gentle.

Kooser: If I'm lucky, someone someday will find my poems and see them as the catalog of the things I found delightful during my life.

Meek: Here's something else that's come to mind in reading *Winter Morning Walks*. I wonder if you think of the poems in your book as fragments, identified as much by their setting in the whole work as within themselves. I'm thinking of Stéphane Mallarme's *A Tomb for Anatole*. It's a gathering of more than two hundred brief poems—fragments, really—after the death of his eight-year-old son from what might have been "rheumatic fever." The pieces are discontinuous, although segments are often roughly attached to one another, in the same disjointed sentence. Who can say they are stanzas merely, or poems, or entirely a poet's notes to himself? One senses in their fragmentation an urgency that comes after a loss, as if it could be recovered by straining for what needs to be said, as if word were deed.

Ted, is it possible the fragment is a poetic form, much as a sestina is a form for cyclic completion? And, if so, what do you see as its formal premise? It's aesthetic and emotional understanding?

Kooser: I'm afraid my answer, like so many of my answers, begs the obvious: If we take for example a poem that appears by itself in a magazine, a part of our experience as readers will be an ascertaining of some sense of the poet's emotional state when the poem was composed. And one of your collections of poems, Jay, or one of mine, might have sixty separate emotional settings or tones because the poems will not have been composed sequentially and will have been pretty widely separated in time. It is part of the reader's work to get a sense of that setting. But in a sequence of poems or perhaps stanzas written one after another, the emotional setting will of course be more consistent. So, I suppose, part of the form of a linked sequence might be seen to be a consistent emotional undercurrent. You introduced Mallarme's book by giving me the emotional setting, which prepared me for my experience with the poems that follow. My prefatory note to *Winter Morning Walks* is designed to do a similar thing, to prepare the reader for the relatively consistent emotional climate of the sequence. In a way, the individual poems or sections are freed from the responsibility of conveying the emotional setting and can be more brief and imagistic. And, of course, I see the fragment as a form just as I see a postcard providing a form for the writer's message.

When Karl Shapiro was writing the prose poems of *The Bourgeois Poet*, he told me he used the sheet of typewriter paper as his form. He would roll it into the typewriter and write till he closed in on the end of the paper, then stop. It was learning *that* that made me start thinking about postcards as defining forms.

Meek: In Oslo's Nasjonalgalleriet, there's a room of fourteen paintings by Edvard Munch. They fight for space, for attention, and *The Scream*—which one thinks he's seen times before—is overwhelmed by powerful paintings of sick rooms, where people are ill. There's a self-portrait Munch made while recovering from flu during the pandemic of 1919. These are all quite moving and recall the double portrait Goya made of himself in his doctor's arms, or the self-portraits Rembrandt made in old age. Do you suppose that as surely as there's a genre of painting we call portraiture, there's a subset about illness and recovery, and if there might be, what are some of the works we should include in it? What are the qualities this art embraces and evokes? And is there a poetry of illness and recovery?

Kooser: I'm certainly not an authority on painting, but on first impression, it seems to me that there are lots of sickbed and deathbed paintings, and I can't think of one that conveys recovery. We might know from another source that someone who was portrayed recovered, but we couldn't get that from the canvas, unless my ignorance prevents my seeing this. This is probably because a recovery would be so difficult to depict. We know when we see Marat's body slumped in the bathtub that he isn't going to get out and towel himself off, but if he were to open his eyes, even, or smile, even, how would we know he was going to recover? Sickness and death are pretty much static and are good subjects for the static art of painting, but recovery is a progress, something in forward motion and very difficult to depict in a static form.

In addition to the visual representations of the sick and dying, there are the paintings of Francis Bacon, in which figures seem to represent states of madness. Bacon's loose brushwork gives these static figures the suggestion of motion, making them all the more frightening. I have seen some of the paintings to which you refer, and Munch sometimes attempts this kind of motion, too, through brushwork or drawing as in *The Scream*. In addition to the oil of *The Scream*, I think there are woodcuts, which to me emphasize by their inflexibility the static nature of the fear.

Since poetry moves forward over a brief segment of time, and can be truly narrative (as opposed to painting, which, when it is described as narrative merely means that a story is present, and all elements—beginning, middle, and ending—are all there at once), a poem could show a process of recovery, could it not? And there are hundreds of poems in which the form seems to be a process of recovery. Or, more accurately, a process from dilemma into hope, a kind of recovery. My book is an extension of this: the dilemma of illness and the recovery or revival of hope.

Meek: What I'm curious about is how you kept your sequence going and how you could ensure that the poems were not only of approximate density and clarity, but that in sequence they might lead convincingly beyond the sum of themselves.

Kooser: For me, the main problem of trying to write a poem every day is that when, after a while, you look at what you've finished, it looks like the work of someone who has been trying to write a poem every day! As I wrote these morning walk poems, I wasn't at all sure that they would add up to more than the mere sum of the parts. I wrote 130 of them and could see when I had finished that I could sacrifice one in four. The ones that failed were often too precious, I thought, or too much like others in the sequence. I do think that my anxiety about a recurrence of cancer during these months, and my anger at finding myself at such a place in life, made me a better writer than I would have been if I had tried a sequence like that under other circumstances. I thought these might be my last poems.

Interview with Ted Kooser

Mary K. Stillwell / 2003

Mary K. Stillwell, author of *The Life and Poetry of Ted Kooser* (Lincoln: University of Nebraska Press, 2013), conducted this previously unpublished interview after taking Ted Kooser's first tutorial at the University of Nebraska–Lincoln, while working on her dissertation on contemporary Nebraska poetry. The interview took place in February 2003, the year before Kooser was named US poet laureate. He had recently completed the manuscript for his Pulitzer Prize–winning collection, *Delights and Shadows*. Permission to print the interview was granted by Mary K. Stillwell.

Mary K. Stillwell: When did you begin writing? Writing poetry, in particular?

Ted Kooser: I started writing when I was in third or fourth grade, but I didn't get serious about it until I was an adolescent. I was beginning to think of myself as a writer when I was eighteen or nineteen, I suppose.

Stillwell: Did you start out writing poetry?

Kooser: Yes. And short essays. The first things I had published were brief nonfiction pieces, a little sugary, published in the student literary magazine at Iowa State.

Stillwell: When did you come to Nebraska? Why?

Kooser: I came in the autumn of 1963 to go to graduate school. I'd taught high school for a year and knew that wasn't for me. Karl Shapiro was teaching here, and I admired what he was writing and had written, and I wanted to work with him.

Stillwell: Did Karl Shapiro influence your work?

Kooser: Oh, yes, very much. There's an interesting article about him by John Updike in a current issue of *Harper's* that emphasizes the fact that Karl was interested in writing about things, and I learned to write about things from Karl. That's things as in objects apart from the poet. The German for a thing poet is *Dinge Dichter*, and Updike picks up on that. I remember Karl describing me as another *Dinge Dichter*.

Stillwell: Literally, a "thing poet," one who writes of things. What made Nebraska a companionable place for you to write?

Kooser: I came here to go to school, and I liked it well enough to stay. After one year in graduate school, I knew I was not cut out to be a scholar, and I got a job in an insurance company. That kept me occupied for the next thirty-five years. There was no creative-writing program back then, or perhaps I might have stayed in school and wound up teaching full time somewhere.

Stillwell: What led you to start a publishing company here? How important has it been to your work?

Kooser: I never really published a great deal with my little company, a couple of literary magazines and a few books, things I wanted to do, books by people who deserved some attention. I'm especially proud of having done Don Welch's first book and Bill Kloefkorn's early books. The literary magazines were a lot of work because I did all the work myself, on my own money. But I made a lot of interesting connections through those magazines, worthwhile correspondences that I've maintained for many years. These days Windflower Press is mostly a nuisance to me, requiring me to keep tax records, etcetera. Short of a miracle, I can't imagine that I'll keep it going much longer.

Stillwell: And your anthology is used pretty widely.

Kooser: *As Far as I Can See* [Charles Woodard, editor, Windflower Press, 1989] has been pretty successful. Yes, yes. But interest in it has faded in recent years, and I doubt if I'll reprint it again.

Stillwell: If you were putting together a course on plains literature, who and what would you include?

Kooser: I'd want to include books on fauna and flora and plains geology and geography and ethnology, and then once the students were steeped in the place, we could look at the standard plains writers we think about Willa Cather, Mari Sandoz, and others.

Stillwell: What poets would you include?

Kooser: The poet I would emphasize the most—he might well be the most important plains poet ever—would be Thomas McGrath. His work is filled with plains history, is very broad and all-encompassing and quite beautiful. His *Letter to an Imaginary Friend* [1970] is a very important book in which he gives us a sweeping picture of the radical AG movement in North Dakota in the early years of the twentieth century. Then, in addition to McGrath, I might pick and choose among all the other plains poets and put together a little anthology of representative pieces. Each of the poets I think of as being of the Great Plains has written at least one or two good poems, and one could draw those works together.

Stillwell: How is place represented in Nebraska poetry? Is there anything that makes it represented uniquely here?

Kooser: I'd be hard put to generalize about that. Every poet is different, every poem. As to uniqueness, I think that maybe one characteristic of our writing here is a prevalence of conversational, idiomatic, anecdotal poems. There's too much of that kind of poem. Bill Kloefkorn manages it very well and has influenced a lot of younger poets, but Bill's imitators don't do it nearly as well and fall back on a kind of corny cracker barrelism.

Stillwell: When did you or how did you—or *did* you—come to realize that place was important to your writing?

Kooser: I really know nothing of the world other than Iowa and Nebraska. People say you have to write what you know, and that's what I know. I don't know how to write in any other way than with my feet firmly planted in place.

Stillwell: Are there, do you think, any pitfalls in writing about a particular place?

Kooser: No, unless you object to being branded a regionalist, which I do not. And, of course, there's a kind of provincial boosterism you need to stand apart from. A number of years ago, a couple of plains poets got the idea of doing an anthology and asked poets they knew to contribute work and essays based on a number of questions the editors furnished. I got the feeling as I read the questions that what these people were looking for were ways in which they could prove once and for all that plains writers were better writers than writers in other places in the country. I wrote a little piece called "Nonsense of Place," in which I said that it really doesn't matter where you're from, that we out here aren't any better writers here than anywhere else. They didn't want to hear that and didn't publish my contribution.

Stillwell: I wonder why [*laughs*]. Maybe they were after what makes us unique?

Kooser: No, no. I know these guys. I know what they were after. They wanted us all wearing yellow blazers with crests on the pockets, like members of a chamber of commerce.

Stillwell: As senior editor for the Plains Humanities Alliance Great Books of the Great Plains, what are the criteria for selecting representative books or authors to represent each state?

Kooser: The work of selecting the books has now been farmed out to general editors in each of the five states. I told the people heading the project that I didn't really want any accountability. I was really too busy to take on the responsibility, so my involvement is minimal at this point. The idea was originally mine, and I did a lot of work on the project when I was going to publish the list as a book. I did a lot of research at that time, and my criteria then were that the book had to be readily accessible at either public libraries or in print, that it be of quality, by reasonable standards, usually by a consensus of readers. The books should not be strictly academic. My concept was that a more general audience might be interested in this and benefit by it. I wanted it to be the kind of thing that, say, if a young woman takes a position at the Wells Fargo bank here and wants to know something about the place she's moved to, she could punch up the website and find books of all kinds. I wasn't interested in it being a tool for research, but rather an introduction to our place.

Stillwell: It seems our state has produced a number of very good writers in a number of genres.

Kooser: Compared to the population. We have about a million and a half people. Tongue in cheek, I did a review a while back of a book of poems and said that you could count on there being about one good poet for every two hundred thousand people or something like that. Since South Dakota has half the population of Nebraska, there should be half as many poets up there. And, generally, that's true—about half as many South Dakota writers are publishing quality work. North Dakota is even smaller, and there are still fewer good writers there. Minnesota has a lot of poets, but they have a much larger population to draw from.

Stillwell: How have your writing habits changed since you retired from the insurance business and now teach at the university?

Kooser: I have a lot more time. I've been very productive in the last five years. Before I retired, it would take quite a while, stealing time from work and responsibilities, to put a book together. Now I can devote a whole day to writing if I want to. Right now, I'm not teaching a class, and I just have a few independent-study students who don't take up much of my time. Even when I'm doing my one-on-one tutorials with graduate students, I don't find it gets in the way of my writing. Talking to students about writing is stimulating.

Stillwell: Are you still an early morning writer?

Kooser: Oh, yes. I usually work from four thirty or five until 7:30, maybe, and then take a little break and eat breakfast and maybe later in the morning come back to it for a little while. I rarely work in the afternoon or evening, when my head has gotten too cluttered up with odds and ends from the day.

Stillwell: Tough life [*laughs*]. Where did the idea for *Local Wonders* come from? How did you set about writing it?

Kooser: Well, there are many other books like *Local Wonders*, in which people wrote their way through the seasons. Hal Borland's *Sundial of the Seasons*, Donald Culross Peattie's *An Almanac for Moderns*, and so on. And I've always liked books about place, like Sue Hubbell's book about keeping bees and Donald Hall's *String Too Short to Be Saved*. Those books are what I like to read. And it came to me that, well, maybe such a book is something I could put together. I had all these little pieces I'd written over the years, and I began to arrange them by the seasons, and they quickly fell into a pleasant order. I never set out to write that book; some of the pieces are ten and twenty years old.

Stillwell: Who is Laura Casari [listed prominently in the book's acknowledgments], and what was her involvement with the manuscript?

Kooser: Laura's an old, dear friend of mine. She taught technical writing at UNL's east campus for years, is retired now. She read the manuscript in a pretty raw stage.

Stillwell: Most people who mention the book, mention in particular the last section, which compares life to a long walk through the cars of a crowded passenger train. Was that written at the end to pull the book together?

Kooser: I wrote it on New Year's Eve, a year before I finished the manuscript. Often around the holidays, I find myself writing a deeply reflective piece like that, and this one fit nicely at the end of the book. I wanted the book to end in an upbeat way, and even though I'm talking about life inevitably coming to an end, at the end of that section, everyone lifts their glasses in a toast, an affirmation.

Stillwell: What is the relationship between *Local Wonders* and *Winter Morning Walks*?

Kooser: Well, obviously, they're both a kind of calendar; they're serially arranged. *Winter Morning Walks* is tighter, which you would expect from poetry, more finely tuned, I suppose, although some of the things in *Local Wonders* I see as being prose poems. And there are pieces in *Local Wonders* that were originally written in verse that I converted to prose because they just felt more accessible that way. There's a piece in there about the spring thaw, for example, that was once a lined-out poem that I changed back.

A woman here in town, who's been a good friend of ours for many years, said that she was surprised that *Local Wonders* was such a spiritual book. It's not anything that I ever intended, but it is certainly there, and somebody here in the English department whose intelligence I really respect said to another friend, who mentioned it to me, that *Local Wonders* is a book about preparing for death. Very interesting. I wouldn't have thought of that or consciously worked that out, but it does make sense to some degree.

Stillwell: It must be interesting to get feedback.

Kooser: I've been publishing poetry now for years, and it seems like I've finally written something that's of use to people. I've always gotten good response from my poetry, but it's such a private art with such a small, dedicated audience. Now I'm getting letters from people all over. I really enjoy it.

Stillwell: Tell me about the Barnes & Noble selection. How did that happen?

Kooser: It's my understanding that University of Nebraska Press took all their forthcoming books in bound galleys back to the New York Book Fair, and it just happened that the Discover New Writers' editor happened upon the book and liked it. She was particularly taken by the passage about my mother sewing, or at least that's what she said to somebody at the press. And from then on, it was part of the Discover Program. As Steve Hillard here in the department said, if you want to pick just two readers, Barnes & Noble are the ones you want.

Stillwell: What are you working on now?

Kooser: I'm working on a little book on how to write poetry. For beginners. Actually, it's on revising poems. I'm also finishing up a manuscript of poems that will be published in a year, *Delights and Shadows*, and a book that Jim Harrison and I wrote together is coming out soon. I just got the bound galleys for that. It's called *Braided Creek*.

Stillwell: Is that Copper Canyon?

Kooser: Yes, and *Delights and Shadows* will be from Copper Canyon, too, on their spring 2004 list. That book has been about ten years in the making. I was looking at it this morning. It's a thicker book of poems than I've done in the past, and the manuscript runs nearly a hundred pages. Most of my books are sixty, sixty-five pages.

Stillwell: What advice would you give an aspiring Nebraska writer?

Kooser: I think the command, "Read," ought to be enough. Every artist learns by imitation. Nobody just starts out—it doesn't just happen. Those people who painted those paintings in the caves of France, someone showed them how to do it. We learn by copying. And the more poems someone reads, the better they get at writing.

Stillwell: Any particular writers?

Kooser: I hesitate to do that. You can learn from just about anything you read. I've never read a book I didn't get something out of. And I'm big on browsing. When I was still at the insurance company, I used to go over to Bennett Martin Library over the noon hours and walk into the stacks at random and just take something off the shelf without thinking about it. Invariably, I'd find something interesting. It's the habit of reading that's so important in the development of writers.

Stillwell: Which leads me back to your book on writing. How are you approaching it?

Kooser: Well, it's called the *Poetry Home Repair Manual.* And I'm doing it by steps. The first step you do this; the second step you do that. It proceeds through titles, openings, working with nouns and verbs, adjectives, adverbs, basics like that, and then I get into things I'm more adept at, working with figures of speech, for example, and throughout the manuscript there are comments about the environment for contemporary poetry. I think it's going to be a useful book. I've got about sixty pages finished, which is just the first two or three sections, and I've got a lot of material that I've yet to organize. I've been working on it a little bit every week. I find that it feels much more rich as far as its depth if I really take it easy and just don't push it, just feed things into it. I might get it done by the end of this year, but who knows what will happen to it from there.

Stillwell: There seems to me there would be a market.

Kooser: It's a very conversational and commonsensical book; there's no effete, literary stuff in it at all, which will frustrate a few people, I suppose, those who thrive on that aloofness. It's very much opposed to elitism in literature.

Stillwell: I like the emphasis on revision. Of the books I've used, Mary Oliver's *Handbook* has been the most successful with students, and they related to it well, but it didn't specifically address revision the way you are.

Kooser: I like Oliver's book, too. Mine is really much more of a manual. Most of the books that advertise themselves as being about writing start out to follow that prescription, then veer off into collections of old book reviews and so on.

Stillwell: Ok, I've come to the end of my questions. Do you have any questions you'd like to answer?

Kooser: No, I don't think so. I'd like to say that John Nims said before he died that a nation only needs a half dozen poets. I'm completely of another mind on that. It seems to me that there couldn't be anything wrong with a nation in which everybody was trying to write poems. Considering the way in which most people use their time, what would be wrong with a world in which everyone was writing? You might say that it'd be awful to have to weed through all that stuff, but, as it turns out, we have to wade through a lot already. Let the literary critics do the weeding; it's their job. As poets, we're just trying to do the best we can. Bill Stafford, used to say that he tried to get the editor within him pushed out of the way. He wanted to let the people who publish magazines decide what was worth keeping. He just wanted to write.

Stillwell: Your students from the last three semesters comment on the little pieces that you send out to them by email.

Kooser: Since I teach tutorially, meeting each student privately, I found the emails were a good way for me to say something to everyone all at once. I'm using some of those emails as raw material for pieces in *The Poetry Home Repair Manual.*

Stillwell: It was helpful and continues to be helpful to them because it helps to hear what you're thinking and provokes them to think about what they're doing.

Kooser: Yes, I'm going to continue to do that kind of thing while I'm teaching. Besides, it's very good practice for me to look at a poem at home, a poem that I like, and then to try to explain why I like it.

"American Life" from Its Poet Laureate

Terry Gross / 2005

This interview aired on NPR's *Fresh Air* on April 4, 2005. It is reprinted with the permission of WHYY, Inc. *Fresh Air with Terry Gross* is produced by WHYY in Philadelphia and distributed by NPR.

Terry Gross: This is *Fresh Air*. I'm Terry Gross. My guest, Ted Kooser, is the US poet laureate, the thirteenth writer to have that distinction. He doesn't like poems that require elaborate explanations, and he doesn't write them. His new book, *The Poetry Home Repair Manual*, offers practical advice for beginning poets. His book *Winter Morning Walks*, published in 2000, is a series of short poems that he sent on postcards to his friend, the writer Jim Harrison, during the period Kooser was recovering from oral cancer. Many of those poems are about mortality; that's a subject he's always written about. His latest poems are collected in his book *Delights and Shadows*. Kooser is the first poet laureate to be chosen from the Great Plains. He grew up in Iowa and lives in Nebraska. The writer Charles Baxter said of Kooser: "He has great gifts for both portraiture and landscape and another gift for dramatizing what is nearly invisible. He is a seer." As Kooser points out in *The Poetry Home Repair Manual*, you'll never be able to make a living writing poems. He hasn't. Until his recent retirement, he worked at a life insurance company. Let's start with his poem "A Death at the Office."

Ted Kooser: This poem is probably almost forty years old. I had my first job in the insurance business working for a company called Bankers Life Nebraska. And this was a woman in our department who had died, and the poem is set on the morning following her death.

"A Death at the Office"

The news goes desk to desk
like a memo: Initial
and pass on. Each of us marks
Surprised or Sorry.

The management came early
and buried her nameplate
deep in her desk. They have boxed up
the Midol and Lip-Ice,

the snapshots from home,
wherever it was—nephews
and nieces, a strange, blurred cat
with fiery, flashbulb eyes

as if it grieved. But who grieves here?
We have her ballpoints back,
her bud vase. One of us tears
the scribbles from her calendar.

Gross: The details in that poem are so recognizable: the Lip Ice in the drawer, "the snapshots from home." I love your description of "the blurred cat with / fiery flashbulb eyes." You write in your book *The Poetry Home Repair Manual* about how important it is to have details in a poem.

Kooser: Oh, yes.

Gross: Can you talk a little bit about the details in *that* poem, about deciding what to put in?

Kooser: The more specific the detail, the more true the experience seems. If I had said—rather than *Lip Ice—lip salve*, it would have been a different thing altogether. But using the brand name even makes it more specific and, therefore, more real . . . *somehow*. I'm not sure exactly how this works psychologically, but this is something I've learned over the years.

Gross: When you say at the end, "But who grieves here?"—here in the office—what were you thinking with that?

Kooser: I'm, of course, speaking ironically at that point. There were people who felt sorry about it, but it seemed as if the management was moving too quickly to just sort of obliterate her from history. So I'm speaking tongue in cheek at the end about, "We have her ballpoints back, / her bud vase." In other words, "After all, we got our things back," that sort of thing.

Gross: The office that you refer to in that poem, the office at which you worked for many years, was a life insurance company. And you worked there until retiring in 1999.

Kooser: That's right.

Gross: How did you end up a poet working in an insurance company for most of your career?

Kooser: Well, I was a poet first, and I came to Lincoln, Nebraska, to go to graduate school because Karl Shapiro, who was a famous, celebrated poet, was here, and I wanted to study with him. And I was given an assistantship as a graduate student and just did a *terrible* job as a graduate student. I didn't do anything I was supposed to. All I cared about was poetry and hanging around with Karl Shapiro. So at the end of the year, they kind of threw me out of the graduate program, said they were cutting off my assistantship money and so on. So I had to find something to do. My first wife had a job teaching school, but I needed some sort of source of income. And I was fumbling through the paper, and I came upon this management trainee job at an insurance company, and I thought, "Well, maybe I could do that, make some money, and I can go back to school on my own tuition," and so on. So for some reason or other, they hired me to do this. I had no business training. I had never had a business course. I didn't even know what insurance was *really*. But they hired me, and I went to work there. And I began writing my poems early in the morning. I'd get up at four thirty or five and write until I had to get ready to go to work. That set me up in a habit that I have persisted in all these years. And I worked for that first company for eight years, and then I moved on to another company and did the rest of my time at the second company. But the job was always, really, to support me as a writer. But I never really returned to academic life. I don't think I would have been good at it, although I am teaching a little bit now in my dotage.

Gross: So what was your position at the life insurance company that you worked at?

Kooser: I started out answering letters from policyholders who were writing in about their beneficiaries and so on. And then I moved into underwriting. The underwriter is the person who reads your application and decides whether or not your medical history will allow you to have the policy. I did that for twenty-five years, probably. And then I moved into the marketing department and public relations as a writer, and I headed up a department of public relations, did the company newsletters and so on. And that's what I was doing. I retired as a vice president of public relations for Lincoln Benefit Life company.

Gross: One of the things I find really fascinating here is that, as a poet, many of your poems are about mortality. Now you worked for a *life* insurance company, which is also about mortality. But, you know, the language that you use in a *life* insurance company to discuss life and death is really different from the language you're going to use as a poet in talking about it.

Kooser: Yes, I think that's right. The language of poetry is not the same sort of actuarial language for sure. Having been an underwriter all those years and reading medical reports day after day about people being ill and having fatal illnesses sometimes was a kind of morbid experience for me that I think must have soaked into my bones a little bit. But in many ways, poetry is really about keeping death in the corner of the room and acknowledging it's there and celebrating life because death is there waiting for us. I think a great deal of literary poetry is that way. So I came to that kind of naturally, I think.

Gross: Well, there's a poem I want you to read that I think perfectly fits the description that you just gave of poetry [*laughs*]. This is a poem called the "Mourners."

Kooser: OK.

Gross: Could you tell us when you wrote it?

Kooser: I wrote this maybe ten, fifteen years ago after a funeral here locally. It was a sunny day, and everybody filed out of the funeral out onto the yard of the church. And it just struck me. I was standing apart from them. I like to be always sort of on the outside looking in. And I was standing apart from this group of mourners thinking about the way they were interacting. Here's the poem:

"Mourners"

After the funeral, the mourners gather
under the rustling churchyard maples
and talk softly, like clusters of leaves.
White shirt cuffs and collars flash in the shade:
highlights on deep green water.
They came this afternoon to say goodbye,
but now they keep saying hello and hello,
peering into each other's faces,
slow to let go of each other's hands.

Gross: That poem is included in Ted Kooser's latest collection of poems, *Delights and Shadows*, and Ted Kooser is the poet laureate of the US. There's no *I* in that poem. You're talking about them, about the mourners, but you're obviously there as a mourner yourself. Why did you not include yourself in the poem?

Kooser: Oh, gosh, Terry, I'm not sure about that. I very rarely use the first-person pronoun in a poem. I much prefer to be observing something at some detachment. And, I don't know. I don't think it would have felt right with me in that group of mourners. I needed to be standing apart looking at them.

Gross: We were talking about mortality and poetry. A few years ago, you really had to deal with your own mortality. You had oral cancer that affected your tongue. Your salivary glands were removed. You don't like to write about your feelings very much. You like to hold things at a distance. But when something like cancer hits you, how much of a distance can you put that? I mean, that's a hard one to . . .

Kooser: Yeah, when I was going through radiation therapy and so on, I didn't write at all. And then as I was coming out of it—since I had had head and neck radiation—I was photosensitive, and I couldn't be out in the sunlight without getting a terrible burn. So I would go for really early morning walks before the sun came up. I was trying to fasten on to life. When you've really looked death in the teeth, you tend to be very attentive to everything in life and want to celebrate even the least thing. So I would find something on my walk, a rock or something like that, and take it home and try to write a little poem. And then my friend Jim Harrison, who's a poet and novelist, was down in Arizona that winter, and I would paste them on a postcard and send them down to him. And it was really very good for me to be doing that. Poetry, for me, is a lot about trying to find some little piece of order in a very disorderly and sometimes chaotic world. And I was really facing disorder and chaos with cancer. But the fact that I could make a little poem every day was very reassuring to me, and it was quite a marvelous experience. I wrote 130 of them day after day. I'd never written like that under any other circumstances. It was a very unique experience. And the book, I think, shows that; it's a sort of a different critter from the rest of my work.

Gross: I think it's interesting that you wrote these poems each day on a postcard, Postcards are so informal and tossed off. You know, you don't labor over a postcard. Did the fact that you were putting them on a postcard help you fuss less and just write?

Kooser: You know, to tell you the truth, Terry, I think I put them on postcards because they only cost twenty-three cents. [*Laughter*]

Gross: That's a practical answer.

Kooser: Yeah, rather than the thirty-seven. But I've always liked a post-card almost as a literary form. Early in my writing career, I wrote poems based on the messages that had been written on old postcards that I'd find in antique shops and so on. They're so marvelously compressed because you have just this tiny, little space in which to write. And so all the poems in that book, of course, are quite small, too. But the messages are sometimes quite marvelous. A typical one would be, "Just a line or two to let you know that everything's all right before the postman comes, and I see him coming up the walk right now. Goodbye." You know, that sort of thing [*laughter*].

Gross: Sickness can make you very self-absorbed because you're monitoring the changes in your symptoms, you're often depressed, and there's not a lot of energy for *engaging* with the world sometimes? So what are some of the things that you found most healing? For instance, you say you took a walk every day before the same came up. Was that a way, in part, of getting out of yourself, of trying to get out of preoccupation with symptoms?

Kooser: Well, I think that, in part, surely, but, you know, I had been very ill, and head and neck radiation is very tough. And I really needed to get my strength back. So the walk was as much for exercise and trying to get my strength back as anything else. And it just happened that I was able—as I have been most of my life—was able to make something out of something else, to get a little bonus out of those walks by writing a little something about them.

Gross: I'd like you to read a poem from *Winter Morning Walks* from February 19. And maybe you could just set it up for us.

Kooser: All right. This is one of those poems I wrote following the walk. At this time, I'm back in the house, sitting in my chair with my little notebook. In this poem I talk about flickers. A flicker is an oversized wood-pecker. We have a lot of them out on the Great Plains. And this particular one is called the "yellow-shafted flicker." They are marvelous big birds. And so here we go.

"february 19"

Thirty-five degrees and drizzling.

When I switched on a light in the barn loft
late last night, I frightened four flickers
hanging inside, peering out through their holes.
Confused by the light, they began to fly

Wildly from one end to the other,
their yellow wings slapping the tin sheets
of the roof, striking the walls, scrabbling
and falling. I cut the light
and stumbled down and out the door and stood
in the silent dominion of starlight
till all five of our hearts settled down.

Gross: What a lovely image at the end. Was there a point when you thought of it that way, of all five of your hearts quieting down?

Kooser: Well, you know what that is, I think? It's being in the natural community. I'm afraid; they're afraid. And it was a frightening experience, frankly, to be up in that attic with these birds flying from one end to the other. They're good-sized birds. So my heart was beating wildly, and theirs were, too. And I just thought, "Well, we're all in this together."

Gross: I want you to read a poem from *Winter Morning Walks*, and this is one is set November 14. And I should mention that each poem starts with a description of the weather that day.

"november 14"

In the low forties and clear.

My wife and I walk the cold road
in silence, asking for thirty more years.

There's a pink-and-blue sunrise
with an accent of red:
a hunter's cap burns like a coal
in the yellow-gray eye of the woods.

Gross: That poem is almost in two parts; one part you're thinking about your mortality, and then the other part is more like a haiku or something.

Kooser: Yeah. Most poems would be the other way around; you'd have the image first and then the more general information afterwards. But in this one I'm with her, and yet I'm looking to the side and seeing something in the world other than us and other than our thoughts.

Gross: You know, the poet Sekou Sundiata once said something to the effect that the most important organ in your body is the one that hurts [*laughs*]. Think, how true. And you had a little tumor on your tongue that had to be removed, and the tongue is already at the center of your body. It's the part that you need for talking, for swallowing, for eating. And it's such a sensitive part of your body, too. As a writer, what was it like for you during that period right after the surgery—and I imagine there was a period like this—when you couldn't talk?

Kooser: Well, we were afraid, going into the surgery, that I'd have to learn to talk again and so on. As it turned out, they didn't have to take as much tissue as they thought they would. But my objective was to try to do everything the doctors told me to get through this, and I could set writing aside and doing poetry readings and stuff. One of the interesting things about this: I had a marvelous doctor at the University of Nebraska Medical Center in Omaha, a guy named Bill Lydiatt. We had our first appointment with him, and he said, "Now I'm going to have to take a piece of your tongue out. Do you do any public speaking?" And I said, "Well, nothing that I couldn't give up if I had to." And my wife was there, and she said, "Well, you know, he *is* a poet. He does poetry readings." So Bill made a note of that, and I didn't think any more of it. And then had another appointment in about a week or ten days, and by that time he had gone to the Omaha Public Library and checked out my books and read them. You know, you don't find doctors like that. It was a really marvelous thing. So it set us up in a relationship of trust that I rely on to this day.

Gross: But was there a period when you couldn't speak?

Kooser: No. Actually, I could speak. I didn't sound very good, but I began speaking almost the minute I came out of anesthesia.

Gross: And was there a period when you felt like the world was centered around your mouth and all the things that it couldn't do quite right?

Kooser: Oh, yeah. And, you know, there was a lot of discomfort with this, if not outright pain. The whole experience was very much day to day and fighting this terrible fear that something's going to happen next, that something more is going to happen and so on. I think cancer patients probably all must spend so much of their time looking over their shoulder, waiting for something to come sneaking up behind them again.

Gross: And I'm going to ask you now to read a poem that's *about* anxiety. And this was also from your book of a hundred poems that you wrote on postcards when you were sick. And this is a poem from December 25. It's a Christmas Day poem.

Kooser: OK.

"december 25"

Sunny and clear.

Sometimes, when things are going well,
the daredevil squirrel of worry
suddenly leaps from the back of my head
to the feeder, swings by his paws
and clambers up, twitching his question mark tail.
And though I try the recommended baffles—
tin cone of meditation, greased pipe
of positive thought—every sunflower seed
in this life is his if he wants it.

Gross: You'd worked your whole adult life in the life insurance business and wrote your poems in the very, very early morning. You quit at about the age of sixty after getting diagnosed with cancer. And now you're poet laureate, something I'm sure you were not expecting.

Kooser: Absolutely not.

Gross: How did you find out the news, and did you have any idea what it would mean, like what it would mean in terms of day-to-day life, what your duties would be?

Kooser: This is something that had *never* occurred to me in my wildest dreams, that it would ever happen to me. And I was at home one night—it was a Friday evening, I remember—and my wife was in Washington, DC, on business. And I got a phone call, and the man said, "Ted Kooser?"

I said, "Yes."

"Ted Kooser the *poet*?"

I said, "Yes."

He said, "I'm wondering how you'd like to be the next poet laureate of the United States." And I was so completely flummoxed by this and sort of stammering and trying to come up with something I could say, and so on, that he finally said, "Well, I think I'd better call you back tomorrow." It was like that. I've told this story: I immediately realized I had a couple of DVDs overdue at this little town nearby, and I jumped in the car and threw the movies on the seat, just completely taken up with all this poet laureate stuff. And I backed out of the garage and ripped the side mirror off on the side of the garage and drove all the way to the body shop and got the price on it; it was going to be $140 to fix the mirror, and went home groaning about having done that, pulled in the garage, and I still had the DVDs on the seat of the car, that sort of thing. It was like that for *weeks*, really.

Gross: Right. Now you're the first poet laureate from Nebraska or from the Great Plains, for that matter. Describe where you live in Nebraska.

Kooser: We are in eastern Nebraska. Lincoln is the state capital. We live about twenty miles north and west of Lincoln in an area of low, rolling hills that were eroded out of the plain by a glacier of some kind, some kind of formation. It's very pretty country. We have sixty-two acres. It's wooded, rolling hills, as I said, prairie grass. I have a little pond, some old farm buildings that I've converted to various purposes. I have a library building, a building where I can paint—I like to paint—things like that.

Gross: As I mentioned, you're the first poet laureate from the Great Plains. Do you think of your poetry as being rooted to your sense of place?

Kooser: Absolutely it is. We tell young writers to write what they know. I've never lived anywhere but Iowa and Nebraska, so that's what I know and that's what I write about. It is interesting to me, though, Terry. At times, people talk about seeing the Great Plains in my work. But if you look at the individual poems, you know, I have a poem about a tattooed man at a yard sale, and there's nothing specifically Nebraskan about that or Great Plains, for that matter. But there must be just enough little pieces throughout that add up to something.

Gross: I happen to really like that poem "Tattoo," that you just mentioned. It's in your collection *Delights and Shadows*. Would you read it for us?

Kooser: Sure.

"Tattoo"

What once was meant to be a statement—
a dripping dagger held in the fist
of a shuddering heart—is now just a bruise
on a bony old shoulder, the spot
where vanity once punched him hard
and the ache lingered on. He looks like
someone you had to reckon with,
strong as a stallion, fast and ornery,
but on this chilly morning, as he walks
between the tables at a yard sale

with the sleeves of his tight black T-shirt
rolled up to show us who he was,
he is only another old man, picking up
broken tools and putting them back,
his heart gone soft and blue with stories.

Gross: Did you know the man you were writing about?

Kooser: No, I didn't. There again, I was watching from afar, from some distance.

Gross: Do you have any tattoos?

Kooser: No, I don't.

Gross: [*Laughs*] I didn't think you did.

Kooser: Do you?

Gross: No, actually [*laughs*].

Kooser: OK.

Gross: No, but I often wonder what it will be like for people who have a lot of tattoos when they do get older.

Kooser: Oh, yeah. When I set that poem up at readings, I often say, "I'm sure that there are people in the audience who have tattoos." Tattoos have become very popular. "But this is a poem about what they look like after forty years."

Gross: Right. You grew up in Ames, Iowa. Your parents met when they both worked at the general store. Did that store exist when you were growing up?

Kooser: Yes. It was a dry-goods store. My father was the drapery manager, and my mother was a clerk who had come to Ames to live with her sister the way young women used to do. And they met there. Recently I had a lovely letter from a woman who remembered them as young people. She had moved away from Ames before I was even born. My parents were very formal. I never saw them embrace. I never saw them kiss. I think they were very fond of each other, but they were very, very formal. And this woman told me, "Your father was so dashing and handsome, and you mother was so sweet and demure. We thought it was the romance of the century."

Gross: [*Laughs*] What did your father end up doing professionally?

Kooser: He was a store manager all of his life, retired in his sixties. He was the first manager of the first branch of the big department store in Des Moines that the Younker brothers opened, back in the days when nobody had even thought of a branch store or any kind of franchising at all. And he stayed with Younkers all his life.

Gross: You write about your mother, that she kept track of every penny the family spent, and she kept track of it in dime-store spiral notebooks.

Kooser: Oh, yes.

Gross: Did you ever use those notebooks to write poems?

Kooser: Well, not the little ones that she used, but I sure used spiral notebooks, of course. Yes, Mother was amazing. She could live for a couple of weeks on a half a head of cabbage and two wieners, you know. She was just like that.

Gross: You say, "She walks beside me through every store I enter, saying, 'Do you really need that?'" [*Laughs*]

Kooser: Absolutely. She'll never let me go. I had her buy a couple of automobiles for me. She was so good at that kind of thing. She would walk into the showroom with her little Mamie Eisenhower pillbox hat on and carrying her little purse that matched, and somehow or other knock the price off several thousand dollars by the time she was done with these salesmen, who were wringing their hands and looking as if they'd been beaten.

Gross: Now I think your mother died while you were getting your radiation treatments?

Kooser: Actually, she died before I'd been diagnosed.

Gross: Oh.

Kooser: She died in March, and I was diagnosed in June.

Gross: Well, that's pretty close.

Kooser: Yeah. I've often thought that perhaps the grief of dealing with her dying, you know, had maybe knocked my immune system or something or other like that. Who knows? You never know about those things.

Gross: Did she live near you, and were you very close?

Kooser: She lived in Cedar Rapids, Iowa, which is about three hundred miles from where I live. But we were very close, and I talked to her a couple times a week. Yes, I was very devoted to her, and she to me, I think.

Gross: Now your father died—what?—about twenty years ago.

Kooser: Uh-huh. He did, yeah.

Gross: Yeah. You have a really interesting poem about your father that's in your latest collection, *Delights and Shadows*, that I'd like you to read for us and to introduce for us, if you wouldn't mind.

Kooser: All right. My father was born on May 19, and there's a story that's told in the poem about how his mother saw lilacs out the window at the moment of his birth. And I wrote this on his birthday.

"Father"

May 19, 1999

Today you would be ninety-seven
if you had lived, and we would all be
miserable, you and your children,
driving from clinic to clinic,
an ancient, fearful hypochondriac
and his fretful son and daughter,
asking directions, trying to read
the complicated, fading map of cures.
But with your dignity intact
you have been gone for twenty years,
and I am glad for all of us, although
I miss you every day—the heartbeat
under your necktie, the hand cupped
on the back of my neck, Old Spice
in the air, your voice delighted with stories.
On this day each year you loved to relate
that at the moment of your birth
your mother glanced out the window
and saw lilacs in bloom. Well, today
lilacs are blooming in side yards
all over Iowa, still welcoming you.

You know, Terry, on what would have been his hundredth birthday, my wife and I drove to Ames and went to that house, and there's a lilac bush in the yard that was blooming on that day, a one-hundred-year-old lilac.

Gross: You know, I'm not really sure how to take that poem, [*laughs*] like at the beginning when you talk about how you're glad he's dead and that he's not going through the indignities of being the ninety-seven-year-old hypochondriac looking for cures and everything. [*Laughs*] I don't know whether you mean that literally or whether you're trying to make him and you feel better about the fact that he had to die so long ago.

Kooser: Probably all of that. I think he probably was spared a great deal of emotional suffering because he really was a hypochondriac. He died of acute leukemia that had not even been diagnosed until he was really on his deathbed. But if someone at that time had told him that there was a cure in Paris, France, for that, he would have insisted on getting there somehow or other—even a quirky cure of some kind, a quack cure, he would have wanted to pursue. I think he was spared a tremendous amount of anxiety by just being taken.

Gross: How did somebody who's a hypochondriac and probably very absorbed in symptoms manage to not get diagnosed for so long?

Kooser: He seemed to be getting weaker and weaker over a number of months, and he'd been to the doctor. And I frankly don't know how it was not diagnosed. But he finally got so weak that he just collapsed, and he died within twenty-four hours.

Gross: What did your parents think about your life as a poet?

Kooser: Mother was more supportive than Dad was. When I was a young man, they thought, "Well, maybe he ought to be doing something a little more productive with his time." But I think they liked the idea. Of course, before they died, I was publishing poems in some pretty good magazines and so on, so they saw me as being somewhat successful, which helped, I think.

Gross: What got you interested in poetry? Did you read it when you were very young?

Kooser: I did read it. When we were in grade school, I had a couple of teachers who showed us how to write poems. And I wrote some little poems. One of them my mother kept, of course. It was "I love my dog, his padded paws. / At Christmas he's my Santa Claus," that sort of thing. I did a lot of that. And then in high school I wrote hundreds of long, tortured poems to my girlfriend. And fortunately, when we broke up, she burned them all, which is good.

Gross: [*Laughs*] No blackmail coming from her now.

Kooser: No, they're out there. They're gone. They're all ashes now. I think having grown up in a very ordinary, middle-class family in an ordinary, middle-class community, I always wanted to be different. I thought, "Oh, boy. How could I be different from the rest of these people?" So I painted and I wrote poems, and I tried to dress differently, all those things that you do in adolescence to try to set yourself apart in some way. And poetry kind of came out of that, in a way. And it was also about girls, you know. I kept seeing these pictures of rumpled old John Berryman with his grizzled beard, and he was surrounded by these gorgeous coeds. And I didn't have much going for me. I wasn't very good-looking. I had no athletic ability. But I thought, well, maybe *poetry* might be something I could do. I'm speaking somewhat tongue-in-cheek. But I think that was a big motivating part of it early on. And then I got hooked and started reading poetry. And before long, I was completely immersed in it, and I've never let up.

Gross: So much of poetry, as you've pointed out in your new book, is about finding the telling details and then describing them as accurately as possible. But, of course, memories fade, and I think that's part of the problem with any kind of writing. You want to kind of grasp those specific details, and you might not remember them anymore. You have a really good poem about memory called "Tectonics." Would you read that for us?

Kooser: Sure.

"Tectonics"

In only a few months
there began to be fissures
in what we remember,
and within a year or two,
the facts break apart
one from another
and slowly begin to shift
and turn, grinding,
pushing up over each other
until their shapes
have been changed
and the past has become
a new world.
And after many years,
even a love affair,
one lush green island
all to itself,
perfectly detailed
with even a candle
softly lighting a smile,
may slide under the waves
like Atlantis,
scarcely rippling the heart.

Gross: Do you think of the loss of memory as being both a good thing and a bad thing because, you know, the pain recedes as well as the vivid memories of joy?

Kooser: Oh, yeah. I've often quoted this line of Mark Twain's that I just love. At one point, fairly late in his life, he said: "I have finally arrived at the age at which the things I remember most clearly never happened at all."

Gross: [*Laughs*]

Kooser: And I've arrived at that age. I'm not sure about those early memories anymore. They may be fictions completely. I don't know.

Gross: Do you write them anyway? Do you work from them as if they were truth?

Kooser: Oh, sure, because they *are* truth to me. They're embedded in me, and they're what I have of the past. I'm sure there's truth there.

Gross: I'd like your last poem to be the poem that concludes your book *Delights and Shadows*. It's a poem called "A Happy Birthday." And there's an image in this poem that echoes an image that you've used to describe your father. Your father used to work in a dry-goods store early in his life, selling fabric for drapery. You have an image of his hand smoothing out the fabric. That's apparently a really strong image for you and a very, I think, in a way, soothing one or pleasing one. And there's an echo of that image in this poem. Why don't you introduce the poem for us. It's called "A Happy Birthday."

Kooser: Sure. Well, that's an interesting observation. I never thought about that, but it is true, and there's a section in my book *Local Wonders*, which is exclusively about my father's hands, and I'm beginning to see them at the ends of my own arms as I get older. Anyway, here's the poem:

"A Happy Birthday"

This evening, I sat by an open window
and read till the light was gone and the book
was no more than a part of the darkness.
I could easily have switched on a lamp,
but I wanted to ride this day down into night,
to sit alone and smooth the unreadable page
with the pale gray ghost of my hand.

Gross: So you weren't thinking about your father when you wrote that line about smoothing the unreadable page?

Kooser: Actually, no, I wasn't thinking about him, but I think a lot of us must have had this experience that all of a sudden, you're startled to see your hands, that they are something you've inherited from someone else, and I have seen my dad's hands on the ends of my arms. It's all mixed up. But in that poem, no, I wasn't thinking about his hands particularly.

Gross: So what are you doing now as poet laureate that you haven't done before?

Kooser: Well, I'm doing a tremendous amount of traveling, flying here and there. I'm not much of a traveler. I'm getting the hang of it, back and forth to Washington, and so on. I have done some things that I think were rather unusual. I invited John Prine to the Library of Congress and sat on stage with him and talked about writing music and songs. Some things like that. We're about ready to release a free weekly newspaper column that I'm going to keep up as long as I can, in which I'll introduce a short, accessible poem and talk a little bit about it. It'll be free to any newspaper that wants to use it, and it'll be posted on a website. It's called "American Life in Poetry." I'm really excited about this, but it has been really like starting a small business. There's a lot of work to this, and I was helped by the Poetry Foundation in Chicago to put it together. So I'm real excited about that, and that'll probably be my big project as poet laureate.

Gross: Well, Ted Kooser, thank you so much for talking with us.

Kooser: Thank you very much for having me. I was delighted to be here.

The American Grain of Ted Kooser

Grace Cavalieri / 2005

This interview was conducted as part of the Library of Congress series *The Poet and the Poem*, produced and hosted by Grace Cavalieri, poet laureate of Maryland, at the time of Kooser's inauguration as the thirteenth poet laureate of the United States. It was broadcast via NPR satellite. It is reprinted by permission of Grace Cavalieri.

Grace Cavalieri: We're at the Library of Congress, looking at the world through the sparkling clean pane of glass: very clear, very exact.

Ted Kooser: Thank you.

Cavalieri: And all the senses are there. We have something to smell; we have something to taste; we have something to see. If I were to say that the one poet that you bring to mind is Stanley Kunitz, would you understand that?

Kooser: Yes, I would. I admire Stanley Kunitz's work a great deal.

Cavalieri: William Blake said the tear is an intellectual thing. Kunitz uses that as an epigraph, and that really brings you to mind, because you have made the tear a perfectly respectable part of the academy. There is always something to feel in your work.

Kooser: If you don't push the edge with your feelings, I don't think you really have much of anything. There's an old Charlie Chaplin movie in which Chaplin is skating along the edge of a mezzanine of a department store during construction, and there's the chance always that he's going to fall into the pit. And the thrill of watching that scene is holding your breath thinking that he's going over the edge. That's where you have to be when you're writing. Out on that edge.

Cavalieri: Would you mind reading one of your new poems for us?

Kooser: Sure. There are a lot of people getting tattoos today, but this is a poem about an older person.

"Tattoo"

What once was meant to be a statement—
a dripping dagger held in the fist
of a shuddering heart—is now just a bruise
on a bony old shoulder, the spot
where vanity once punched him hard
and the ache lingered on. He looks like
someone you had to reckon with,
strong as a stallion, fast and ornery,
but on this chilly morning, as he walks
between the tables at a yard sale
with the sleeves of his tight black T-shirt
rolled up to show us who he was,
he is only another old man, picking up
broken tools and putting them back,
his heart gone soft and blue with stories.

Cavalieri: I have to comment on that poem, "The Diminishing Tattoo." "The Law of Diminishing Returns" is a haunting theme in your work. In another one of your poems, a man's head is now too small for his hat. Always the impending loss. But you are there right before it goes away. All of your poems are there, right in a rest home before the death, right at the elderly woman's living room to speak of your mother's death, before her *own* demise. You are there at the brink of diminishment.

Kooser: Grace, I really appreciate the way you've read my work. I'm often interviewed by people who have not really studied my work, and you are dead right with that: I am standing at that point.

Cavalieri: And I'm sure you can't think of it when you're doing it. But it is a haunting aftertaste in your work. So let's continue on and see if I'm right.

Kooser: This poem is called "A Rainy Morning." Again, this is a situation where I saw someone on the street.

"A Rainy Morning"

A young woman in a wheelchair,
wearing a black nylon poncho spattered with rain,
is pushing herself through the morning.
You have seen how pianists

sometimes bend forward to strike the keys,
then lift their hands, draw back to rest,
then lean again to strike just as the chord fades.
Such is the way this woman
strikes at the wheels, then lifts her long white fingers,
letting them float, then bends again to strike
just as the chair slows, as if into a silence.
So expertly she plays the chords
of this difficult music she has mastered,
her wet face beautiful in its concentration,
while the wind turns the pages of rain.

Cavalieri: One more poem about a glimpse of a person, "Skater."
Kooser: Okay.

"Skater"

She was all in black but for a yellow ponytail
that trailed from her cap, and bright blue gloves
that she held out wide, the feathery fingers spread,
as surely she stepped, click-clack, onto the frozen
top of the world. And there, with a clatter of blades,
she began to braid a loose path that broadened
into a meadow of curls. Across the ice she swooped
and then turned back and, halfway, bent her legs
and leapt into the air the way a crane leaps, blue gloves
lifting her lightly, and turned a snappy half-turn
there in the wind before coming down, arms wide,
skating backward right out of that moment, smiling back
at the woman she'd been just an instant before.

Cavalieri: We could look at that poem and say, "That's a perfect portrait of a skater. He's caught her freeze frame." But we could also look at that poem and say, at that second, that you've compressed time, and mortality, and then it fans out again. That's magic. That is *magic*. And we do see, in all your work, that you are a noticer of people.

Kooser: I try to pay attention to people and things. The poet Linda Gregg said one time that she asks her students to notice six things a day. And I think that's a marvelous practice. It's very difficult for most of us to pay attention to just six things a day.

Cavalieri: You even notice bugs.

Kooser: I'm kind of taken with bugs.

Cavalieri: I've learned more about bugs from your memoirs. The leaf-footed bug?

Kooser: The leaf-footed bug is a kind of a squashed beetle.

Cavalieri: And I must admit, I did not know how to move an outhouse until I read your work, either.

Kooser: And now you know, in case it's ever necessary.

Cavalieri: It's very illuminating. I'll tell you, you have brought a whole new dimension into the world of poetry. And we're going to hear some more of them. And I'll tell you a little bit more about him. He has won several awards and honors. The Pushcart Prize. Do you remember which poem that happened to be for the Pushcart?

Kooser: The Pushcart Prize was for a poem called "As the President Spoke." It was about watching Ronald Reagan at the podium.

Cavalieri: And you teach as a visiting professor in the English department of the University of Nebraska. What is your teaching load, is it one course?

Kooser: One course a semester.

Cavalieri: Creative writing?

Kooser: Yes. Graduate students.

Cavalieri: And how long has that been going on?

Kooser: Oh, I've been doing that about five years now. Since I retired from the insurance company.

Cavalieri: Yes, I forgot to say that, like Wallace Stevens, you were a man of the world. You counted money, and you dealt with paper, and you were an executive at a life insurance company. But always a poet?

Kooser: Always a poet. The life insurance job was mainly to support my writing. And I would get up very early in the morning—before I had to get my suit and tie on—and do my writing from four thirty to about seven.

Cavalieri: Like [Arnold J.] Toynbee, or like a mother with small children. I think between five and seven is really when the muse comes to call. Some more poems, Ted Kooser?

Kooser: Sure.

"At the Cancer Clinic"

She is being helped toward the open door
that leads to the examining rooms
by two young women I take to be her sisters.
Each bends to the weight of an arm

and steps with the straight, tough bearing
of courage. At what must seem to be
a great distance, a nurse holds the door,
smiling and calling encouragement.
How patient she is in the crisp white sails
of her clothes. The sick woman
peers from under her funny knit cap
to watch each foot swing scuffling forward
and take its turn under her weight.
There is no restlessness or impatience
or anger anywhere in sight. Grace
fills the clean mold of this moment
and all the shuffling magazines grow still.

Kooser: I showed that poem to my doctor, and he made a copy of it and had it framed for the nurse's station at the University of Nebraska Medical Center. I felt, "Oh boy, I've written something that someone is getting some use out of." He had me do a reading to the staff at the medical center once, which was a very short reading, but at a big meeting. They had all the staff there.

Cavalieri: I call you "The Poet of Affirmation." And I think that is what the doctor wanted to have happen. I mean, as much good will as you can bring in, that people can understand. I think that's why you're being applauded. Because we've waited a very long time to have something that belonged to everyone.

Kooser: Thank you.

Cavalieri: And your poetry, on the literal level, will belong to every nurse in the back ward but can also be, I see, subject for some very philosophical thought. So, I'm looking forward to the rest of that book on your lap. But I want to say some things that people have talked about. *Poetry* magazine says: "Kooser documents the dignities, habits and small griefs of daily life. Our hunger for connection, our struggle to find balance." And the *Minneapolis Star Tribune* says, "Kooser will one day rank alongside Edgar Lee Masters, Robert Frost, and William Carlos Williams."

Kooser: I'll either rank beside them or be lying beside them. Williams taught me to look at things like that. I've written several poems about these little moments in life, that there's a little bit of tension that passes. I would guess that most of the audience has experienced this.

Cavalieri: You have one poem that ends, "with no one to tell" ["After Years"].

Kooser: Oh, yes.

Cavalieri: And now, I was wondering, that you are going to be heard by millions of people, does that feeling change? Do you feel you'll be heard? That what you have to tell will be heard?

Kooser: I certainly hope that I'll get some more readers out of this. It's not a matter of wanting to make money selling books. I really enjoy having readers, and especially having people write letters to me and tell me a poem has meant something to them.

Cavalieri: I wish people would know that the poet really does want to hear from them. They always think, "Oh, I wouldn't want to bother him." But, you know, it's quite the contrary. You don't know anyone's out there unless they tell you.

Kooser: And I try to do that myself. I try to write a card to somebody when I see a poem that I like.

Cavalieri: You're reading from *Delights and Shadows*. And that is just out, 2004. Charles Baxter said: "Ted Kooser has great gifts for both portraiture and landscape. And another gift for dramatizing what is nearly invisible." That's the part I like. "He is a seer, and we are lucky to have him among us, and blessed to have these beautiful new poems." It's about being in touch with the invisible.

Kooser: This poem, however, is about a thing. I've written a lot of poems about things.

"A Spiral Notebook"

The bright wire rolls like a porpoise
in and out of the calm blue sea
of the cover, or perhaps like a sleeper
twisting in and out of his dreams,
for it could hold a record of dreams
if you wanted to buy it for that,
though it seems to be meant for
more serious work, with its
college-ruled lines and its cover
that states in emphatic white letters,
5 SUBJECT NOTEBOOK. It seems
a part of growing old is no longer
to have five subjects, each
demanding an equal share of attention,

set apart by brown cardboard dividers,
but instead to stand in a drugstore
and hang on to one subject
a little too long, like this notebook
you weigh in your hands, passing
your fingers over its surfaces
as if it were some kind of wonder.

Here's another poem about a thing, a moth that drinks tears. The title of the poem is the species *Lobocraspis griseifusa.*

"*Lobocraspis griseifusa*"

This is the tiny moth who lives on tears,
who drinks like a deer at the gleaming pool
at the edge of the sleeper's eye, the touch
of its mouth as light as a cloud's reflection.

In your dream, a moonlit figure appears
at your bedside and touches your face.
He asks if he might share the poor bread
of your sorrow. You show him a table.

The two of you talk long into the night,
but by morning the words are forgotten.
You awaken serene, in a sunny room,
rubbing the dust of his wings from your eyes.

Cavalieri: As far as your process goes, did you have the center of the poem already committed to a page so that when you wrote about the event you plugged it in, or did you write that poem in all one process? There seems to be a centerpiece there, a little light at the center, that you may have been harboring elsewhere.

Kooser: Well, I might have. Frankly, I don't remember exactly the process of that poem, but my usual process would be pretty linear. I would write from front to back, and then go back into it with countless revisions and see what I could make of it, and my guess is what you're referring to is something that came in through the revision.

Cavalieri: I see. You don't keep a little messy box with dirty pieces of paper you scramble through when you can't get an idea?

Kooser: No.

Cavalieri: You have to get one.

Kooser: I'm too Germanic and compulsive to have a box of little scraps of paper.

Cavalieri: Good. That's a good segue, Germanic and compulsive. Now, to your memoirs, which are about the place of Germans and Czechs, the Bohemian Alps. And I'm just going to take a short detour and get back to your poetry because we have to congratulate the new book, *Local Wonders*. It is subtitled *Seasons in the Bohemian Alps.* The book is separated into seasons, and it is your view of living among your people, peppered with these wonderful folk sayings. Now, are these folk sayings something you collected on index cards, or do they just come to you?

Kooser: As I mentioned earlier, I'm kind of a devotee of garage sales and yard sales, and there was a book that I found at a yard sale. It was called *International Proverbs*, and it had a section of Czech and Bohemian proverbs, and I got most of them out of that. The marvelous one that heads the book—"When God wishes to rejoice the heart of a poor man, He makes him lose his donkey and find it again"—I just love that.

Cavalieri: And you speak of that when you recovered from a very serious illness, and you found your donkey again. So you've come full circle with that idea. That's really important. And, when we think of the people who you talk about in this book, we know so much of your life intimately. I'll give you an example. You talk about how busy you're going to be this winter. And you say in *Local Wonders* that winter is your favorite season because you can stall all day in your long flannel shirt that your mother made you, looking out over the snow over all the chores that you don't have to do.

Kooser: That's right.

Cavalieri: Ted, this is going to be a different kind of winter.

Kooser: Yes indeed, it will be.

Cavalieri: No flannel shirts in Washington.

Kooser: No, this year is going to be quite a disruption, but I'm willing to accept it.

Okay. My grandmother, my mother's mother, had a set of pink Depression Glass dishes, and I wrote this about those.

"Depression Glass"

It seemed those rose-pink dishes
she kept for special company
were always cold, brought down
from the shelf in jingling stacks,
the plates like the panes of ice
she broke from the water bucket
winter mornings, the flaring cups
like tulips that opened too early
and got bitten by frost. They chilled
the coffee no matter how quickly
you drank, while a heavy
everyday mug would have kept
a splash hot for the better
part of a conversation. It was hard
to hold up your end of the gossip
with your coffee cold, but it was
a special occasion, just the same,
to sit at her kitchen table
and sip the bitter percolation
of the past week's rumors from cups
it had taken a year to collect
at the grocery, with one piece free
for each five pounds of flour.

Cavalieri: You had two grandmothers. You had a nuclear family. And Grace Kooser was your father's mother?

Kooser: Yes.

Cavalieri: And I know because her name's Grace. She was a large woman.

Kooser: She was a very large woman. I remember sitting, when we were very small, she made paper dolls for us. My sister and I sat at her knees, and she would make these paper dolls, and I'd look up at these enormous knees, and they were like the faces on Mt. Rushmore.

Cavalieri: And you liked your mother's mother better.

Kooser: Well, actually my grandmother Kooser died when I was about ten, but my grandmother Moser lived on for many years. So we really spent much more time with the Mosers than the Koosers.

Cavalieri: But the characters in your life will live longer than you do. It's kind of impressive that they've been made immortal.

Kooser: The University of Nebraska Press is about to publish a little book of mine, a kind of special edition called *Lights on a Ground of Darkness*. It is a reminiscence of my grandmother Moser's family. I had written it as an essay and published it in the *Great River Review*. The press came to me and said they were looking for a book that they could give to donors at the university, a sort of special edition. So they were interested in looking at this. In print it only runs about forty-five pages, so it'll be a very slim book, but I was delighted by this because it was a real labor of love. My mother was dying when I was writing it. I wanted to finish it and show her the manuscript before she was gone. And I thought it would make her terribly sad, but in fact she liked it. But it was exactly as you say. It was an attempt to keep some very ordinary people alive.

Cavalieri: You have to mention that there is another book. You're keeping the University of Nebraska up late! They have another book from you called *The Poetry Home Repair Manual*. There are no loose hammers here? You're going to tell us how to do it.

Kooser: Well, it is not a book of real specifics. They're my ideas about the things I do best: working with metaphor, fine tuning metaphor. It's more of a philosophy of writing. Initially I say that I believe in writing as communication. If you don't believe in that, then you have no business with this book because it's not for you, and so on. But there are readers out there, and we have to think about what we are giving an audience.

Cavalieri: What do you do with your dreams?

Kooser: Sometimes I jot dreams into journals, and from time to time I have written about them.

Cavalieri: Maybe little droplets. It feels as if you carry everything you felt with you at all times. That's what it feels like when I read your work.

Kooser: I don't know how other people operate psychologically, but, at some given moment every day, I momentarily review every person I have ever known, I think. It's as if there's a constant parade. Not everyone I've ever known; I shouldn't say that. But the people who really mattered to me. I sort of check in with them every day at some point.

Cavalieri: Alive or dead.

Kooser: Oh yeah, mostly dead, actually.

Cavalieri: Me too. That's where the best communication's happening.

Kooser: Yeah, isn't that interesting, the way that works. Now this one is a little longer poem, but it's very interesting, I think. It's a narrative. I don't write a whole lot of narrative poems, but it's a story that was told to me by Keith Jacobshagen, a very dear friend of mine who's a noted landscape painter. This is about his family.

"The Beaded Purse"

for Keith Jacobshagen

Dressed in his church suit, and under
the shadow of his hat, the old man
stood on the wooden depot platform
three feet above the rest of Kansas
while the westbound train chuffed in
and hissed to a stop. He and the agent
and two men, commercial travelers
waiting to go on west, pulled mailbags
out of the steam, then slid out
his daughter's coffin, canvas over wood,
and set it on a nearby baggage cart.

Not till the train had rolled away
and tooted once as it passed the shacks
at the leading edge of the distance,
and not till the agent had disappeared,
dragging the bags of mail behind,
did the old man pry up the nailed-down lid
with a bar he'd brought in the wagon.

Hat in hand, he took a long look.
He hadn't seen her in a dozen years.
At nineteen, without his blessing,
she'd gone back east to be an actress,
now and then writing her mother
in a carefree, ne'er-do-well cursive
to say she was happy, living in style.

A week before, the agent sent word
that there was a telegram waiting,
and the old man and his wife rode to town

to read their daughter had died
and her remains were on the way home.
Remains, that's how they put it.

She was wearing a fancy yellow dress
but was no longer young and pretty.
She looked like one of the worn-out dolls
she'd left in her room at the farm
where he would sometimes go to sit.

A bag of women's private underthings
had been stuffed between feet,
and someone had pushed down next to her
an evening bag beaded with pearls.

He opened the purse and found it empty,
so he took a few bills out of his pocket
and folded them in, then snapped it closed
for her mother to find. Then, with the back
of the bar he tapped the lid in place
and went to find the station agent.

The two of them lifted the coffin down
and carried it a few hard yards across
the sunny, dusty floor of Kansas
and loaded it onto the creaking wagon.

Then, clapping his hat on his head
and slapping the plump rump of his mare
with the reins, he started the long haul home
with his rich and famous daughter.

Cavalieri: What a cinematic moment. I can just see a Mike Lee film
where they open the purse and put the money in.

Kooser: It's a whole movie, isn't it?

Cavalieri: It is. A film. Hearing you, I thought, "Well he's got a really
good voice, and he reads very well." But then I got in touch with your vowels.
I know that you cannot prescribe this ahead of time, but "one of the worn-
out dolls." I can follow your vowels through the line "the plump rump." I

think that this is the remarkable thing that makes you read it so easily. I'm sure you don't know ahead of time that your vowels are aligned that way. What *are* you aware of?

Kooser: I think I'm very much blessed with that gift. One of the first poems I wrote when I was a very young man, twenty years old, was an exercise that a teacher had given me in writing rhymed couplets. I described a cemetery and a mole underground tunneling through the cemetery, a gothic sort of scene. But I look back at the poem now, and I see all these vowels and internal rhymes. They just seem to flow into the poem, and I am very much blessed with having had that happen to me. I don't think about those things when I write. They're just there.

Cavalieri: I think writers are wired a certain way. When you're born, your brain just has vowels in it.

You've written about snakes in poems such as "Snake Skin" and in *Local Wonders*.

Kooser: Yes, we have a little pond on our acreage, and down by the pond I have a building with windows where I keep a lot of the books that won't fit in the house. I go down there to sit a lot. And next to it is a well pit, and the snakes come up. Bull snakes and blue racers and garter snakes come up out of the well pit. They love it there. And one of the bull snakes comes over to the library when I'm not there and goes after the mice if there are any in there, and all I've ever seen of him are these snake skins that he leaves around.

Cavalieri: You recall in *Local Wonders* an electrician coming to fix your circuits, and he's afraid of snakes. So you reach down and retrieve the two snakes that are residing in a pit and carry them across the frozen yard to keep them safe. Then after he fixes the circuits, you pick the snakes up because you're afraid they'll freeze, and they're gone.

Kooser: That's right.

Cavalieri: My husband didn't believe that story. He hates snakes. But every living thing matters to you.

Kooser: Yes, it does. We let the spiders live in our house because we live in the country where there are a lot of those little German wood roaches that live in stacks of firewood. The house probably would have cockroaches were it not for the spiders in the house. The spiders hunt the cockroaches. It makes it sound like we're living in terrible circumstances. Actually, our house is practically brand new, but living in the country, there's a lot more insect life around.

Cavalieri: But for you to spend fifteen minutes looking at a bug. I think that's a man who does not race with the clock.

Kooser: Yes. I try to take notice of things.

Cavalieri: Now is a good time to take another really quick detour, because I would hate to leave this program without mentioning your good friend Jim Harrison. We won't really have a chance to read from your book with him, but we can mention it. It's called *Braided Creek: A Conversation in Poetry*. It came out in 2003. And it is simply pages with little poems on them, and the author is not identified. We don't know whether Ted wrote them or his friend Jim Harrison. They're just thrown in the mix. How did that book come about?

Kooser: Well, when I was recovering from radiation, I wrote a poem every day and pasted it on a postcard and sent it to Jim, and they were about things that I would find on the road when I was out walking before dawn. These little poems are actually poems that we corresponded with for over a longer period than that. Some of them were interspersed in that period, but he and I have been exchanging poems for many years. And I arranged the book myself. They are not literally sequential. I had them all on three-by-five index cards, and I had two strips of three-by-five index cards probably thirty-five feet long, and I went up and down and up and down, until I could finally braid them together in a way.

Cavalieri: And they are braided. The funny thing is, you don't know who wrote what, so it's like a detective game. I thought, well now here's somebody who says he finishes a bottle of wine in thirty-three minutes. That is not Ted.

Kooser: That indeed is not Ted.

Cavalieri: No. You're the odd couple: the wild and crazy guy and the conservative. I almost could tell which sounded like you, just by the content. But it doesn't matter. Why doesn't it matter?

Kooser: In a book of several hundred poems like this, to have the name of the poet underneath each poem would really interrupt the whole experience. Also, we decided, why call attention to the fact that Ted wrote this poem or Jimmy wrote this one? We just decided we'd try it this way. Of course, everyone is trying to figure out who wrote what. People say, "Well, I know that you wrote that one," and I say, "Well, you know, I didn't write that one." And one of the interesting things about it was that there were a couple of poems in that bunch of three-by-five cards that I couldn't remember. We were close enough, and *are* close enough, that I couldn't remember which of us had written that one.

Cavalieri: Well, I can understand that. Where does he live?

Kooser: He lives in Montana in the warmer months and Arizona in the winter.

Cavalieri: Does he like the fact that he's famous now that you're poet laureate?

Kooser: Well, I think Jim was very famous long before I became poet laureate.

Cavalieri: His name is certainly well known.

Kooser: Particularly for his novels, and his movie work, and so on. Jim sees himself as being a poet. It was his first love, and he writes beautiful poems. But his reputation has been made in fiction, really.

This is an elegy I wrote for my mother about a month after she died.

"Mother"

Mid April already, and the wild plums
bloom at the roadside, a lacy white
against the exuberant, jubilant green
of new grass and the dusty, fading black
of burned-out ditches. No leaves, not yet,
only the delicate, star-petaled
blossoms, sweet with their timeless perfume.

You have been gone a month today
and have missed three rains and one nightlong
watch for tornadoes. I sat in the cellar
from six to eight while fat spring clouds
went somersaulting, rumbling east. Then it poured,
a storm that walked on legs of lightning,
dragging its shaggy belly over the fields.

The meadowlarks arc back, and the finches
are turning from green to gold. Those same
two geese have come to the pond again this year,
honking in over the trees and splashing down.
They never nest, but stay a week or two
then leave. The peonies are up, the red sprouts
burning in circles like birthday candles,

for this is the month of my birth, as you know,
the best month to be born in, thanks to you,
everything ready to burst with living.

There will be no more new flannel nightshirts
sewn on your old black Singer, no birthday card
addressed in a shaky but businesslike hand.
You asked me if I would be sad when it happened

and I am sad. But the iris I moved from your house
now hold in the dusty dry fists of their roots
green knives and forks as if waiting for dinner,
as if spring were a feast. I thank you for that.
Were it not for the way you taught me to look
at the world, to see the life at play in everything,
I would have to be lonely forever.

Cavalieri: You were very close.

Kooser: Oh yes.

Cavalieri: You are accused of having a happy childhood.

Kooser: Yes, that's right. All this business about artists having to have terrible childhoods doesn't play with me. The painter Keith Jacobshagen, whom I mentioned in regard to the poem "The Beaded Purse," had a blissfully happy childhood, and he's a marvelous painter. His folks, whom I've been around, adore him. And you can tell. They've adored him since he was born. He's an only child.

Cavalieri: Well, you say that your mother's sun shone on you.

Kooser: Yes, that's right.

Cavalieri: Who would you say was another Great Plains poet? McGrath? Was McGrath a Great Plains poet?

Kooser: Tom McGrath is probably one of the greatest of the Great Plains poets, I think. And it's a shame . . .

Cavalieri: He's not known.

Kooser: He's not known. His, sort of, magnum opus was *Letter to an Imaginary Friend*, which comes up out of the plains experience. McGrath was way over on the left politically.

Cavalieri: Yes, he was.

Kooser: He got blacklisted, and one thing and another, and I think that may have done some long-term damage to his career. But his poems are really beautiful. There's a Whitman conference coming up in the spring at Nebraska, and I'm to introduce that conference, and I'm going to read a poem of McGrath's, because they're so much like Whitman and so much influenced by them, I think.

Cavalieri: That will be very good because you're the only two that are known for that region really.

Kooser: Well, of course there are others that are not quite as well known.

Cavalieri: Of course.

Kooser: I've been extremely lucky with my career. I think literary careers are about 40 percent skill and 60 percent just dumb luck. And I've been very lucky with mine.

Cavalieri: And then we go even more north, and we get Robert Wrigley and so many fine poets.

Kooser: Bob Wrigley's a wonderful poet. That's true.

This is a poem I wrote after seeing a student walking across campus one day and realizing how much students with backpacks on look like sea turtles.

"Student"

The green shell of his backpack makes him lean
into wave after wave of responsibility,
and he swings his stiff arms and cupped hands,

paddling ahead. He has extended his neck
to its full length, and his chin, hard as a beak,
breaks the cold surf. He's got his baseball cap on

backward as up he crawls, out of the froth
of a hangover and onto the sand of the future,
and lumbers, heavy with hope, into the library.

Cavalieri: May we have a final poem?

Kooser: Here's a self-portrait. And the places that are mentioned in this poem are small towns near where I live.

"That Was I"

I was that older man you saw sitting
in a confetti of yellow light and falling leaves
on a bench at the empty horseshoe courts
in Thayer, Nebraska—brown jacket, soft cap,
wiping my glasses. I had noticed, of course,
that the rows of sunken horseshoe pits

with their rusty stakes, grown over with grass,
were like old graves, but I was not letting
my thoughts go there. Instead I was looking
with hope to a grapevine draped over
a fence in a neighboring yard, and knowing
that I could hold on. Yes, that was I.

And that was I, the round shouldered man
you saw that afternoon in Rising City
as you drove past the abandoned Mini Golf,
fists deep in my pockets, nose dripping,
my cap pulled down against the wind
as I walked the miniature Main Street
peering into the child-size plywood store,
the poor red school, the faded barn, thinking
that not even in such an abbreviated world
with no more than its little events—the snap
of a grasshopper's wing against a paper cup—
could a person control this life. Yes, that was I.

And that was I you spotted that evening
just before dark, in a weedy cemetery
west of Staplehurst, down on one knee
as if trying to make out the name on a stone,
some lonely old man, you thought, come there
to pity himself in the reliable sadness
of grass among graves, but that was not so.
Instead I had found in its perfect web
a handsome black and yellow spider
pumping its legs to try to shake my footing
as if I were a gift, an enormous moth
that it could snare and eat. Yes, that was I.

Cavalieri: The voice of Ted Kooser, poet laureate of the United States.

An Interview with Ted Kooser

Stephen Meats / 2005

This interview appeared in *Midwest Quarterly* 46, no. 4 (Summer 2005), a special issue commemorating the life and work of Ted Kooser. It is reprinted with the permission of Stephen Meats.

Stephen Meats: How would you say your parents influenced your becoming a poet?

Ted Kooser: My father was a storekeeper, loved the public, and was a marvelous storyteller. I remember a woman once said to me that she'd rather hear my dad describe a person than see the person herself. He had an interest in the theater, too, and he and Mother belonged to a group that got together to read plays. Sitting in our living room listening to those plays was, I think, my first experience of literature as fun. We also had a few books, a collected Balzac, a collected plays of Ibsen, the novels of John Fox Jr., the works of Dumas père. I read them all.

Meats: Same question about the landscape and the people of the Great Plains, particularly your region of Nebraska-Iowa. What role have they played in your becoming a poet and in your work?

Kooser: I have never lived anywhere else, and I've always written about what I've experienced. I might have written about different landscapes if I'd lived somewhere else, but I think the poems might have been much the same. My interest is in writing about the ordinary, and the ordinary is everywhere.

Meats: What poems by other writers have served as touchstones for your own writing?

Kooser: I have been thinking lately how much I may have been influenced by May Swenson's poems. I think *To Mix with Time* was one of the first books I read and reread. Several years ago, someone brought out a posthumous book of her nature poems, and when I read it, I recalled how much I'd been inspired by her. I also remember being very interested in the poems of John Crowe Ransom. Also E. A. Robinson and [Robert] Frost. I read anything and everything when I was young, and I couldn't possibly list all the poets who've had some influence on me. Today I look to Nancy Willard and Linda Pastan and other Americans, and Thomas Tranströmer and Rolf Jacobsen, the two last in Bly's translations.

Meats: You mention that your father was a marvelous storyteller. I've heard from some of your close friends that you love to tell stories and to hear stories, as well. What role does narrative play in your work?

Kooser: I have written very few poems in which narrative seemed to be leading. There's a poem in *Delights & Shadows*, "The Beaded Purse," that is indeed a narrative, but it seems quite unlike most of my work, which works with single moments rather than sequences of moments. Poets have tried to write narratives in verse, and some of them are quite effective, at least to me as a literary person, but I have always wondered how they might be received by everyday readers. Novels are much less intimidating than poems, and if I were to choose between reading a good story in verse and one in prose, I think I'd go for the prose. Literary people have interest in narrative poetry, but it's my guess that most narrative poems wouldn't compete very well in paperback on an airport book rack. David Mason has a new poem about the Ludlow Mine disaster that is very well done, and a part of it has been in *Hudson Review*.

Meats: Still dealing with influences, but in a different vein. Was religion a significant part of your life growing up? Has religious belief been important to your poetry?

Kooser: We were Methodists but only went to church a few times a year, on holidays usually. I am not a traditional believer by any means, but I do believe in a universal order. But it doesn't have a personality. I don't think I have been much influenced by anything in any way churchly.

Meats: Your work has sometimes been described as "accessible." What is your view of such labels? I ask this because I find your work accessible, but not at all simplistic, yet I believe that some readers, and even some critics, have trouble separating the two.

Kooser: I don't object to my poems being called accessible, and I work hard during the process of revision to make them clear. I revise away from difficulty and toward clarity and simplicity. It doesn't matter to me what critics say about it. There's no way to control what people want to say about your work. It's best not to pay any attention, and I don't read reviews of my work.

Meats: It's also been said that you write for the "common reader." Do you write with an "ideal reader" in mind? And could this reader in any sense be termed "common"?

Kooser: I talk about imaginary readers in my *Poetry Home Repair Manual*, and the idea is to have an imaginary reader for each poem we write. My imaginary reader is usually someone who has read a little poetry, has a couple of years of college or more, but is not a literary sophisticate. I don't think there is a common reader, if that means one imaginary reader for all work. If I've used the term *common* I have meant it in the sense of ordinary.

Meats: How did you get started writing, and at what point did you realize writing poetry would be a life-long calling? [Interviewer's note—In response to this question, Mr. Kooser referred me to his recently published *The Poetry Home Repair Manual*, where he suggested I would "find some ready-made sentences."]

Kooser: "I don't remember the specific date when I decided to be a poet, but it was during one of my many desperately lonely hours as a teenager, as I set about establishing myself as a poet with adolescent single-mindedness. I began to dress the part. I took to walking around in rubber shower sandals and white beachcomber pants that tied with a piece of clothesline rope. I let my hair grow longer and tried to grow a beard. I carried big fat books wherever I went—like Adolph Harnack's *Outlines of the History of Dogma* and Kierkegaard's *Fear and Trembling*. I couldn't have understood a word of those books if I tried, but they looked really good clenched under my arm and, as a bonus, helped me look as if I had big biceps. There were, it seemed to me, many benefits accruing to a career as a poet. There were fame and immortality. . . . There was also the delicious irresponsibility of the bohemian lifestyle. . . . But best of all was the adoration of women. . . . It didn't occur to me for a long time that in order to earn the title of Poet, I ought to have written at least one poem. . . . I was an artificial poet, a phony, when, by rubbing shoulders with poetry, I gradually became interested in writing it. I'd begun to carry books less cumbersome than Harnack and Kierkegaard, and one day I picked up the New Directions paperback edition of William Carlos Williams's *Selected Poems*. It weighed no more than a few ounces and fit in my pocket. I began to read Williams and soon discovered other poets whose work I liked: May Swenson, Randall Jarrell, John Crowe Ransom, to name a few. I began to read poetry when I had a moment free from pretending to be a poet, and soon I started to write a few poems of my own. The two sides of being a poet—the poet as celebrity and the poet as writer—began to fall into balance. I read poems, I wrote poems, and at times, sometimes for hours on end, I was able to forget about trying to attract women." [Excerpt from Ted Kooser, *The Poetry Home Repair Manual* (University of Nebraska Press, 2005, 3–5); reprinted with the permission of the author.]

Meats: Your first collection [*Official Entry Blank* (1969)] was published by a university press and came out when you were a very young poet. How did that collection come to be published?

Kooser: My friend, mentor, and teacher, Karl Shapiro, took the manuscript to the University of Nebraska Press, which then had an ongoing poetry series. His influence must have been helpful.

Meats: How else did Shapiro influence your direction as a writer?

Kooser: He taught me, by his example, that it was possible to write interesting poems about inanimate things.

Meats: How do you go about putting a book together?

Kooser: Most of my books are little more than collections of poems that have appeared in journals over a period of years, sometimes arranged by theme or point of view. It takes between seven and ten years for me to get around sixty poems that have been published and/or that still please me enough to include. *Winter Morning Walks*, written over just one winter, was a different kind of project, and this was also true of *The Blizzard Voices*, which I wrote as a book, rather than as a compilation of single poems. *Braided Creek*, with Jim Harrison, is a compilation of about fifteen years' worth of little poems he and I sent back and forth with no intent to make a book. The idea for a book came about quite suddenly, when we realized how many poems there were. We had about four hundred to choose from. But all three of my books from Pitt and *Delights & Shadows* from Copper Canyon were put together as I've described, as compilations of published work.

Meats: Besides creating poems, I know you also make paintings. When did painting become an active part of your creative life?

Kooser: I was interested in drawing and painting as a child, long before I got interested in poetry. I still love to paint. I consider myself a dedicated amateur. I don't show my work or sell it, but I sometimes spontaneously give it away. It's nice to have something like that, something that I can be naive about.

Meats: Near the beginning of your essay "Riding with Colonel Carter," you mention briefly in passing that your poems resemble Disney animated films. Could you explain what you meant?

Kooser: I don't have a copy of what I said, but what I meant to suggest is that my use of metaphor is something like those Disney films in which the forests have personalities, the trees have faces, etcetera.

Meats: Do you feel that your work as an insurance executive helped you or hindered you as a poet (I'm thinking of your short poem, "They Had Torn Off My Face at the Office")? Maybe a different way of asking the same question is, how did you balance those different parts of your life—businessman and poet—that may seem to an observer as unrelated, or even incompatible?

Kooser: That poem arose out of resentment for office work, but I managed to put that resentment behind me quite early. Later poems, like "Four Secretaries" in *Weather Central,* are better indicators of how I felt about the workplace. Lots of people have asked me about how I was able to do that kind of work and write poems, and my answer is that I did both. I wrote every morning from four thirty or five till I had to get my necktie on, and then I went to work. The two occupations never seemed incompatible to me.

Meats: You're not a teacher by profession, but I know that you have often taught poetry-writing classes. What led you to want to teach while you were pursuing a successful business career, and what—as a writer have you learned from teaching?

Kooser: I have always liked to teach, and probably would have stayed in the profession if I'd been a better scholar, but all I cared about was writing poems, and when I was in graduate school, creative writing as an academic pursuit hadn't arrived in Nebraska or most places other than Iowa and a few other schools. Now I teach tutorially. I take a dozen graduate student poets and see each of them for an hour each week, privately, in my office. It's a fine way to teach, and I've had a lot of success with it. *The Poetry Home Repair Manual* owes a lot to what I've learned from teaching.

Meats: How did making the transition from being a poet working for an insurance company to being a poet working in an academic setting affect your writing?

Kooser: I don't think it has affected it at all.

Meats: Many people have lamented the fact that poetry writing in America has become institutionalized in creative-writing programs and the infamous workshop. As someone who has observed this phenomenon from both outside and inside the academy, what is your view of its effects on the development of American poetry?

Kooser: We owe many good contemporary poems to the workshops, and many bad ones. I think if we were able to look back at this period from a hundred years from now, we'd mostly notice that there were lots more poems being written than during the period before creative writing took hold on campuses. Nothing wrong with lots of poems being written. I say in the *Manual* that I wouldn't see anything wrong with a world in which everybody was writing poetry. It's a good thing for us to do with our time, and while we're doing it, we're not causing anybody any trouble.

Meats: Teaching isn't the only way you have offered a helping hand to poets and to poetry. I'm thinking of your journal—back in the seventies, wasn't it—the *Salt Creek Reader*? Could you give a brief history of the journal and your reasons for starting it?

Kooser: I began my little publishing business in the sixties with poems on single sheets of paper that I sold for a penny. I stole the idea from Jon Bracker, as I recall, who had done a similar thing. I then founded the *Salt Creek Reader*, a more typical journal, and kept it going for a while. Then I let it lapse for a few years and picked it up again as the *New Salt Creek Reader*. After I got tired of that, I published a couple of issues of a new magazine, the *Blue Hotel*, and then tired of that.

Meats: You also conducted Windflower Press for a time. Could you give a brief history of your press and your reasons for starting it?

Kooser: Windflower Press went hand in hand with the magazines. I started by publishing a couple of books by Bill Kloefkorn, one by Don Welch, one by Steven Osterlund. Later, I did an anthology called *The Windflower Home Almanac of Poetry*, which I really liked and have thought of reprinting. Then a pretty successful one called *As Far as I Can See: Contemporary Writers of the Great Plains*. Windflower was never a very serious publishing enterprise. I didn't want to throw that much time or money into it. I do think it performed a small service for a time. I was able to keep Bill Kloefkorn's *Alvin Turner as Farmer* and *Uncertain the Final Run to Winter* in print for example.

Meats: Now, besides your teaching and publishing, you have another very rare opportunity, as poet laureate of the United States, to do something of benefit to poetry and poets. What do you hope to accomplish in this job?

Kooser: I'd like to try to expand the audience for poetry, if even just a little, by showing people that poems need not be intimidatingly difficult. My major project is a weekly newspaper column, to be issued at no cost to the papers, in which I'll present a poem by an American poet with a few lines of introduction and the proper acknowledgments language. The poems will be examples of the kinds of works I am talking about: understandable yet having something unique to offer. By the time your issue comes out, this ought to be up and running.

Meats: From the viewpoint of where you are now, what does the future of poetry look like in this country? For example, a friend of mine recently told me about seeing fabulous television programs on poetry in London. Do you think it's possible that we might see poetry programs on TV in this country?

Kooser: We make a mistake, I think, in talking about American poetry as if it were one big thing. In fact, it is Balkanized, with clearly separated communities that thrive in their own fashion. There is the rap poetry community, the slam poetry community, the cowboy poetry community, the literary poetry community. None of these has much to do with, or interest in, the others, and each is healthy in its own way. The literary poets are never going to persuade, say, the cowboy poets to write literary poems, and the cowboy poets aren't going to start writing literary poems because someone tells them that the literary poems are better. Because the success of TV programs has to do with advertisers, I am not optimistic about TV poetry programs having any kind of endurance. There was quite a good series back maybe fifteen years ago, on public TV, called *Anyone for Tennyson?* and it seemed to have an audience. But, of course, it didn't last more than one series of maybe eight programs. And I'd guess there have been others.

Meats: In your view, what are the biggest threats today to the expansion of poetry's audience?

Kooser: Intentional obscurity and difficulty.

Meats: I take it from your answer that you place the primary responsibility on the shoulders of poets. Does anyone else share the responsibility with them, even if it's to a lesser degree?

Kooser: Readers are consumers, and I suppose one might say that they need to become more sophisticated, but if we were talking about sushi, would we tell people who don't like sushi that they ought to become more sophisticated?

Meats: What's your view of federal support for individual poets, poetry programs, and poetry publishing? Has it been helpful, harmful? Should there be more, less?

Kooser: I am for funding for all the arts, at a level Congress will support. I don't think there's been any harm done by past funding.

Meats: Do you think your service as poet laureate is having, or will have, any effect on your writing?

Kooser: I have been too busy to write poems, and I doubt if I'll have time for it until I've completed my term and can get back into my usual routines. But I am not upset about this. I've written lots of poems, and nobody's holding their breath waiting for one or two more.

Meats: Many of your poems deal with the subjects of old age and death. Has this always been true of your work?

Kooser: Yes, I think it has. I have been thinking about the lives of the old all my life.

Meats: I know that you value the well-conceived and well-honed meta-phor. Do you go looking for the striking figure, or do you depend on chance and coincidence?

Kooser: I have never consciously designed a comparison to fit a situation. I am lucky to have the kind of mind that seems to come up with metaphors quite spontaneously.

Meats: How important is it, in your opinion, for a poet to indulge experimentation?

Kooser: Artists of all kinds receive support for something they've done, and then because they enjoy success, the tendency is to repeat what they've done. I think we need to be aware of the dangers of receiving praise so that it doesn't begin to shape our artistic lives.

Meats: Do you find it necessary to write under any special conditions?

Kooser: I just need to have peace and quiet. Part of the advantage of writing early in the morning is that everybody else is still in bed.

Meats: Do superstitions or rituals play any role in your writing, the way, say, a baseball pitcher wears the same cap all season or takes care not to step on the baseline?

Kooser: No superstitions.

Meats: How did your recent battle with cancer affect your writing?

Kooser: Actually, I guess we have to quit thinking of it as a recent history because I have six years going on seven of good health. But, of course, something like that does change you forever. For one thing, I had spent my share of time worrying about something terrible happening to me, and then it did, and I had to ask myself, "OK, now what? Now how do you intend to live your life?" In my case, the nearness of death made me very aware of everything in the world around me. There's a poem in *Delights & Shadows* called "Surviving" that is about this awareness.

Meats: What role did writing poetry play in your beating the disease and in your recovery?

Kooser: I don't know that it actually helped with beating the cancer, but it did help me cope with it in that I was able to create a few little packets of order out of a chaotic time.

Meats: If you had a second life to live but had to exclude poetry from it, what would you choose to fill the void it would leave?

Kooser: Painting. I love to paint, and wish I had more time for it.

Meats: Is there such a thing as a "Kooser poem"? If you had to choose a single poem to represent you (as the editor of an anthology might, for example), which poem would you choose?

Kooser: I think "Etude" in *Weather Central* is a representative Kooser poem.

Meats: You've just published an entire book of advice for aspiring poets, so this may be asking the impossible, but if you were only able to offer them a sentence or two of guidance, what would you say?

Kooser: The best advice I could give is READ.

Meats: My final question may seem a little "off the wall," but if you were suddenly to recognize your first car, parked on some side street and evidently back in circulation again, how would you feel?

Kooser: I had a strange experience about twenty years ago. My first car was a forty-nine Ford coupe, and I lowered the front end, put in an Oldsmobile grill, and pinstriped it. I did a lot of pinstriping for hotrodders when I was a teenager. I was driving on I-80 across Iowa and came up on the back of a coupe just like the one I'd had, and the pinstriping looked like mine. The license plate on the back said "ANTIQUE."

On the Outside Looking In:
An Interview with Ted Kooser

Harbour Winn, Elaine Smokewood, and John McBride / 2006

Ted Kooser was the featured poet at Oklahoma City University's annual Thatcher Hoffman Smith Distinguished Writer Series in April 2006, supported in part by a grant from Oklahoma Humanities. This interview, conducted during that visit, was previously published by Oklahoma Humanities in the Fall 2006 issue of *Humanities*. It is reprinted with the permission of Oklahoma Humanities.

Harbour Winn: Ted, what does it mean for a poet laureate, for the first time, to be from the Great Plains? What does that mean geographically, culturally, historically?

Ted Kooser: Well, there are some qualifiers there: Bill Stafford, of course. So much of his work was written about Kansas. When he was named poetry consultant, he was living in Oregon, so I'm the first person who actually was living out here when this happened. And you know, I think it was an enormous risk on the part of the librarian to do this.

Of course, to me, it means a marvelous opportunity to do some things. I do think that it's good for an official body like the Library of Congress to recognize that there are writers and artists living out here in the Great Middle and that some of them are doing pretty good work. The Library of Congress is the people's library. I think the librarian has that in mind, that this is not the property of the East Coast and so on. One of the things that happened was I said, "If I'm going to be the first one named from this area, I had better do at least as good a job if not a better job than anyone's ever done." So I really threw myself into it, and it's been pretty much seven days a week since then. I've done around two hundred appearances, about one hundred interviews. I think I've been in front of maybe thirty thousand people.

Elaine Smokewood: Did you know that offer was coming?

Kooser: No, I had no idea.

Smokewood: What were you doing, and how did you react?

Kooser: Well, this is a pretty good story. My wife was in Washington—she's a newspaper editor, and she'd gone there for business. It was a Friday evening about six fifteen, and I was trying to figure out what I was going to cook for supper, and the phone rang:

"Ted Kooser?"

"Yes, this is he."

"This is Prosser Gifford. I'm the director of Scholarly Programs for the Library of Congress, and I am calling to ask if you'd like to be the next poet laureate of the United States."

I was just staggered. I stammered around and tried to ask some questions, and he finally said, "I think I better call you back tomorrow." I got off the phone, and I'm thinking I couldn't get hold of Kathy. I tried to call her, and she was in a meeting or something. So I'm trying to figure out how I can come to terms with this, and I notice that we had a couple of DVDs checked out from the little town of Seward, about fourteen miles away. I thought, "Well, if I get those over there in time, maybe they won't fine me. And while I'm driving, I'll think about what it's going to be like to be a poet laureate, what I'm going to say." So I got in the car, backed out, and ripped the side mirror off the car on the center post of the garage. It's one of those mirrors that has a power cable, so it's hanging on the side of the car, swinging like a skillet all the way to Seward. I pull into Seward and I think, "Those guys at the body shop work late on Friday nights. I'll go see what this is gonna cost." So I drove to Bernie's Body Shop, and they did all the stuff with the computer and said, "Well, it's gonna be $138.43," or something like that. I get back in the car, and all the way home I'm thinking about being the poet laureate and about having to put out the money for this mirror, and I pull in the garage, and the DVDs are still in the car.

It was like that for weeks. I remember when the first press release went out, I got phone calls from newspapers from all over the country. I remember lying on the bedroom floor, looking up at the ceiling thinking, "I am never going to be able to do this. This is so foreign to me." And then, of course, the first trip to Washington. I hate to fly, so I drove. They made quite a bit out of that in Washington, that I had driven all the way, because for them it's the other end of the solar system. It was amazing. There still is, at times, the feeling that I may wake up, and this has never happened.

Smokewood: Do you feel that this happened at the right time in your life and career?

Kooser: Probably did, yeah. I had the time and still had the energy. I had my health back after having been very ill in ninety-eight and ninety-nine, so, sure, it was good.

Smokewood: You're famous for having talked about liking poems with more *eye*, e-y-e, than *I*. How do you deal with students who are writing in a very confessional mode in your classes?

Kooser: Well, without overtly saying that I don't particularly like that, I've said things like, "You ought to do a version of this poem in third person, just to see how that sounds." That, again, is personality, and you're never going to turn some people away from that, from writing where *I* is the most important part. I remember a review of one of my contemporaries—it was in the *New York Times Book Review*, maybe ten years ago—and the reviewer said, "There could be an earthquake in Ethiopia, and 150,000 people would perish, and so-and-so would feel she had to take her temperature."

Winn: You have a variety of poems that are your response [to] looking at a painting: one on Winslow Homer, one on Washington. There are others, but you look at portraiture and painting. As I read your poems, I find so many of them are portraits in words, portraits of people that usually are not famous beyond the way that they impact the people in their everyday lives. You've talked about the cover of *Braided Creek*; you painted that, and I'm wondering about your view as a person who looks at portraiture and, then as a poet, who creates portraits.

Kooser: I have a very strong visual orientation. I've drawn and painted all my life, and sometimes I have to remind myself to get the other senses in those poems because they're so very visual. I do like the idea of being on the outside looking in; that's the point of view I prefer.

In the Sheldon Memorial art collection on the campus of the University of Nebraska, we own a very famous Edward Hopper painting. Hopper was very influenced by photography, and this is what looks like a telephoto shot through an apartment window. On the left, there's a man on a couch reading a newspaper on an overstuffed chair. On the right, is a woman sitting on a piano bench, touching one key of the piano. To me that is the ideal point of view: across the street, looking through the window at something happening. That's where I'd like to be as a poet. I do appear in some of my poems, but I like the idea of being on the outside looking at things.

Smokewood: What can you do as a painter that you can't do as a poet, and the other way around?

Kooser: Well, I think poetry has to be more exacting than painting. Since painting doesn't have anything as precise as language to go along with it, it can be freer. You notice that particularly when you hear people talking about paintings, about how the painting goes beyond language in some way. I do think the visual orientation of my poetry comes out of my having been interested in drawing and painting for years.

Smokewood: Do you think those two activities complement each other for you, that painting makes you a better poet?

Kooser: I don't know about that. I find it very useful to have something I can do when I don't feel like writing, something that is engaged with the arts in some way. I don't like wasting time; there's not enough of it. Although when I'm traveling, I must say that sometimes in motel rooms I like to watch television.

John McBride: You said this morning that regarding your painting, you don't show it; you don't sell it. Presumably, there are enough of [your paintings] around that they're just starting to pile up if you don't give them away?

Kooser: I've given away a lot of them—as a matter of fact, most of them. I keep them around for a while to pat myself on the back for having painted something, and then somebody will come by to visit and complement me on a painting and I'll say, "Here, why don't you take that one?" It's great fun to do that.

McBride: You don't really have any intentions beyond that?

Kooser: No, I don't think so. I've been friends with Debra Winger for twenty years, and I gave her a big painting of a barn burning. Copper Canyon Press decided they wanted to use that painting on the cover of a book of some writings of Roethke that is coming out, so I let them do that. My book *Winter Morning Walks* has a painting of mine on it, but that's different from really being engaged in the profession.

McBride: Some of the poets that we've talked to, we try to get into some of their craft. A lot of them talk about the difference in writing versus editing and it's a completely different mindset; they're a different person, they are approaching it in a different way. You're the first that we've talked to that seems to be more integrated, that editing and writing—there's not that big of a difference.

Kooser: To my sense, a poem is at play not only as I'm writing it but as I'm editing it. Maybe I'm the peculiar duck in that sense.

McBride: Is most of your editing subtracting?

Kooser: Subtracting almost always. That's a good question.

McBride: We've heard that before. I'm thinking of Michael Ondaatje. He, too, was taking away more than he adds.

Kooser: The poem that I read this morning, that memory poem where I talk about all of these things coming in, is very much the way for getting my students to look at writing. I want them to get all the detail they can possibly get in the first draft and then go through and select the detail that is the most effective in conveying whatever they want to do, getting it all in there and then starting to compress it down.

One of my colleagues in the English department is very much on the idea "We'll add to this" with her students. She'll say, "You need to put more in this part of the poem and blow it up a little bit and expand it." To me, it's unbelievable to go at it that way. It's very interesting to have two people working with the same students. They've been taught for a semester to expand, and then they come to me, and I'm telling them to compress it and take the hot air out of it. Maybe between the two of us, they come to some sense of themselves.

Winn: I don't know if it was just the moment in time when I was reading it, but *Winter Morning Walks* struck me as much as any of your books. Tell us about that. Did you write a poem for every day?

Kooser: I wrote one every day.

Winn: But your average, you were saying, was to get one good poem a month and twelve a year. This was a demanding time, wasn't it?

Kooser: Well, it was me really fighting for life, you know, and hanging on to these poems like I was sliding down a rocky slope and grabbing at handholds. At that time, I had no idea whether I would be alive in six months. Going through a near-death situation was reawakening to the world and appreciating all those little details. There's a poem in *Delights and Shadows* called "Surviving" that it is very much like that, too, about seeing the ladybug on the windowsill, the kind of thing that you're suddenly aware of and appreciating in life that might have otherwise been gone.

I really think that this writing business is a lot about trying to find order. At a time when you've had cancer—you've gone through this devastating treatment, everything is chaos, you're scared to death, in two weeks it might be back—the idea that I could put together a little square about the size of a playing card of order every day was very helpful to me.

Winn: In a number of these poems, there's personification, metaphor, but also you assume the point of view of animals. I write "Walden Pond" in the margins often when I'm reading this book. There's a Thoreau-like appreciation, for want of an analogy or a comparison.

Kooser: I've always been very interested in the natural world. We live in the country, so it's all around us. I wasn't running into people on those walks,

I'm running into rabbits and birds. There's a hunter that appears in one of those poems, and some other things like that, but generally that's what I had available to me to write about. In one of the poems that I like very much, a person appears, the one about my wife going off to work and twirling into her coat. It was a lonely time, and I wasn't well enough to spend a lot of time in town with my friends; so I was alone with nature, watching it very carefully.

Smokewood: I was thinking that's one of the things I love about your poetry, that over and over again your poems seem to be coming from someone who is not afraid to be alone with himself and not afraid to be alone with nature. That's so sustaining to just be connected to that person through those poems.

Kooser: I have thought that when it comes time for me to die, if I could find a place where I would like to be, it would be in October when the fruit is overripe on the apple trees, and we have a lot of wild plums. I want to go into the corner of a field in the deep grass that has not been plowed, under a thicket of plums that are overripe and falling down with that fruit smell on a crisp October day, all by myself, just crawling in under one of those bushes and lying there looking up at the sky. To me, that would be the ideal way to go.

McBride: One of the questions I like to ask of people is on the subject of fear because it's something I've noticed with poets: they tend to be fearless, which probably is because of their poems. Do you ever come across anything in your writing that has scared you off, you just can't go there, or do you find a way through that?

Kooser: I can think of instances when I was in my twenties and thirties where I wrote things that made me feel kind of crazy, and that was scary to me. I drank way too much when I was young, and that was part of it, but that hasn't happened to me in a long time. I haven't found myself drawn into an area in writing that had that kind of darkness. I probably write differently about death now, having come close to it, than I would have when I was younger. One of the things about being terribly ill is you worry all your life about some terrible thing happening to you, and then it happens, and you think, "Well, okay, now what am I going to do? It's already happened. I've gotta live now; I've gotta go on living." That's a really important thing to have happen. It changes you.

Do you know about Lorca's idea of the *duende*? He wrote about the idea that the height of Flamenco dance is to dance out to the edge of death—in other words, out to the edge of complete physical collapse—and then to draw back from that. It gives you an aura. By extension, persons who have looked death in the teeth and have turned away from that have a different kind of character or something about them—not necessarily an aura but something like that.

Winn: You mentioned the poem from *Winter Morning Walks* with your wife and the twirling of her coat. One thing recurrent in your poems is movement. You have a gift for looking at the sequence of how something moves.

Kooser: I like writing that way. I have a poem called "In Passing" about two people who are meeting on the sidewalk, not knowing whether they really recognize each other; then that moment when they pass without speaking, there's a sort of charge there. I like that kind of subject matter. I don't think I've ever thought about this until this moment, but in landscape painting, it's always good to have suggested motion, wind blowing. When the trees are bent into the wind, the painting has a lot more to it than if they're just standing there; so there I'm picking up on motion in a visual way.

Smokewood: When reading your books end to end, it's like the book of changes, it's all flux. I feel as if I'm riding the wave of change and the wave of time.

Kooser: Thank you. I don't know that I've ever consciously sought that. I like the sound of it, that we are all astride this ribbon of time. The classic imagistic poems that have lasted the longest, the ancient Chinese poems, have that. It seems to me that the poems that have lasted the longest— although the ones in the Greek anthology are not like this particularly—are the poems which establish place and weather almost right off the bat. I think that happens in human conversation. We say, "You know, Harbour, I got up this morning, it was raining a little bit, looked out the window, and I could see whatever snow was left melting," and then I introduce my story.

Winn: You talked about your view of the confessional poet, the preference for the third person, the observer; and yet there are the poems about your mother, the poem about your father, and "Pearl." Those are like anomalies to your other poems, and yet to me they're some of the most memorable ones.

Kooser: Well, I was willing to take the risk of letting my feelings out in those poems, particularly the one about Mother. Whenever I come to my family, I've done that. I had an email this morning; it was a teacher, and one of her students had a question about those poems about my father and my mother, wondering if those were real, or if I'd made those up. I thought, "Who would make up something like that?" I really think we trust the lyric poet to be telling the truth. Of course, this is a kid; he's in school; he doesn't know that yet; but I mean I couldn't have made those poems up.

Winter Morning Walks is much more open to expressions of feeling than anything I'd ever done before. Mother had died just before that book was started; Dad had been dead twenty years, but I was still writing about him from time to time. I really liked my family. I mean they were extremely ordinary in every way, but if we can write about family, then they gain a little edge on mortality. Every time somebody reads that poem about my mother, [she] comes into the light for a little bit. That's part of what I'm trying to do, keep them in the light a little.

Winn: Do you do poetry readings for corporations? Having worked in the insurance world or business world, you would seem to have the credentials to address them.

Kooser: I would do it under some circumstances. One of the groups I really like reading to is the medical personnel. There's an awful lot of emphasis now on healing and the arts, and I'm trying to be a part of that. I've done maybe three or four things at the University of Nebraska Medical Center where I've read poems and talked about how good it was for me to have poetry at hand when I was trying to recover. That's really satisfying work because I so admire people who are in medicine and really doing something of worth like that.

Winn: The whole phenomenon of anthologies is interesting. I think that poets are saved or damned because of the poems that are anthologized. What would you anthologize of yours? What are you pleased to see has been anthologized?

Kooser: My experience has been that most anthologies copy each other, so that a poem of mine about an abandoned farmhouse has been in dozens of anthologies, primarily because someone saw it in another one. It would be nice if newer work was, for that poem was written in 1969. You think, "Well, Jesus, haven't I written anything good since then that's worth being anthologized?"

I think that anthologies tend to preserve a kind of poem associated with someone's name. For instance, "Those Winter Sundays" is the only poem of Robert Hayden's that anyone knows. He wrote a number of good poems, but that's the one that is anthologized over and over and over again. Maybe that's not all bad. Maybe if that poem can live a hundred more years, that's all right.

Smokewood: You are often compared to Robert Frost, or your poetry's compared to Frost's poetry. Do you think that's an apt comparison?

Kooser: Oh, I don't know. It's flattering, I think. I really like Frost, but he's not somebody that I think I've been profoundly influenced by. I wonder if part of that just doesn't come from the fact that I write about rural life and so did he.

Smokewood: I want to ask you about metaphor in one of your poems, "Etude," about the heron. It starts out being a poem about a bird, and the bird is compared to a man writing a love letter; but then it becomes a poem about a man writing a love letter that's compared to a bird, and it's like the whole literal/figurative distinction is completely ungrounded. I almost get dizzy when I'm reading that poem, and it seems like that's a kind of mood that you're attracted to in your poetry.

Kooser: I think it's sort of like daydreaming. You're in the present, here's the heron, and then you dream off into this other thing and then eventually you have to come back. Another poem in *Delights and Shadows*, very much like that, is "Bank Fishing for Bluegills." I talk about the boat as if the boat were a man, and then the man becomes very real, and then I've got to get it back to the boat. I had a student recently send me an email saying he couldn't quite figure out which was the real thing, the man or the boat. I do a lot of that. It's great fun.

Winn: When I look at *Weather Central*, the table of contents shows seven parts; *Delights and Shadows*, four parts. How do you structure these?

Kooser: If I have sixty poems that I think could be in a book, then I start trying to arrange them on the floor. I see if there are similarities between certain poems. As it turned out in *Delights and Shadows*, there's the section of poems that are largely about my family; there's a section of portraits; there's a section of poems about things. Another advantage of having sections is that you use up four pages of signature, so you don't have to have quite so many poems. I have never wanted to put a poem in that was filler. That could be the one poem somebody sees first, and it's not going to represent the book's better stuff.

Winn: What's so interesting is that a year ago at this time the three of us sat here with Billy Collins, and he described the very same process of how he puts books together. He has them all on the floor; they're in a couple of rooms; he walks around them for several days, and he rearranges them.

Kooser: I rearrange them by shape and length, too. I don't want to have a whole string of poems that are long poems together. I like to have it feel kind of eclectic. I didn't know that about Billy, but I'm not surprised.

McBride: You describe poetry itself as making order out of something that doesn't have inherent order. It's kind of the same process. It's like the book itself is a poem of sorts.

Kooser: I think that's right. I think a book should add up to being more than the sum of its parts. That's what usually goes wrong with chapbooks. Many chapbooks just look like twenty poems stapled together; they don't really ever come to more than that.

McBride: What has been some of the fun of getting to be poet laureate?

Kooser: Getting John Prine to come to the Library of Congress for a concert. He was the first folk singer to perform there since Woody Guthrie in 1936. What I love about Prine is if any other singer in the country had a verse in a song, "There's a big old goofy man / Dancing with a big old goofy girl. / Ooh, baby, it's a big old goofy world," it would have come out as a sneer or looking down on those people. Not Prine. He is right at their level, and he respects them and loves them, I think. He's right there, but what a huge presence he is. I told my wife when I got home that it was as if I were sitting onstage with a huge chunk of the universe that had been drifting for a billion years; he had that kind of gravity to him. It was marvelous. That was the most fun, I think.

I also have liked going to the National Council of Teachers of English meetings both years, hanging around with the English teachers for four or five days, talking to them about poetry. Those people who go NCTE are the best of the best. Those young women and young men have gone to those things on their own nickel; the school boards won't give them a dime; and they're paying two hundred bucks a night for a hotel room in Indianapolis just so they can be there and participate. It's really quite marvelous.

Winn: Well, we appreciate you being here, Ted.

Kooser: Thank you, I've enjoyed it.

The Crossing Over:
The US Poet Laureate on the
Aesthetic of the Simple Poem

Andrew Varnon / 2006

A version of this interview originally appeared in the *Valley Advocate*. The full interview was later reprinted in *Guernica* in 2006. Reprinted with the permission of Andrew Varnon.

This interview was conducted in Pittsburgh, PA, outside a bar in the Hilton Hotel downtown. Kooser was in Pittsburgh for the annual conference of the National Council of Teachers of English, where he read to a banquet hall of seven hundred teachers from around the country. For Kooser, it was an opportunity to reach out to the people who are the front lines in the effort to get more Americans to read and enjoy poetry: schoolteachers.

Andrew Varnon: I get the "American Life in Poetry" delivered to my e-mail. I sensed an attempt to show the geographical range of the poets in the United States.

Ted Kooser: In some degree I am, and that's why in many of those introductions, I'll mention where the person is from, for that very reason, to show that all those people aren't from Nebraska.

Varnon: Poetry has these sort of hot spots—New York, Los Angeles, and Chicago—where the huge poetry institutions are. It's nice to see that poetry comes from everywhere and not just there.

Kooser: It's pure demographics, in a way. If you look at *A Directory of American Poets and Fiction Writers*, there are hundreds of poets in New York City. So therefore, just by specific gravity, it seems like a more significant place. Robert Wrigley is a poet who lives in rural Idaho—I think it's really backcountry Idaho—and he writes beautiful poems.

Varnon: I saw a quote from you, I think it was in the *New York Times*, where somebody had asked about both you and Wallace Stevens working in the insurance business. You said, "Wallace Stevens had more time to write as an insurance agent." Can you talk a little about that?

Kooser: Well, he was a bond lawyer, and I know that insurance company lawyers don't have to do nearly as much as we had to do. We were out more in the production area. I was writing sales materials and publishing brochures, and I was an underwriter for years and years. I was being tongue in cheek about that—I'm not condemning Stevens for having had a better job than I did, but that's one of the many places where I differ from him.

Varnon: Many of Stevens's colleagues in the insurance agency didn't know that he was a poet. Do you feel you've had a double life in a way?

Kooser: They knew I was writing poems. I never hid it from them. I don't think they ever thought I was cheating on them. So, I think they probably saw it as being rather peculiar, that I was doing that sort of thing, but nobody ever suggested I shouldn't be doing it. I think that would be different on Madison Avenue or Wall Street, where you're really expected to be doing 110 percent for the company.

Varnon: How was it that you got into the insurance business as a young man?

Kooser: I really stumbled into it. I had in effect been thrown out of graduate school because I was a lousy graduate student, and I had to find a job, and I took the first job that came along. It happened to be a management trainee job in a life insurance company, and I just stayed. The idea was that I would support myself as a writer, and I knew I would have to have some sort of work, and it didn't make a whole lot of difference to me what it was. I mean, I could have been a paper hanger or something for that matter. But this job, it had good benefits, the salary was good, good working conditions. So it seemed to be something that I could maintain myself by. I thought it was an okay job. But I never invested my ego in it.

Varnon: How do you find teaching now? I understand many poets teach—not sure what the percentage on that is but . . .

Kooser: It's a huge percentage. I have a full professor's rank—I have a 0.5 appointment—which means I only have to teach one section a year. I'm not really around the department or involved in the department as much as you would be if you were a tenured faculty member, and that was your career. So, it hasn't really affected me all that much, except as a source of some pretty nice income in my retirement. And I really enjoy teaching a lot. I think I'm pretty good at it.

Varnon: Do you talk to your students at all, as they're trying to figure out what to do with their lives? Do you tell them whether they should get a job doing something else?

Kooser: You know, I try to be realistic with them and say that there's a good chance that they're not going to get a creative-writing teaching job, that there aren't enough jobs to go around, and the university faculties are cutting back on staff, and that they may have to get some other kind of work. None of them wants to hear that, but it is true, you know, and I think I'm a good example for them of somebody who took the other route. So it is possible. I think part of it is that many of them don't want to give up the perceived luxuries of a teaching career. Summer off, that kind of thing.

For a while, you know, the creative-writing community sprung out of places like Iowa and Syracuse. The graduates sort of went out, and they would found creative-writing departments in the little colleges where they went, and then some of those would found other ones. I mean every college has got a creative-writing department, so where are the jobs coming from? Well, there are a few people retiring, and some of the programs are increasing their load because they have more enrollment, but generally, there are not any jobs out there.

Varnon: What does Nebraska mean to you?

Kooser: It may very well be that people in San Francisco don't think we have any culture in Nebraska, but we have a different culture, and it's a very deep culture. We have these Czech immigrants, who are making this marvelous ethnic food and their Catholic lives, and it's very fascinating stuff.

Varnon: I want to ask you the Dana Gioia question. It's something that you're addressing with your work as poet laureate, the idea that people have been sort of scared of poetry, and there's an itch to reclaim itself. Tell me about your own poetics and your push for clarity.

Kooser: Every poet gets to choose what kind of community he or she serves with the poems, and it's true that there is a community for very difficult, challenging poetry. It's a community that's established itself over the last eighty years, that was originally, in effect, really started by Eliot and Pound. They believed that poetry ought to contain learning, that it ought to rise upon all the learning that went before. But there's always been the other strain; there's always been what I would call the William Carlos Williams strain, in which poems of simplicity and clarity are valued by a different community. I was talking to Galway Kinnell one day, and he said that there was an audience for poetry up until about 1920, and then, from that point on, the poets and the critics drifted.

Varnon: Do you have a sense that in some ways, maybe these two different strains of poetry—if you want to think about it in that way—will be reconciled?

Kooser: I don't really know that they need to be reconciled. There are going to be poets in the middle ground—and, frankly, I've written some poems that are in the middle ground—who are in between very challenging and abundantly clear, but there's a tremendous investment in the challenging poem, and it's been going on so long that the whole infrastructure supporting it, a lot of critics and theorists and so on, is deeply invested in maintaining that status.

I predict, though, that there's going to be some adjustment of some kind. Every time somebody writes a theory about where literature's going, that person is not only contributing thought but nudging things to happen in one way or the other. Just as in painting, there's much more interest in the American scene painters and the early American . . . like the Ashcan School of painters. Who would have thought, fifty years ago, that Norman Rockwell would again be considered a serious painter? And yet, there are a lot of people who are saying Rockwell was a very accomplished technician. These things are constantly moving.

Varnon: I understand that you do some painting, too. That seems very appropriate from reading your poems, that there's this same sense of observation that you have.

Kooser: Actually, when I was a kid, I suppose I got more praise for being able to draw things and paint things than I did for my little amateur poems I was writing. But the thing that I'm trying to do with my painting is to keep it in the realm of pleasure. I don't show my work, I don't try to sell it. If somebody comes to my house and admires what I've done, sometimes I just give it to them. I don't want to get tied up in all that professional stuff because I have to do that as a writer. I don't need that. I need something like painting, where I can just play.

Varnon: It seems in some way an exercise in noticing. In the way that you write your poems, there's a way of having a painter's eye and noticing the small details.

Kooser: There's a very interesting essay. Have you ever read any John Berger? He's a British writer who's written a lot of art criticism, some novels, very bright guy. I suppose Berger's eighty years old now. He has an essay about drawing. Let's say that you and I are doing a drawing of that pot or that plant in it. At first, the subject is what we are trying to render on the piece of paper, and our attention is on the subject. And then there comes a point where there's a crossing over, where all of a sudden the drawing itself becomes of interest. We quit looking at the subject and we begin to look at the drawing. With writing, that same thing can happen; there's a certain amount of subject can come out of the direct observation of things, and then suddenly it shifts into the other realm, where the poem itself becomes of interest. I can always feel that happening, you know. I start with a subject, and then I feel myself sort of forgetting about the actuality of the subject and letting the poem develop.

Varnon: You've had a long career as a poet. Your first book came out in the 1960s.

Kooser: Yeah, I was thirty.

Varnon: This happens to a number of poets, but you've had recognition late in your career. I'm wondering what that has been like.

Kooser: Well, of course, it's been good. It's felt good. It came as a complete surprise, you know. I was pretty much resigned to not being noticed, other than in literary circles. And this happened, and then everything changed. It changed my life. Two years ago, if somebody told me I'd be addressing seven hundred people at a luncheon like this, I would have been terrified. But I've learned that audiences are generally welcoming and pleasant, and they want you to succeed.

Varnon: Has it changed your writing at all? I'm thinking of the poem that you read called "Success" and wondering if there is some warning or wariness in that?

Kooser: Yeah, I've written two or three, actually three, poems that I can think of about my current situation. I've been working on a poem while I've been here. The image is of one of those telephone poles you see on the street on which a lot of notices have been stapled and then torn away, and they leave little triangles of paper, held by staples. On those notices were things lost and things found and the photos of people missing, and now even the photos are missing as a metaphor for what happens in life. All this experience is tacked upon us and then torn away, and we become a residue of all this experience. I wouldn't have written that poem under other circumstances.

Varnon: You said you've collected thousands of poetry books. How do you find new poets?

Kooser: Well, over the years, I've judged a few contests, so I've gotten huge boxes of books; my library's filled up with that sort of thing. I have three hundred books published in the year 2005 at home, and I'll keep them all, even the ones that I don't like. I feel a need to have a place for these books, and I suppose some time, years from now, I'll donate them all to some library. But I look through them, and every once in a while, I find a poem that I like, and I put a piece of paper in there. So I'm reading all these people all the time. I just drift from book to book.

Varnon: Anything going on that excites you?

Kooser: One movement that I find interesting—this is not a movement in poetry necessarily, but there's a movement on a lot of campuses now called ecocriticism. It's a body of theory based on how nature is treated in literary works. That sort of interests me. We have a discussion group at the University of Nebraska, and I've sat in on what they're doing.

Varnon: Who is out there reading these books? I'm interested in poetry, and I'm lucky if I get to read a few of them.

Kooser: If you can find two poems in a book, it could be a pretty good book for you. You know, two poems you really like. There are some poets who are fairly big names in contemporary poetry and who write a book, and I might like three or four poems in the book, but the rest of them don't appeal to me personally; but I think that's the way it really ought to be. It's really a rare thing to like everything that somebody has written. And often— you've probably had this experience—you see a poem in a magazine that you really like, and you order the book, and it happens that that's the only poem in the book you like. But that's probably the way it ought to be. It would be the same way in buying paintings. You find a painting that you really like, and you don't necessarily like the rest of the person's work at all.

Something Just Happens:
A Conversation with Ted Kooser

David Baker / 2008

This interview was begun at Denison University in March 2007 as a public conversation with Kooser, conducted by David Baker, poetry editor of *Kenyon Review*, and Tim Hofmeister, professor of classics at Denison. The interview was completed in November 2007 through a series of email exchanges. It appeared in *Kenyon Review* in 2008, funded in part by a grant from the National Endowment for the Arts, and was collected in *Talk Poetry: Poems and Interviews with Nine American Poets* by David Baker. Copyright © 2012 by the University of Arkansas Press. Reprinted with the permission of the Permissions Company, LLC on behalf of the University of Arkansas Press, www.uapress.com.

David Baker: Ted, thanks so much for the chance to talk about your five poems in the new *Kenyon Review* and about your work as a poet and poet laureate of the United States. Tim and I will step in and out with questions for you. I'd like to start with "Success" since it suggests issues relating to the public service of the laureate. Is it true that these five poems are the first you wrote and published since the laureateship?

Ted Kooser: Yes, that's right. While I was poet laureate, I had very little time for writing, and these five are among a few that I felt worth publishing.

Baker: Let's look at the poem here. This is "Success":

I can feel the thick yellow fat of applause
building up in my arteries, friends,
yet I go on, a fool for adoration. Do I care
that when it sloughs off it is likely to go
straight to the brain? I am already showing
the first signs of poetic aphasia,
the words coming hard, the synapses
of metaphor no longer connecting.

But look at me, down on my knees
next to the podium, lapping the last drops,
then rolling in the stain like a dog,
getting the smell in my good tweed sport coat,
the grease on my suede elbow patches,
and for what? Well, for the women I walk past
the next morning, the ones in the terminal,
wheeling their luggage, looking so beautifully
earnest. All for the hope that they will
suddenly dilate their nostrils, squeeze
the hard carry-on handles, and rise to
the ripening odor of praise with which I have
basted myself, stinking to heaven.

This is one of my favorite new poems of yours. I like it in part because of features that I admire in all your best poems—intensity of observation matched with a casual idiom, self-effacement alongside your obvious delight in making, and maybe most, your genius for image and metaphor—metaphor sustained like a metaphysical poet achieving that high trope of conceit. Here, the conceit is of self-basting, celebrity as high cholesterol.

Kooser: I wrote it in fun, to answer all my friends, who kept asking what it was like to be thrust into celebrity. They knew I am an introvert and that it would be difficult for me to be a public figure.

Baker: For all the obvious good of the laureateship—both for us and for yourself—we can't ignore the complaint in "Success." I think about your larger body of poetry, where the typical Kooser hero or persona is alone, that single soul out in the vast universe of nature and of others. There's a lone student carrying his heavy backpack through the hard wind; there's a man in awe of a stormy landscape; on and on. The pressure on the protagonist of this poem is, of course, public service. He is ironic and reluctant. But he is also delighted by the "ripening odor of praise," even though he knows it will be, so to speak, the death of him.

How did you manage such public life, so many appearances? You have spent a lifetime in a kind of quiet anonymity in Nebraska. Was this a shock to your system? Or did the honor override the shock?

Kooser: I guess you might say that the honor overrode the shock. I was at first terrified, but I decided that if the Library of Congress was willing to take a chance on a poet from the Great Plains, I'd better do the best job I could. So I threw myself into it and pressed forward. In the twenty months while I was in the post, I made around two hundred appearances and did a hundred interviews. I talked to little groups and big ones, local book clubs and Rotary and Kiwanis groups and, of course, to lots of schools, both secondary and college. That activity continues, and I've made another fifty appearances, I'd guess.

Tim Hofmeister: The laureateship gave you a unique opportunity to look at poetry across the country. I know we want to talk more about this in a minute. But first I want to ask a little more about your work as laureate. In fact, what is the nature of the laureateship? Are there official responsibilities and obligations?

Kooser: The actual obligations are few. The laureate is asked to give a public reading at the opening of each term, in October, and a lecture at the close of the season, in May. In between, the laureate has the privilege of giving away two Witter Bynner Fellowships of ten thousand dollars to promising poets. It's optional, but you can also bring poets to read at the Library of Congress, where they're recorded for posterity. Again, I took on a whole lot in addition to these basics. One of the most pleasurable things I did was to invite the singer-songwriter John Prine to the library to talk about writing songs. I interviewed him on stage in the Coolidge Auditorium, and he was the first folksinger who had been there since Woody Guthrie in the 1930s. You can see that interview on the library's website.

By the way, the laureateship is in no way connected with the presidency, the executive branch, or even with Congress. Congress appropriates no money for it. It is a privately endowed program at the Library of Congress. I suppose that if the laureate were summoned to the White House and asked to write a poem for the president, somebody might want to do that. Not this guy. I did have one similar opportunity. I had an email one day from a group of Cheney supporters asking if I would be willing to write a poem for Dick Cheney's birthday. And I responded that I would not be available on that occasion. And then after I hit the SEND button, I realized that there was no date in the invitation at all.

Hofmeister: Did you realize you could've had some fun forwarding that email?

Kooser: I guess it didn't occur to me to do that. I wanted it out of the house as quickly as possible. But the thing is, actually, even if it had happened to be a politician I respected a great deal, I couldn't write a poem like that. Occasional poems simply do not work, and I don't like writing poems on request. I have written a few things for people's weddings, and they're OK for that one moment, but as works of art, they just don't hold up.

Baker: But that is one of the features of the British poet laureate, isn't it? They are obliged to do poems on command and for occasions. That may be—I looked this up—why we no longer remember the work of Laurence Eusden, Colley Cibber, Henry James Pye, and some of the other less famous laureates from Britain.

Kooser: And they do it for, I think, a small keg, or butt, of sherry. Yes, well, we'd all agree that the laureates in America have it a lot better.

Hofmeister: I'd like to ask what you felt you've learned about the state of poetry from being poet laureate.

Kooser: I became convinced fairly early that there is an enormous audience available to us as writers if we want to approach them, to bring them back. These are people who had poetry ruined for them in the public schools by teachers who said, "The following poem has a meaning that I want you to dig out. I have it written down in the back of my *Teacher's Guide.*" And so we fell upon poems as if they were walnuts we had to crack—rather than seeing poems as pleasurable experiences that we can take into our lives and use however we wish. A poem does not have to have a *meaning*!

I don't want to disparage all English teachers because lots of them do wonderful jobs with this kind of thing and really should be sainted. Everywhere I went when I gave a reading—and my work, for those of you who don't know it, is that I really work hard to make it available to kind of a broad, general audience—anyway, everywhere I went, someone would come up after the reading, some guy in the back, with his thumbs in his belt, and say, "My wife dragged me to this thing, and you couldn't have gotten me to go to a poetry reading for anything, but I want you to know I had a good time, and I'm going to give this poetry stuff a chance." Modernism, the poetry of the twentieth century, beginning at about World War I, did its best to exclude a lot of readers by its difficulty, its elitism.

Hofmeister: I know you've said that there are different kinds of poetry in the United States. Don't you think that's a healthy thing in the United States?

Kooser: Absolutely. I was saying somewhat facetiously that people will, from time to time, ask a question about the "state of American poetry." You can't really talk about it that way because you have these various groups doing things. You have the cowboy poets who are perfectly happy doing what they are doing. They have this big meeting in Nevada every year, and they have a wonderful time. You have rap poets who have a big following; you have hip-hop. You know, all these various groups. All of them are thriving within their groups, and they really don't have too much interest in each other.

Shortly after I was named poet laureate, I thought, "I'm going to go to the National Cowboy Poetry thing in Elko, Nevada. That ought to be fun." So I called up the Western Folklife Association that runs it and said I was just appointed poet laureate of the United States, and I'd like to come to the Elko thing. And the response was, "So what!" They don't care about the poet laureate of the United States; they've got their own thing going. All those groups are there, and they are *thriving*. The only group that thinks everyone should be writing like them is we literary poets.

Baker: Let me ask something related to that. We're talking about school. We're all working in schools. And now you're talking about what happens to poetry in schools. Here are two passages I want to read for your response. This is from Jerry Thompson in the *Yale Review*: "Nabokov wrote that 'Art consists of specific details and not the general ideas Americans are taught from high school to look for in works of art.' He's unquestionably right; the difference between art and commonplace expression is in the last five percent of rigor." And this is Paul Kane: "Since virtually all literary themes can be reduced to commonplaces, there is clearly something other than cognitive content that attracts us."

I'm interested in what that other thing *is*. We get good at asking our students to find the theme of this or that poem. We take a beautiful poem and reduce it to its theme. You know: "Nature is awful, nature is beautiful, we are all silly people doomed by fate or culture. . . ." So what is it that we're missing in the treatment of poetry in school? What is that "thing" that makes the poem more than its testable content?

Kooser: I think we respond to poems the same way we respond to works in a gallery. We walk through a gallery; we may not be crazy about abstract expressionism, but we turn the corner in a gallery, and there is an abstract expressionist painting, and there's something that just happens to us, and this is an individual, a private response. There are poems that will immediately move us, emotionally move us. And we don't need to know exactly why that happens. I mean we can, upon analysis, figure it out: What is it about that painting that makes it so thrilling? But we have to use language to do that, and our response to a painting is not in language but in the viscera, in the heart.

Allan Grossman has a beautiful poem called "Two Waters." It's one of my favorites. On this farm he's talking about, there are two kinds of water: the water that drained into the cistern from melting snow and falling rain and then the well water, which is of a different character. I think the reason that I love that poem so much is because that's the way it was at my grandparents' home. They had a cistern and a well. It's beautifully written, but it also seems to be written for me. I bring my own experience to the poem. I don't know whether that's a decent answer.

Baker: It's a fine answer. Your illustration about understanding poetry uses the example of an art gallery. Does your own work as a painter affect your poetry? Are your paintings miniatures, too, like the poems?

Kooser: I do often paint very small paintings, five inches by seven, say, even smaller. I think a big part of making art of any kind is an attempt to secure order, and there can be a lot of pleasure in making something small and orderly.

Hofmeister: I'd like to get back to the issue of audience again, as well. I guess my question would be: How do we get more people to come out to poetry readings?

Kooser: Well, people will read and enjoy poetry and go to poetry readings as long as those experiences are pleasurable. We have to remember that pleasure is an important thing to human beings. We all want to have a pleasurable experience, but to go to a reading where you're sitting in the audience for sixty minutes, and someone is reading and not saying anything that you understand in any way is an altogether unpleasant experience. That has happened to a lot of people because of the difficulty and obscurity that evolved in the twentieth century.

In building readership for poetry, we have to think of having fun with little children. I really do believe children will be lifelong readers of poetry if we will spend time showing them that it is fun when they are small. A lot of teachers are very good at that, and poets like Shel Silverstein and Dr. Seuss can provide material. Their work shows that poetry can be fun.

But all too often what happens is that Ms. Smith in the eighth grade says that the meaning of this poem is not what you said it is; in fact, you get a D today because you didn't get the meaning right. So everybody gets out of school, and they see a poem in the *New Yorker* and they go, "Ahh, I don't have to do that anymore. I got a D in that."

Baker: I want to ask you more about this, the issue of availability. I am thinking about your own style and clarity, the simplicity of style in your poetry. I wonder whether you might agree with this little sentence of Edmund Burke. Burke says that "a clear idea is another name for a little idea."

Kooser: No, I would not agree. It's great fun not to agree with Edmund Burke.

Baker: I thought that is what you might say. Let me trace the tendency toward simplicity back a little further. Your own style is a plain style or colloquial style, where the lyric poem is stripped down, image driven, and narrative based. So I'm thinking of the American appeal to simplicity that runs all the way back to William Bradford, the first governor of Plymouth. In referring to the need for simplicity in his own language, he says, "As by the scriptures we are plainly told." He extols the virtue of simplicity or plainness. This is embedded in our national character, even our politics and religion, and of course in one strain of our poetry.

Kooser: That Shaker song "'Tis a Gift to Be Simple" might make a good thing to tack up over a writing desk. One of the most influential books for me as a writer is the Strunk and White *Elements of Style*. That book puts a lot of emphasis on the virtues of clarity and simplicity.

Baker: Let me ask you to respond to one last quotation. This is Helen Vendler. And the question again is about style, your own. Vendler says that "a writer's true vision lies in the implications of his or her style." Now, as you think about what your style is or what you hope it is, do you see a connection between style and something larger, like vision?

Kooser: That's very interesting. I'm not sure what Ms. Vendler means, but I do think that style is an extension of personality. I am comfortable, as a person, with the style of my poems, if that makes any sense at all. I am saying poems out of my heart, and this feels harmonious with the person who I am. I tend to be someone who writes with a great deal of sentiment. I'm willing to take that risk at a time when people are suspicious of sentimental poetry. But I think that is what I need to do as a poet.

Baker: Do you think your vision, then, is a social one? Or at least, do you think your style is crafted to be more available and public, rather than exclusive or academic?

Kooser: Yes, absolutely. Let me turn back to this problem we have with excluding audience. I'd like to be on record as saying that anybody can write a poem that nobody can understand. That's really easy. On the other hand, it might be really hard to write a poem that everyone in a room found meaning in. I would fail at that, even though I would like to reach out to everyone in this room.

Hofmeister: I have a question that relates to these issues—of the poet's ability to reach a broad audience, to speak or write in ways that are inclusive versus exclusive. "Availability" doesn't necessarily equate to "ease." Some of your poems that seem accessible are also challenging. I'm thinking of poems like "Praying Hands." You write a lot about hands, but here the hands are a made object. They are akin to particular objects in other poems—broken-down rural churches, odd roadside shrines—with some religious connotation. I wondered why these objects keep coming back into the poetry. My first guess is that they have something to do with what David calls the "midwestern social text"; these objects are a part of the community, and they need to be represented.

Kooser: I'm not a traditional believer in any manner of speaking, but I do go to church; I go to different churches. I like sitting with a group of people for about an hour who I imagine are thinking in the right direction. The denomination means nothing to me; it's the idea of being in a community, people who are actually spending some time thinking about their spiritual life.

When I was younger, I was extremely intolerant of people who were devout believers. I have come to believe that nearly everyone is trying to live a good life, and this may be tremendously Pollyannaish of me to think this. There are a few evil people in the world, and they cause a lot of trouble, but nearly everyone is trying to live a good life despite ignorance and poverty and the worst kind of circumstances.

Several years ago, I went to a wedding where the brother of the bride was a jailer in Texas, at the county facility that processes all the prisoners going to their executions at Huntsville. Now as you know—I hope you know—Texas executes maybe a hundred and fifty people a year, and Huntsville is where that happens. So these prisoners are coming to this county facility to be processed before they are sent on to death row. I said, "How many of these people are genuinely evil?" He said, "Ted, maybe one or two out of one hundred." He said the rest of them have just made stupid choices.

We might make fun of somebody with a *Praying Hands* plaque on his wall. But I'm for kindness and tolerance toward all of those things; they're part of what we have and who we are. The world is too short of kindness.

Hofmeister: You write quite a few poems about nature and seem to imply there is an order of things in nature. By contrast, in "The Red Wing Church," there's a sort of comedy going on. The church is all busted up; it's disintegrating, and you find the pews on everybody's porches around town, and the cross is God knows where. On the other hand, in a passage from *Local Wonders*, you carefully depict the Mennonite women, whose community is intact, and you invest them with a lot of respect. You begin by saying, "A person needn't be fearful of sixty-five-year-old Mennonite women in white lace caps." This implies, correctly, I think, that there is a lot of fear on the part of many people of other people who are like the Mennonite women.

Kooser: I know nothing about the Mennonite religion really. All I have to draw on is that when I go into the store, and those women are behind the counter, I like the way they count out the change. They're so careful not to cheat me of a penny. We really have a wonderful country full of lots of fascinating, beautiful people. I think we have a lot of stupidity in our leaders, but most of the people, I think, are pretty good people, doing as best they can.

Hofmeister: A certain kind of poetic approach can challenge a reader with a vision of inclusion, and at a time when the country is divided in so many ways—NASCAR Nation, *New Yorker* Nation, and so on. It's as if we've reached a point where people want to say thanks to social stratification or the legal system or whatever, we are finally immune from one another. A sad view, really, which I find your poems often subvert.

Baker: These issues—of clarity, inclusion, public utility—must be related to your work with "American Life in Poetry." Would you say something about that? How did your project get started? What have been your goals? And what do you see for the future of the project?

Kooser: My wife is in the newspaper business, and for years she and I had been talking about how one might get poetry back into the papers. There was a time when lots of newspapers printed poetry. It was her idea to let papers use the column free. She didn't think that, on the lean budgets upon which newspapers now operate, many could pay even five dollars a week. We wanted it to be free. After I was made poet laureate, I approached the Poetry Foundation. Without them, it couldn't have happened. They were behind the creation of the website, and they continue to maintain it. And they have given me enough money to pay for a halftime assistant editor and a graduate assistant. I get no money from them, but that's fine. I am a volunteer. The column has been very successful, and at the time of this interview, we have about four million readers. We have been published in around three hundred papers. I plan to keep the column going as long as I can, and, of course, as long as the Poetry Foundation continues to support it. What the column accomplishes is to show American newspaper readers that poetry is not something they need to fear, that there are poems that can be understood and appreciated.

Baker: Let's backtrack now—to before the laureateship and the Pulitzer. Once upon a time, you were an insurance man back home in Lincoln. How did your work in business affect the poetry?

Kooser: I believe that writers write for perceived communities and that if you are a lifelong professor of English, it's quite likely that you will write poems that your colleagues would like; that is, poems that will engage that community. I worked every day with people who didn't read poetry, who hadn't read it since they were in high school, and I wanted to write for them. I am not looking for an audience of literary professionals, though it's nice when some of them like what I'm doing.

Baker: And you retired, I think, around 2000?

Kooser: In mid-1998 I was diagnosed with a squamous cell tongue car-cinoma that had spread into my neck. I never returned to work after that. I was able to retire at age sixty about six months later, after an extensive sick leave. I'm delighted to say that I am cured now. I'm well, but it was a bad thing to go through. And it was the end of my insurance career, but I have never missed it for a minute.

As I began to come out of that illness, the University of Nebraska asked me to do some more teaching. I had, from time to time, taught as an adjunct. So they brought me in as a visiting professor. Later, I was made presidential professor and given a renewable contract. Anyway. the insurance career was over in 1999. I had been just doing what I do, writing poems and painting pictures and doing a little bit of teaching. Then this poet laureate thing came out of the blue, and I decided it was an opportunity to make some statements about poetry and talk to people in the world about American poetry. I took this on, and I worked pretty much seven days a week for two years. It was very important for me to show that someone from Nebraska could do that kind of work.

Hofmeister: That's a pretty amazing commitment of time and energy. Are you still working so hard?

Kooser: Now that I am out of office, I feel a little bit more able to say "no" to things even though I am always honored when I am asked to come to some civic group or something or other like that. I still do a lot of that. But I'm trying to say "no" a little more because I need to get back to doing some writing and quiet down a little. I keep my calendar on a word processing document, and at the height of my activity, I had five pages of things to do, single-spaced. It's down to about two and a half now. Over the next year or so, I hope to get back to where I can spend more time at home, where I write best, and I can do some painting. I'm still teaching. I teach once a year in the fall semester, just one class, and I'll keep doing that. And then my newspaper column is something that doesn't take up a great deal of time, but I do have to put regular time on that during the week.

Baker: So now, what is a normal day like for you? What is your habit, and what do you expect out of yourself?

Kooser: Well, all those years when I was at the insurance company, I learned that if I was going to do any writing at all, I had to do it early in the morning. And I got up at four thirty a.m. every day, and I would write until maybe seven. Then I would get in and out of the shower and get my suit and tie on and go off to the insurance company. And I have continued that all these years. You know, once you get used to getting up at four thirty in the morning, that's when you get up. My dogs are used to getting up at that time, and if I don't get up, they're usually bothering me to get up. So I get up every morning, and I sit in the same chair every morning, with my coffee pot at hand, and write in a notebook. And I am a dismal failure as a writer twenty-eight days out of thirty. It's just junk when I'm done, after my two or three hours at it. But I've learned that unless I'm sitting there with my notebook, on the day when the good one comes, I'm never going to get it at all. So I have to show up for work, which is one of the important things about doing this kind of work, or doing really any work.

Here is a little anecdote. This happened just before Thanksgiving one year. I had broken an overhead door in one of the outbuildings on my farm, and I went to the lumber yard to find a part for it. Here was this older guy who knows where things are, and he's sorting through all these boxes, and we started to talk about Thanksgiving coming. He said it was going to be a warm Thanksgiving, and so he was going to pitch horseshoes after Thanksgiving dinner. I said something about horseshoe pitching and about the fact that I had an uncle with cerebral palsy who could barely walk but who could pitch horseshoes. He said, "Yeah, my uncle Ed was Tri-State Horseshoe Pitching Champion three years running, and I asked my uncle, 'Uncle Ed, how did you get so good?' And he said, 'Son, you gotta pitch a hundred shoes a day.'"

That's what it takes to get good at anything. You've got to be in there pitching horseshoes every day. If at the end of the year I've written ten poems that I think are really effective, then it's a really good year for me—six to ten.

Baker: How do you *know* your good poems? How do they assert themselves or stand out from the other ones? In horseshoes, it's clear. The thrower hears the ping and sees the shoe around the peg.

Kooser: Sometimes I don't know. I have a sense of the quality of the work when it's finished. Maybe it's a ping. I want every part to snap into place at some point and become a whole. That poem "Success" is a good example. Or a poem David has written about, "Etude," which is as strong a poem as I've ever written. From the minute I wrote it, I was delighted with it, with finishing it. I remember thinking, "Did I just write this thing?" I was astounded at the way it all came together. So you have the feeling every once in a while when it all comes together, and it feels like more than itself somehow.

Baker: On those two poems, can you say what it is that came together, or why a particular poem may seem like your best one?

Kooser: I think what happens is in that extended metaphor. The power is in having its parts, its vehicle and tenor, greatly separated and then moved into a relationship. In "Etude," we have a bird, a blue heron, and we have a guy sitting in a blue suit at a desk. It's a big stretch to make. And if you try a stretch like that with a metaphor, and you can't hold it up, it will just sag and fall away. It happens that in that poem I was somehow able to make it work. I do believe that a lot of this material or connection comes forth by dictation—something deep in me, something that I'm not really in control of. If I knew how to write a poem like that, I would do it every day. But I can't. What happens in my favorite ones is that, toward the end of the poem, the metaphor makes a circle; it goes way out here, way at this guy at the desk, and it comes back at the point where I say "his pencil poised in the air like the beak of a bird." Back we'll go to the heron, and then it's all over. The figure is complete. I have no idea how I wrote that, but I had to be sitting there for a long time to do it just so.

Baker: We have talked a lot about plainness. But in some way, your best poems move beyond conventional definitions of the plain. I am thinking of what you have described just now, that sustained or pushed metaphor. Isn't that a very fanciful figurative metaphysical conceit, where you take an image and push it into a metaphor and take the metaphor and push it into a pattern, and push the pattern as far as it will possibly go until it nearly breaks? That's the way you were talking about the heron poem, and that's what I see in "Success" and, really, the other four poems in the new *Kenyon Review*. "Success" is not an imagist poem so much as a poem of conceit. "Two Men on an Errand" works that way, too. It develops an image—the men waiting at an auto repair shop—but pushes the whole image into metaphor and the metaphor into sustained conceit. There's a "foam rubber sandal," which seems like a car tire, and the older man "steering with his cane," and much more. This extends far beyond the simplicity of an isolate image. It seems to me, in some way, not plain at all. Is that a fair thing to say, or is that an insult?

Kooser: No, it isn't plain in the common sense, and I thank you for describing it so clearly. I think one thing about working with metaphor this way is that you want both sides to work perfectly well together. It's a matter of paring away the things that won't work in the comparison and being sure that the only things in the comparison are ones that play on both sides. Often, most of my work goes into fine-tuning the central metaphor.

Baker: You pare away? So perhaps you achieve a kind of plainness or economy even in the way you construct patterns of metaphor. No waste, even in elaboration.

Hofmeister: It almost seems as though the breaking point between a plain style and another kind of style is metaphor. But maybe you're saying it's more the way you manage the metaphor?

Kooser: I don't know, Tim. I guess the plain style is there in that I'm going for simplicity and plainness and clarity.

Baker: The rhetoric is plain, the idiom. That's the virtue of the plain style in your poems. But the application of the metaphor, the pushing of metaphor into extended conceit, that's the thing I like, that sort of irony, that pull of those two polarities. What we think of as usually different kinds of rhetoric. It shoves the image beyond its economical spare use.

Hofmeister: I'm thinking of a passage in *Local Wonders* where you're talking to your postman. Your postman has seen one of your poems and also some mention of your poetry, and he reluctantly says, "They say you have a gift for metaphor. What exactly does that mean?" What I like about that passage is you work through with him what metaphor is and what metaphor does. And that contributes to a step in his understanding of what you're about.

Kooser: I can't remember exactly how that passage goes, but the mailman had stopped me by the side of the road and said he read on the back of a book that I was a "master of metaphor," and he said, "What does that mean?"

I said, "Well, you know, a metaphor is a kind of comparison of things."

He said, "You mean when I say such and such was like, it was like . . . well, you know what I mean."

I said, "Yeah, that's right."

Hofmeister: Do we have a natural gift for metaphor, and to what extent, do you think?

Kooser: No, all of us don't have a natural gift for metaphor. I happen to be blessed with an imagination that leans in that direction. I've worked with a lot of students who have learned to write poems that exclude metaphors because they are just no good at it. You cannot deliberately construct a metaphor. It arises in the process of writing. It always comes as a marvelous surprise when it arrives. Just like that "Etude" poem, you think, "Where did that come from?" A student will show me a poem and say, "Don't you think I ought to put a metaphor right about there?" As if you could go to Circuit City and buy one and plug it in. I am immensely grateful that I was given an imagination that has the associative side to it.

Hofmeister: You have a wonderful way of sharing it in the poems. This partly has to do with what we are talking about, with that style. I also think about a device you use, which I think we have touched on. Where you say to a reader "You've seen how . . . ," and then you lead them into a scene. But you have a tension there, too, a tension where you expect a person to say, "Yes, I have seen that."

Kooser: You have to be careful with that kind of "lead-in" phrase. In the poem we're talking about—it's the one about the woman in the wheelchair, in which I say "You've seen how pianists bend forward to strike the keys, then lift their hands." I can assume when I write like that everyone here has seen a pianist do that. I wouldn't say, "You've seen how a man can repair a carburetor on a chainsaw." I couldn't expect you to know that.

There is another poem, the kind of poem that we've been talking about, a poem with an extended metaphor, that I sometimes read in public. It's called "A Washing of Hands." This is what happens to me when I'm working. I try to pay attention. This is the important thing in being a writer, trying to pay attention to what's going on. I was watching my wife at the sink washing her hands under the water and then flicking her fingers to get the water off.

Baker: Great. Let's take a look at "A Washing of Hands":

> She turned on the tap and a silver braid
> unraveled over her fingers.
> She cupped them, weighing that tassel,
> first in one hand and then the other,
> then pinched through the threads
> as if searching for something, perhaps
> an entangled cocklebur of water,
> or the seed of a lake. A time or two
> she took the tassel in both hands,
> squeezed it into a knot, wrung out
> the cold and the light, and then, at the end,
> pulled down hard on it twice,
> as if the water were a rope and she was
> ringing a bell to call me, two bright rings,
> though I was there.

Kooser: I love the idea of playing your way into that sort of associative stuff: just a braid of water. Those are the kinds of poems I really love to write because I am always so thrilled when they work and let down when they fail.

Baker: This poem again is a single conceit, or rather, a poem whose metaphor keeps transforming into another version of itself. There's the cocklebur, and then the seed of the lake, and then the tassel, the knot, the rope. These images aren't exactly cognitively connected; it's more about the magic, the leap of an associative imagination.

Kooser: Yes, it's me following my imagination as it plays and writing down some of that play, but not all of it. In a poem like that, I will usually have deleted some of the play if it doesn't seem to enhance the effect. I like your use of the word *magic* because when those metaphors come to me, unbidden, it feels magical.

Baker: What do you see as the most hopeful movements in contemporary poetry? You are right, earlier, when you point out so many fields and schools and types. A poetry for every audience. There is a loud din in the small world of poetry. What do you foresee?

Kooser: I am not much of a scholar, and no cultural historian, but I hope time will somehow preserve the poems that have real meaning for broad groups of people, not just for literary professionals. Sir Thomas Beecham once said that he thought composers should write music that chauffeurs and delivery boys could whistle. Elsewhere he said that unless composers write music that organ grinders can play it will never be immortal.

Baker: What are you working on now? I know—the "American Life in Poetry" project. But how about your poems? Are you writing? Do you see a new collection in the future?

Kooser: I am slowly assembling a small stack of poems I'm pleased with, and the ones in the *Kenyon Review* are part of that, but I think it will be five or six years before I have another book ready. I don't want to publish anything that isn't at least as well done as *Delights & Shadows*. Right now, I could get just about anything published because my name is well-known. But it would be stupid to use that celebrity as a way of getting inferior work published. Others have done that, and it's a mistake.

Hofmeister: I wonder if you have any final things you'd like to say—about your work or the wider state of poetry?

Kooser: Poetry has meant a great deal to me for almost fifty years, and I have been immensely lucky with my poems, to have them noticed and appreciated. I have a happy writing life, and I am thankful.

The First Order of Wonders: An Interview with Ted Kooser

William Barillas / 2008

This interview was conducted at Ted Kooser's home in Garland, Nebraska, in August 2007.
It was first published in *Bloomsbury Review* in the January/February 2008 issue. Barillas
has written widely about Kooser, including a discussion of the poet and his work in his 2006
critical study, *The Midwestern Pastoral: Place and Landscape in Literature of the American
Heartland*. Reprinted with the permission of William Barillas.

Recent years have been good to Ted Kooser. He received two of the high-
est honors that can be given to an American poet. He served two terms as
United States poet laureate (2004–2006), and he won the 2005 Pulitzer
Prize for Poetry for his book *Delights & Shadows*. These accolades brought
Kooser, who has had a long and distinguished career, to a much larger
national readership. There is a kind of justice in these events, as Kooser
has always written poetry with a diverse, nonacademic audience in mind.
As Dana Gioia has said of him in *Can Poetry Matter? Essays on Poetry and
American Culture*, "There is to my knowledge no poet of equal stature who
writes so convincingly in a manner the average American can understand
and appreciate." Accessibility, clarity: and the transformation of ordinary
experiences by means of startling metaphors: these are the distinguishing
characteristics of Ted Kooser's poetry.

It is also notable for its origins in small-town, rural Nebraska, where
Kooser makes his home. He gives voice to a region known by many readers
only in the fiction of Willa Cather, or perhaps the nonfiction of Mari Sandoz. In announcing Kooser's appointment as poet laureate on August 12,
2004, librarian of Congress James H. Billington said: "Ted Kooser is a major
poetic voice for rural and small-town America and the first poet laureate
chosen from the Great Plains. His verse reaches beyond his native region to
touch on universal themes in accessible ways."

William Barillas: Your poetry has done pretty well lately. You received the Pulitzer Prize and served two years as US poet laureate.

Ted Kooser: It has been a surprising time for me. Ten years ago, I didn't know if I would be alive in six months. I was really sick, and then all of this wonderful stuff happened. It's quite miraculous.

Barillas: To begin, I'd like to ask about your early years in Ames, Iowa.

Kooser: I was born in 1939, so by the time I was really awake to the world, it was the postwar period, the Eisenhower years. Looking back, Ames seems idyllic, in a Norman Rockwell kind of way. We had huge elm trees and a park three blocks from where I lived where they had band concerts on summer nights. We had little makeshift parades on Memorial Day.

As a teenager I was obsessively interested in automobiles. I built hot rods and did a lot of drag racing. I didn't think much beyond that. It was all about hot cars and girlfriends, like in my poem "Hometown," where I describe myself wearing Levi's, boots with chains, a leather jacket, and duck's ass hair. Ames was populated with a lot of professors' families, whose children we called the popular kids. We hot-rodders were on the other side, getting in trouble, smoking cigarettes.

Barillas: What started you writing as an adolescent?

Kooser: One of my primary motivations was girls. I didn't have much else going for me. I didn't have athletic ability. I couldn't play any instruments in the band. I thought being a writer would make me interesting and mysterious.

Barillas: Your first book, *Official Entry Blank*, was published in 1969. When did you start working on the poems that appeared in it?

Kooser: Around 1959. I had a couple good friends, outsiders, in Ames. One was Jim Stevens, who went on to success in electronics and telecommunications in Seattle. The other was Jack Winkler, who was a history major. The three of us were interested in the Beat movement. Jim had a little house, and I spent a lot of my time there trying to be a beatnik. I wrote the first poems I was serious about while squatting on Jim's living room floor, drinking beer. In 1960, I was the editor of the student literary magazine at Iowa State [*Sketch*]. I published some things in that.

Barillas: What led you toward writing about the life around you rather than more arcane subjects?

Kooser: It was Karl Shapiro's influence, mostly. I had come to Nebraska because Karl was here; I wanted to study with him. I talked to him a great deal about William Carlos Williams. So Shapiro and Williams writing about ordinary life—they were my touchstones. If I was going to write about ordinary life and ordinary things, I was going to do it about what was right under my nose, which was the Great Plains and the life we have here.

Barillas: Of all the poems in your first book, *Official Entry Blank*, only one made it into *Sure Signs: New and Selected Poems*, and that was "Abandoned Farmhouse." What distinguished that poem in your mind?

Kooser: Of all my poems it's the one that appears most frequently in anthologies. It has stood the test of time. Many other poems in my first book are clearly derivative of Williams and other poets I was copying. But that one does seem very much my own. It's an experience I've had again and again, hanging around abandoned farmsteads and picking up things and looking at them.

Barillas: The image of abandoned buildings on the plains appears in a number of your poems. Is it a metaphor or a synecdoche for the history of the Great Plains?

Kooser: Who knows exactly why I was attracted to those things? For one thing, I was an architecture major as an undergraduate. I was always interested in buildings. I have always drawn pictures of old farmhouses. In *The Poetry Home Repair Manual*, I tell a story about how important reading Walter de la Mare's "The Listeners" was to me. It has a scene in which a man rides up to an empty house and hammers on the door, and no one is there. There was a wonderful mystery about that poem that I liked. In a way, I've been rewriting "The Listeners" all of these years.

Barillas: I'd like to ask about your desire to write for a wide audience. Where does that come from?

Kooser: I like the idea of being of some use to a broad, general community, including people who live around me here in the country. I love the idea of writing poems the guy right down the road would appreciate. I've been thinking quite a bit about this lately. What is it about a popular song that makes people remember lines from it? Or even be able to sing the whole song? The music aside, it's that the lyrics supply useful language to people who may never have been able to articulate a certain feeling. They pick up on a phrase from a song, and it becomes a part of their personal vocabulary. I would like to do that in poems. I would like to provide language people can use in daily life.

I had John Prine come to the Library of Congress because I so admire his lyric writing. He writes with tremendous respect about ordinary people. There's no sneering whatsoever in Prine's work. He has a wonderful song that goes,

There's a big old goofy man
Dancing with a big old goofy girl
Ohh baby
It's a big old goofy world.

That could be done in a sneering way, but Prine does it with respect, and wonder, even. There are marvelous lines in popular music that as a poet I wish I had written. Kris Kristofferson has a line: "Maybe I'll never believe in forever again." That is the kind of phrase people all over the country could be packing around with them and using. I'd like to be of service in that way.

Barillas: What qualities make for good poets, the kind of poets you admire?

Kooser: Jim Harrison, who is one of my best friends: The personal characteristic Jim has that makes him a very attractive writer is, he is an extraordinarily generous man. He wants to give something to the reader, something of use, but he never condescends. I like that about his work.

Barillas: How did you get to know him and start a correspondence?

Kooser: When he was working on his novel *Dalva*, he came to Nebraska to do research at the Historical Society. He was looking through boxes of old photographs there, and John Carter, the photo curator, got to be friends with him and eventually introduced us.

Barillas: Very few poets cowrite a book with another poet How did you and Harrison come to collaborate on *Braided Creek*?

Kooser: We had no idea we were writing a book; we were just sending poems back and forth. At some point Jim mentioned we might have a collection. Although those poems appear to be sequential, I arranged them all. I had them on three-by-five cards in two long strips going into the bedroom and out to the far wall of the living room. I kept moving them around until I got them into an order that had a movement to it. One of the reasons readers can't identify which of us is writing what is that I didn't just alternate between Jim and myself. I used two by Jim, one by me, three by Jim, two by me, that sort of thing. We were so closely in tune that there are a few poems neither of us remembers who wrote.

Barillas: The poems resemble haiku; each has two to four lines and conveys a single image or idea. How did the two of you get into that?

Kooser: Both of us have been interested for years in the Asian poets. And there is a pithiness to haiku that works well in a letter. In the fall and winter of 1998 into 1999, I was also sending Jim the poems that turned into *Winter*

Morning Walks. The two books developed at the same time. The intent with *Winter Morning Walks* was not necessarily to correspond, but to prove to myself I was well enough to write a poem every day and stick it in the mail.

Barillas: Does *Winter Morning Walks* suggest poetry is about survival?

Kooser: Poetry can be a way of identifying and preserving order in chaotic times. When I was desperately ill, trying to get back my health, writing poetry helped me identify a little area of order about the size of a postcard. I could make that much order every day out of my world, which was in great disorder. The same thing happened to many people who responded to September 11 by writing poems. I see that as their attempt to make order out of chaos.

Barillas: You often take a seemingly ordinary subject and transform it through metaphor. Have you written a poem that achieves what you are after in using metaphor?

Kooser: One of the better of that type is "Etude," in *Weather Central,* which I begin by talking about a great blue heron and then move into the image of a man in a blue suit at his desk writing a love letter. I reel in the metaphor at the end, with the man holding his pencil in the air like the beak of a bird. I often use that poem as an example of working with metaphor.

Barillas: So it is a matter of introducing the connection, developing the actual subject, and then returning?

Kooser: Yes. A metaphorical poem won't work if it just flies off and stays there. You have to ground it again; you have to pull it back. Writing with figures is like tying a knot in a rope. You begin the poem with one strand, and then you tie in a little figure. Then you go a little farther and tie another little figure into it. Many failed poems are just catalogs of knots. The trick is to run a little thread through the whole poem so that when you get to the end, you pull the thread, and all the loops unite into one big knot. After the reader has been captive of the comparison throughout the poem, he or she is released at the end of the poem.

Barillas: What do people outside of the Great Plains most misunderstand about the region?

Kooser: People say, "You have no culture out there," as if there is one culture everyone should share. But we have a marvelously rich culture here on the plains; it is just based on different things. We may not have the Museum of Modem Art, but we might have a beautiful Catholic church in a small town, or tractor pulls and county fairs and small-town parades. It is just a different kind of culture. I don't know that many people out here hanker for something else. You could walk through Omaha, Nebraska, and talk to everybody on the streets and ask them how many people wish they could go to see the

Bolshoi Ballet that evening, and you probably wouldn't find very many people interested in going. They have other things they want to do. People tend to be provincial wherever they are. They like what they have. People in Manhattan like what they have, and they have their own provincialism, just as we do.

Barillas: How would you characterize people who live on the Great Plains?

Kooser: Self-effacement is very important out here. We generally do not put ourselves forward. It is a culture of diffidence.

Barillas: Soon after being named poet laureate, you executed something of a jujitsu flip on the *New York Times* interviewer who pestered you about not studying European poets. You replied, "Think of all the European poetry I could have read if we hadn't spent all this time on this interview."

Kooser: Well, that interview is only one page in print, but we had been working on it for ten days by email. The way the interview was printed, it looks as if I am being impatient with her over a few questions, when actually we had been going on like that for days. A lot of people told me, "You really got her," but I wasn't being short. I really did like working with her. It was a very interesting process.

Barillas: Her questions seemed to typify a coastal view of the interior. Many East Coast intellectuals are attached to Europe and are dismissive of the interior of the United States.

Kooser: Yes, I think there is something to that. It is all part of modernism. T. S. Eliot said all art ought to build upon the art that went before. In order to make art, you had to have a deep education. That thinking has been with us for about a hundred years now and will persist. It has a lot of vitality. But the audience I am after does not have that sophistication.

Barillas: I have written about Midwestern cultural archetypes, such as the tinkerer—the person with practical knowledge about how to invent things, or build them, take them apart, or repair them. In the public imagination, the tinkerer is embodied in Edison, Ford, and the Wright brothers, all Midwesterners, but it is also reflected in people's lives and in Midwestern writing. The title of your book, for example, *The Poetry Home Repair Manual*, strikes me as a very Midwestern way to think about poetry. Does that make sense to you?

Kooser: Yes, I am very much a part of that tinkerer culture. When Jim Harrison met me, here at my house in Garland, one of the first things he said was, "I'll bet you have a couple buckets of bent nails in your barn you're going to straighten someday." And I said, "I do, as a matter of fact." When you live in the country, you don't throw anything away because on any given day you might need to find something, and you're not going to drive twenty miles to the hardware store to find it. I have a barn full of miscellaneous stuff: pieces of furnace pipe, fittings, and tools of all kinds. I can fix just about anything myself if I have to. The air-conditioner repairman is here today because that is a little beyond my learning. Given time, though, I would take on an air conditioner just to see if I could figure out how to do it. I've built buildings; I've done wiring and plumbing. You're right; tinkering is very much a part of this culture.

Barillas: In terms of the writing process, how is writing for you like tinkering, whether that be building something, repairing something, or keeping spare parts? What would be the equivalent in your writing process of the bucket of bent nails in the barn?

Kooser: For me writing a poem involves making use of available materials in the locality where I am. I'll make the poem out of whatever I can grab up. I'm not going to go to the library and check out *The Golden Bough* when I can make a poem out of available things. Some modernists would go to *The Golden Bough* and install something from it into the poem. I'm not interested in that.

Barillas: Your newspaper column, "American Life in Poetry," which was your project as poet laureate, seems to have come out of the same ideas about poetry and audience. How did the column come about?

Kooser: You can be poet laureate without doing any projects at all. But it seemed to me this was a great opportunity. For years, Kathy and I had been thinking about how to get poetry back into newspapers. My laureateship gave me the authority to pursue that, and the column has been very successful; we are in more than 150 newspapers with a combined circulation of over eleven million readers. I took my idea of the average newspaper reader largely from my wife's experience in newspapers. I looked for poems that would be understandable to that kind of reader. I also looked for short poems because I know newspapers won't print a very long column; they don't want to give that much space. So I worked with twenty lines or less.

Barillas: What other duties were required as poet laureate?

Kooser: You give an initial reading in October to open the library's reading series and a speech at the end of May. In February, you select a couple of poets to receive the Witter Bynner Fellowships, which are $10,000 apiece, and you introduce the winners when they come to Washington to read. You can invite other people to the library to read as well and be there to introduce them. Really, the duties are minimal. The rest of the work comes in correspondence and appearances and so on. I made a point right away to contact the National Council of Teachers of English, to tell them I wanted to come to their convention. It was a wonderful experience, talking to English teachers about poetry. I went to the American Library Association meeting in Chicago as well. I've done quite a few traditional readings on campuses and that sort of thing. But I prefer to talk to people who are not already in the poetry camp, as a way of extending the reach of poetry. For instance, there is a lot of emphasis in medicine now on healing and the arts. So I arranged to talk to medical schools.

Barillas: Do you read reviews?

Kooser: No. I find them upsetting one way or the other. I feel terribly hurt by the critical ones, and the ones that praise me make me think, "Oh come on, this is way over the top. I'm not that good a writer." I have friends who are writers who don't read their reviews either.

Barillas: By now you are beginning to get some scholarly interest. Do you give an eye to that?

Kooser: Yes, but I find it amusing when people draw preposterous conclusions about my work. Perhaps they are right, but the ideas never occurred to me. Somebody wrote to me and said, "I noticed you often use the color blue in your poems. Why is that?" I responded, "I didn't realize I was doing that, but it is my favorite color." It is logical that I would use it. In the issue of the *Midwest Quarterly* devoted to my work (Summer 2005, 46, no. 4), there is an essay in which the writer says a person familiar with my writing can identify the poems I wrote in *Braided Creek*. Then the writer cites a poem that is not one of mine but one of Jim's. I think that is hilarious.

Barillas: Would you talk about the genesis of a poem? I'm thinking about "Fort Robinson."

Kooser: That is the place in northwestern Nebraska where Crazy Horse was murdered. It was also the scene of the Cheyenne outbreak of 1879. The army had captured Dull Knife and his northern Cheyenne and kept them in a barracks in the dead of winter with no heat and little to sustain them. On a very cold January night, they broke out of the barracks and ran. They had some arms they had hidden under their clothes, but they were outgunned, and many of them were killed.

Fort Robinson is now a historical park; it has all been restored. What happened was I took my young son on a vacation trip. When we pulled in, the grounds crew was poking the magpies out of the trees, I suppose because they mess on the sidewalks. The nestlings fell to the ground, and the crew was stomping on them, killing them, and it was horrible. The matted bunches of feathers on the ground and in the grass connected with the memory of the Indians who had been killed there. The poem is a juxtaposi-tion of two times. It is quite different from a lot of my work. Over the years, people told me they remember that Fort Robinson poem, even when they don't remember anything else I've written. So it has a different effect. It is something of a history lesson, with a social message that is a little bigger than the topics I usually take on.

Barillas: The poem ends:

We didn't get out of the car.
My little boy hid in the back and cried
as we drove away, into those ragged buttes
the Cheyenne climbed that winter, fleeing.

Kooser: Fleeing, of course, meaning my boy and myself as well as the Cheyenne.

Barillas: Which of your recent poems has caused strong reactions at readings?

Kooser: The poem "At the Cancer Clinic" is one. I read it a lot in public because it is an example of me standing on the outside of things looking in, not identifying myself with an *I*, yet being a participant. It is based on an experience I actually had at the cancer clinic in Omaha, in an oncol-ogy waiting room, watching a cancer patient, a woman, being helped by two other women, who may have been her sisters. It would be easy to slip into irony in such a poem, but I counter the ironic impulse by saying, "There is no restlessness or impatience / or anger anywhere in sight." That is how it was; everybody in that room was on that woman's side. The part of the poem I like the best is the part that is most closely observed, how the woman watches "each foot swing scuffing forward / and take its turn under her weight."

I gave a copy of that poem to my doctor in Omaha, and he had it blown up and framed for the nurses' station in the cancer ward. It hangs on the wall, not in the patients' area but behind where the nurses are, where they put their stuff. I thought that was something; I had been of use with a poem. It was wonderful. There couldn't be a better way to be published. That's what I would love to happen with my work, to have somebody take it into their life and make some use of it. The doctor must have sensed that by where he put it. The poem is about the dignity of medical care. The nurses are not restless or impatient or angry with anyone. They are there to serve. So the poem honors them as well as the patient. I found the people in those waiting rooms were almost beatific in their affirmation of life. Here were people who had lost their hair, people who had to have parts of their faces reconstructed. But they glowed with a love of life that was marvelous. Plenty of people had given up and gone home to die. But the ones in the waiting room, who were working on it, who were going through treatment, really wanted to live. It radiated from them. I have no idea what happened to the woman in the poem, but she was a good example of someone who was struggling to live, leaning on a community to do that.

Barillas: "At the Cancer Clinic" might be called a love poem for a community. That feeling for community emerges from many poems in *Delights & Shadows*, along with a kind of gentleness. They are quieter than many of your earlier poems. There is a new patience there.

Kooser: Postcancer, I've become much more patient and tolerant of all kinds of things. In Jim's new book of novellas, *The Summer He Didn't Die*, he cites someone who wrote that 80 percent of people are trying to live as best as they can, and 20 percent are not. It serves the book he is writing very well, but I think a much greater percentage are doing the best they can. I went to a wedding ten years ago in which the brother of the bride was a jailer from a county facility in Texas that processes all the guys who are on their way to death row at Huntsville, where they are executed by the hundreds. I asked, "How many of those guys are genuinely evil?" and he said, "Maybe two or three out of a hundred are evil. The rest just made stupid choices." I believe that most people try to live a good life, but they just screw up monumentally. They're up against enormous odds. But most people are trying to be good.

"Simple, Clear, Direct": Ted Kooser Talks Poetry with AP Literature Students

Charleston School of the Arts / 2010

This interview was conducted on March 11, 2010, via conference call between John Cusatis's AP English Literature class at the Charleston School of the Arts (SOA) in Charleston, South Carolina, and Ted Kooser, who spoke from his home in Garland, Nebraska. Interviewers were Cusatis and the following students: Catherine Bowler, Lauren DiNicola, Jacob Fanning, Austin Jur, DeAnna Kerley, David Nicholson, Collins Rice, Graeme Rock, David Sass, Schuyler Seaborn, Kayla Watts, and Seth Zimmerman. Cengage Learning Inc. Reproduced by permission. www.cengage.com/permissions.

School of Arts: Hello, Professor Kooser.

Ted Kooser: Hello.

SOA: How are you doing today?

TK: I'm ready to go.

SOA: Great. Thank you. There are twelve Advanced Placement English Literature students here. Everybody has a question for you. Do you happen to have a volume of your poetry nearby?

TK: I have a few poems here.

SOA: We were hoping you could read a poem to us to start off, one of your choice.

TK: Sure. I have a longer poem that will be coming out in the *Hudson Review*. It's kind of timely. It's called "A Morning in Early Spring." It's the way it is here today: half rain and half snow and mud. I'd be happy to read that.

SOA: That would be great. We'd love to hear it.

TK: Okay.

"A Morning in Early Spring"

First light, and under stars
our elm glides out of darkness
to settle on its nest of shadows,
spreading its feathers to shake out
the night. Above, a satellite—
one shining bead of mercury
bearing thousands of voices—
rolls toward the light in the east.

The Big Dipper, for months left
afloat in a bucket of stars,
is starting to leak. Each morning
it settles a little into the north.

A rabbit bounces over the yard
like a knot at the end of a rope
that the new day reels in, tugging
the night and coiling it away.

A fat robin bobs her head,
hemming a cloth for her table,
pulling the thread of a worm,
then neatly biting it off.

My wife, in an old velour robe,
steps off a fifty-yard length
of the dawn, out to the road
to get the newspaper, each step

with its own singular sound.
Each needle in the windbreak
bends to the breeze, the windmill
turns clockwise then ticks to a stop.

No other day like this one.
A crocus like a wooden match—

Ohio Blue Tip—flares in the shadows
that drip from the downspout.
This is a morning that falls between
weathers, a morning that hangs
dirty gray from the sky,
like a sheet from a bachelor's bed,

hung out to dry but not dry yet,
the air not warm nor cool,
and my wife within it, bearing the news
in both hands, like a tray.

Along the road to east and west,
on the dark north by the fence posts,
thin fingers of shadowy snowdrifts
pluck and straighten the fringe

on a carpet of fields. Clouds float in
like ships flying the pennants of geese,
and the trees, like tuning forks,
begin to hum. Now a light rain

fingers the porch roof, trying
the same cold key over and over.
Spatters of raindrops cold as dimes,
and a torn gray curtain of cloud

floats out of a broken window
of sky. Icy patches of shadows
race over the hills. No other day
like this one, not ever again.

Now, for only a moment, sleet
sifts across the shingles, pale beads
threaded on filaments of rain,
and the wind dies. A threadbare

pillowcase of snow is shaken out
then draped across the morning,

too thin to cover anything for long.
None other like this.

All winter, the earth was sealed
by a lid of frost, like a layer
of paraffin over the apple jelly,
or the white disk of chicken fat

on soup left to cool, but now,
in cold tin sheds with dripping roofs
old tractors warm their engines,
burning the feathery mouse nests

from red exhausts, rattling the jars
of cotter pins, shaking gaskets
on nails and stirring the dirty rags
of cobwebs. And young farmers

who have already this morning
put on the faces of ancestors
and have shoved the cold red fists
of grandfathers, fathers, and uncles

deep in their pockets, stand framed
in wreaths of diesel smoke,
looking out over the wet black fields
from doors that open onto spring.

Twenty miles east of where we live
the day blows out the candles of the city,
street light by street light,
and the thin smoke of rain drifts away,

while a quarter of a million people
go to their windows to peer out into what's coming,
holding their cups like beggars
asking for little.

In first light I bend to one knee.

I fill the old bowl of my hands
with wet leaves, and lift them
to my face, a rich broth of browns

and yellows, and breathe the vapor,
spiced with oils and, I suspect,
just a pinch of cumin. This is the life,
none other like it. [*Applause*]

TK: Thank you.

SOA: Thank you for sharing that. So when can we expect to read it in the *Hudson Review*?

TK: I just read the galley proof, so it will be in the next issue [Spring 2010].

SOA: We'll keep an eye out for it. Would you mind commenting a little bit on the poem before we begin with our questions? We've talked about how your poetry is very expansive, reaching back through generations and into the cosmos, but also focusing on the magnificence of here and now, as this new poem seems to do.

TK: This poem is unusual in that, ordinarily, my poems that run twenty lines or so start with an image or a metaphor, and then I expand upon that single image or comparison to some degree. In this instance, the poem is really a compilation of a lot of short poems that are just strung together. I tend to write a lot of short things, and I just noticed one day that if I could organize them, I might have a poem about spring. And that's how it came together. But I don't think consciously about whether or not I'm addressing the cosmos or ordinary things close at hand. I don't make those kinds of rational decisions when I'm writing. I just write about whatever comes to mind and what I'm enthusiastic about at the moment. I suppose my personality, to some degree, directs my choices. But the worst thing for me as a poet is to think too much about what I'm doing. It's better, in my instance, to have my poems respond to the emotional state that I might be in at a given time.

SOA: You mentioned in an interview that in order to perfect a poem, you often write thirty to forty drafts.

TK: Yes.

SOA: You've already said a word or two on this subject, but can you elaborate on how you begin writing the first draft, and also what elements are you looking to perfect as you revise?

TK: Yes, as I mentioned, ordinarily some little image or comparison will stick in my mind, and I start writing about that. For instance, in the poem

I read, I might have begun by noticing the way robins pull worms out of the ground and then thought that I could compare that with a woman pulling a thread through a piece of cloth. Then I would try to build a poem for that image with some other language. In other words, expand it from there. Whatever I can do with that image really determines the shape and size of the poem. Then I begin the process of revision. I'm always trying to revise toward simplicity and clarity and away from difficulty and obscurity. This is the choice that I make as the literary artist, and it is certainly far different from what another poet might do. I have graduate students who want to make their poems more and more difficult. I think that comes out of the fact that we are trained to read poems as if they have hidden meanings that need to be discerned, and that their worth has something to do with the depth of the hidden meaning. Of course, that's something I don't really subscribe to at all. At any rate, my revisions are always trying to be as graceful as I can make them: simple, clear, direct. And I want them to sound like me. I wouldn't put a word in a poem that would cause you to go to the dictionary and look it up. I don't want you to break away from my poem to do research to understand what I'm doing. I want you to have the experience right there as you're reading the poem. I want the whole thing there. If I used a word that you might not be familiar with—let's say I referred to a myth or a mythical character. If I referred to Vlad the Impaler, I would say in the poem that he was a Transylvanian man from whom our interest in vampires descends. That's a really terrible example. [*Laughter*] But if I put something in a poem that I think you need help with, I'm going to give you help in the poem rather than ask you to go somewhere else to find it.

SOA: How do you know when you've finished the poem, when you've reached that final draft?

TK: Well, it's usually when I can't think of anything I can do to make it any better. It just comes down to that. I spend hours working on a poem. When I come to a point where I can't think of anything to do to make it any better, I'll let it sit for a couple of days and look at it again. Sometimes by then I will notice certain things that I can do to improve it. But, generally, there comes a point where I simply can't think of anything else to do to make it any better, and that's where I stop.

SOA: Your poem "Memory" describes the process of writing through memories. As a writer myself, I've often contemplated the role of memory in a writer's life. How is memory important to you as a writer?

TK: Well, it's really all important. In addition to all those poems I've written that come out of memory, in essence, I wrote a whole nonfiction book about memory. I have actually written two. One just came out not too long ago called *Lights on a Ground of Darkness*, which is basically an extended memory of when I was a little boy visiting my mother's parents. I use memory for everything. Even a poem that would appear to be immediate, something that happened right now, very often comes out of a memory, a shorter-term memory. Let's say I saw a particular bird on Monday of this week, and today is Thursday. Now I'm starting to write about it. Well, that's working memory. It's really very important. I can't imagine being a writer without that.

SOA: I was reading about your morning writing routine in an interview you did with NPR. You said, "Nine days out of ten, nothing good comes of it at all. Maybe on the tenth day, if I'm lucky, some little thing will start a poem." How do you know when a poem is actually getting started?

TK: Usually what happens is that I might write a complete poem and look at it and think, "This is absolutely stupid." [*Laughter*] Or I'll think, "You've written poems like this before. You ought to be writing something new." And on the good day, perhaps it's a really fresh comparison of two things, something that really comes at me and startles me with its interest. And that is good. Those little events that happen when I'm writing are the things that I thrive on. I love it when that happens. You're sitting there, and something comes into your head, and you think, "Ah, where did that come from?" It's a real rush. So those are the good things that happen, again, once or twice a month. You have a morning like that when something happens, and, as I probably said in that interview—I've said it a million times—if you're not sitting there on that morning trying to write, you won't get it at all. It's important to show up to work and sit there. And it's probably important to write stupid stuff as well as things that are not. I've had some celebrity as a poet, but I still get my poems rejected by magazines when people think something I've written isn't any good. That's just part of the way it works.

SOA: Is there anything in particular that you find inspiring, that sparks your writing?

TK: Not really. I do like writing about very ordinary things and very ordinary occurrences. I've been writing a good many poems in the last few years in which I simply observe a couple of people doing something across a room. Although I am a part of their community, in a way, I am outside of what is happening, and I can just watch it happen. And I am very comfortable doing that kind of thing. I really prefer that point of view rather than being in the poem myself, talking about myself.

SOA: Some of the greatest poets of the past century, such as William Carlos Williams and Wallace Stevens, worked in other professions while they wrote. Before retiring from your position at the insurance company, did you draw ideas for poems from your work experience?

TK: Sure. There's a poem in my book *Weather Central* called "Four Secretaries," which describes, pretty accurately, four young women who were working in my department. I also wrote a series of short poems, looking out the window of my office at the things that were lying around on a neighboring roof. There was an old mop that somebody had used to put some tar on the roof and other things people had left there. And then, of course, our building was right in downtown Lincoln, so when I would go out for the noon hour, there were a lot of people on the street, a lot of things going on. One of my Valentine poems [*Valentines*, 2008], for instance, was written across the street in the alley where I saw a couple of guys digging through a dumpster behind a flower shop, pulling out roses. I tend to use everything that happens to me in some way or another.

SOA: So, the work itself wasn't a source for material?

TK: No. I had a very uninteresting job. It was nothing that I ever cared for a great deal. I had a pretty good income, and there was some security in it. But the reason I had a job was because I was a writer, and I needed some way of paying the bills. I knew that there was no money in writing, so I just took a job that I could do eight hours a day and be done with. And it turned out I was pretty good at it. I was a vice president in the company when I retired. But my heart was never in it, basically. It's interesting, your generation and the generation just ahead of you have the privilege of talking about finding fulfilling work. But the generations up to mine, for instance, my parents' generation, if you had mentioned "fulfilling work" to them, they would have looked at you like you were from Mars. That never occurred to them that there was work like that. You just got a job, and you did it.

SOA: The accumulation of wisdom that is part of the aging process seems to be a prominent theme in your work. Do you feel it's worth it, trading youth for wisdom? Is it a fair trade?

TK: Well, [*Laughing*] I never thought it was particularly fair that we had to grow up and die. [*Laughter*] It didn't seem to me like that was the deal that we should have gotten, but that's just the way it works. You really do gain some wisdom by growing older. I'm sure there are people who don't, but we all learn things as we grow older. I'm now seventy years old, and every once in a while now, I get a real insight into something about life. I can't give an example of that, but all of a sudden, I will realize something about life at my age that would have been pretty useful to know when I was twenty or fifteen. There are all kinds of good things about growing older as well as being young.

SOA: Well, thank you. The reason I ask is because we're a class of eighteen-year-olds who think we know what's right about everything, but sometimes we're wrong.

TK: I'm sure you've heard this from your parents and grandparents, but there will come a time for all of you when you will look back at your life when you were eighteen years old and think about all the stupid things you said and did. [*Laughter*] That will happen when you are thirty and when you're forty. When you're fifty, you'll look back at things you did when you were forty that will seem stupid. [*Laughter*]

SOA: You stated that if your poems were read one by one, they could have been written anywhere or about any place, but considering that many of your poems are vividly connected to the heartland, what is it, do you feel, that makes them universal?

TK: Oh, gosh. [*Laughter*] I don't try to make them universal. I don't have that as a goal. If any universality shows up in those poems, it's because I am writing about an experience that people all over have had, rather than just people in Nebraska. For instance, the poems I was talking about where I'm observing two people. I have a poem called "Splitting an Order," which is about watching an older couple cut a sandwich in half in a restaurant. The man cuts it in half and gives half of it to his wife on an extra plate. The whole poem is about that gesture and watching them do that. I saw that happen in a restaurant in Lincoln, Nebraska, and I've seen it happen elsewhere, of course, too. But there are lots of you in that room who've seen that happen, as well. You've been in a restaurant somewhere and seen some older people splitting an order. You may not have noticed it with the specificity that I did, but it happened. So that's the kind of universality I'm talking about. It's nothing bigger than that. It's just simply knowing that we're all a part of one great big community, and we all have like experiences.

SOA: How do you maintain originality while also writing about a universal experience?

TK: Well, originality is a difficult thing to talk about. We all have original experience. Your experience right here talking to me is an original experience. The way that you would write about that in an original manner would be to talk about the things that could only have happened to you in this conversation that we're having. You raised your eyes while we were talking and saw something across the room, or you felt some physical sensation when I said, "Boo!" [*Laughter*] So it is the specificity of your personal experience. Everyone in that room, and I'm including myself, has eaten an apple, but none of us has eaten an apple in exactly the same way. To write a good poem about eating an apple, you simply have to pay a lot of attention to the way that the experience is uniquely yours. And that's where the original-ity comes in. Sometimes poems are too original, and they become merely clever. That's another issue. You don't want your reader to think that you're showing off with your originality. But again, it's a pretty complicated thing.

SOA: I enjoyed reading your poem "Tattoo," and I was especially moved by the opening image, in which you depict a tattoo on the shoulder of a male who "looks like someone you had to reckon with" but is in actuality "only another old man." Have the ideas you held about aging when you were younger changed as you've gotten older?

TK: Well, I'm quite sympathetic with the guy in that poem. I don't look anything like that. I've never had a tattoo. But I know what it's like to be past your prime, which he is. I've seen lots and lots of those guys with their T-shirt sleeves cut off, showing off tattoos that are old and blurred. How many people in your room there today have tattoos?

SOA: I don't believe any of us do, but some of our classmates do.

TK: As they get older, tattoos turn into bruises, like on that man. I'm giv-ing you a little bit of a message about that in the poem. [*Laughter*] At any rate, I'm not looking down on that guy. I'm one with him in that place in his life.

SOA: When you were younger, did you ever imagine yourself growing older?

TK: It's interesting, there's a point in our lives, maybe at about your age, where we would love to be mysterious and romantic figures. That's one of the reasons that I started writing poems when I was a teenager, because I wasn't good at anything else. I had no athletic ability. I wasn't particularly good looking. I was just a kid with acne, and I decided somehow or other that poems would make me interesting, and drawing pictures, as well. At any rate, we all have that quest to be unusual and different, and that's a pow-erful thing. I was thinking the other day about when I was a teenager and thought it would be really cool to walk with a cane, to have a really interest-ing hand-carved cane with an interesting knob on it, maybe in the shape of an eagle's foot or something. Now I'm seventy years old, and, if I really wanted to, I could be walking with a cane, but all of a sudden, it's not as interesting as when I was a teenager. [*Laughter*]

SOA: How did you begin teaching at the University of Nebraska, and were there aspects of the academic world that you felt conflicted with your love of writing?

TK: What happened was that until I was sixty, I worked full time at a desk job at the insurance company, and I would occasionally teach a night course at the university as an adjunct, usually in poetry writing. They needed some people to teach that in the evening. So I would do that off and on, and when I retired, they put me on as a visiting professor for a couple of years. I took two years off when I was being poet laureate because I didn't have time to teach. Now I'm back doing a little bit of teaching. I just teach one course a year. But I haven't left it completely. As to whether or not the academic life conflicts with what I'm doing as a writer, I think there's a time that it would have, if I had been involved with it years ago. Now I'm pretty well set in my way of writing, and what happens to me at the university doesn't make much difference. But I do think that we all tend to write toward a perceived community of listeners. For instance, if you wrote a poem that you were going to show to your class, you would shape that poem for that audience. Maybe not a whole lot, but some. And when I was working for a life insurance company, some of my poems were shaped for that kind of an audience, people who didn't read poetry regularly, and for those secretaries in my department, and so on. And the same thing happens at the university. If you are a professor in an English department, the chances are very good that the kind of work that you write would be things that appeal to professors in an English department. But, as I say, I'm advanced enough in years that that's not going to happen to me, but it would have happened to me when I was thirty or twenty-five.

SOA: You mentioned that you started writing poetry when you were a teenager, but could you explain how you became interested in poetry? Were there poets that you read when you were young who captured your attention?

TK: I had some good high school teachers and junior high school teachers that picked up on the fact that I had something that might be developed. I remember, particularly, one high school English teacher who was very good at that and encouraged me. I was reading poetry, not a lot of it. We had a little newsstand in my hometown that sold books, and they had a few volumes of poetry. It's very important for those of you who decide you want to be writers to do a lot of reading. Reading is the way we learn to be writers. I tell my graduate students at the university that they ought to read a hundred poems for every one they try to write. I learned a lot that way. Of course, it's a long time ago. I don't remember exactly how it all came together.

SOA: Your poetry often features yard sales, garage sales, and thrift stores. Could you comment on the use of these settings and your interest in discarded items?

TK: I happen to be wearing some right now. [*Laughter*] I love thrift shops and garage sales and yard sales and things like that. I have a children's book that just came out [*Bag in the Wind*, 2010]. It's about a plastic bag that gets recycled into different things. The story has a thrift shop in it. I don't know exactly what it is that attracts me to those places, but there's a lot of humanity there. In my book *Local Wonders* I talk about garage-sale visiting sort of like theater. The curtain goes up, just like the garage door goes up, and inside some people are sitting on the set smoking cigarettes and drinking coffee. But I've always liked that sort of thing, and I really can't explain it. You can buy some wonderful things at garage sales and thrift shops.

SOA: The Midwest is the setting of many of your poems, including "So This Is Nebraska" and "Memory." What characteristics of your home region have had the greatest influence on your work?

TK: It may be that this is a lonely environment out here. There's a lot of space between people. Not in the city. I lived for years in Lincoln, Nebraska, where there are 220,000 people. But, generally, the Midwest is a big, wide-open place. There is a lot of loneliness to it, and I think that figures in my work. I grew up among people who were farming, and were it not for their families, they wouldn't talk to anybody for weeks on end. So all that is a part of it. It's kind of hard to convey this to people who live elsewhere, but it's really quite a beautiful place. I love these enormous skies, and I love the weather. I'm very much at home here, but I've really never lived anywhere else. I've traveled, and I've been to the Carolinas and so on. I liked it there, but this is home. And this is what I know best. That's why I write pretty well about it, I think.

SOA: The poet and critic Dana Gioia said, "Kooser has written more perfect poems than any poet of his generation." Are there any poems you've written that you hold in particularly higher regard than your other poems?

TK: Yes, there are poems that are favorites. They shift from time to time. Ordinarily, I think the last poem I wrote is really wonderful for a very short time, and then it starts to change. But there is a poem in *Delights & Shadows* called "Screech Owl" that seems to me to be the kind of poem that I've been trying to write all my life: very small, very precise, nothing extra in it at all. And it's a poem about hope. So that's a favorite of mine right now, but there have been others from time to time. I think what we try to do as writers is to write the kind of poems that we like to read. We try to discover within ourselves something to read, and, for me, "Screech Owl" is that kind of poem.

SOA: Do you read much fiction? If so, what do you prefer?

TK: I read all kinds of writers. One of my best friends is Jim Harrison. He's a very good fiction writer, writes wonderful novels and novellas. I also like reading detective novels just for entertainment. There's a novelist by the name of James Lee Burke, whose work I admire immensely, a really good writer. His hero is a cop in a parish in Louisiana. His work is filled with lots of sensory stuff, odors and sound, very good. There's a writer of espionage novels by the name of Alan Furst, whose work I like a lot. I read fiction for pleasure, not because it balances me or anything like that. I have a huge collection of short stories. I love short stories. But there's nobody in particular that I think is superior to anyone else. I sort of just dabble around. I'm also the kind of reader who very often doesn't finish a book. If it's a novel, and I'm interested in it, I will press on to the end, but if it doesn't interest me the first fourth of the way through, I'm not going to read it. I just don't have time to press on just because it's in my hands. And I usually have a dozen books that I'm reading all together, going from one to another.

SOA: You mentioned in an interview that you asked your coworkers in your insurance office to read your poems, so you could keep your writing accessible, but you commented that you did that without "pandering to a larger audience." How do you balance those two ideas?

TK: That's a really good question, and I'm not sure I can answer it precisely. I don't think that I am dumbing down my poems that far. What I'm trying to do is reach for you as a reader, and I only want to reach as far as I need to. I don't want to overreach. I don't want to be oversimplistic, which would be an insult to you as a reader. So it's a touchy thing. Looking at a single poem, I could probably show you decisions that I have made, the end of which was to make the poem accessible, without going over the top to be accessible.

SOA: You mentioned your friend Jim Harrison earlier. Harrison was friends with Richard Brautigan. Are you familiar with much of Brautigan's work?

TK: Oh, sure.

SOA: Your skillful use of figurative language and your attention to clarity and detail remind me of his writing. Is he someone you like to read?

TK: I read Brautigan years and years and years ago and have not read him for a long, long time. If he had any influence on me, I would have forgotten it by now. I have a great deal of difficulty with reading writers who have committed suicide. I'm really uncomfortable with that. And I think it's because I believe that art is affirmative, and that there is such negation of life with a suicide that it makes me extremely uncomfortable. I can't read Brautigan. I can't read Sylvia Plath for that reason.

SOA: It does color the way you read the work.

TK: Yes.

SOA: It's been very generous of you to spend this time with us. Thank you. This has been wonderful.

TK: It sure has.

SOA: Good luck with all your work in the future. [*Applause*]

An Interview with Ted Kooser

Judith Harris / 2010

This interview first appeared in the October/November 2010 issue of *Writer's Chronicle*. It is reprinted with the permission of Judith Harris.

Judith Harris: Eudora Welty wrote that "place will endow," and she saw the virtues of rootedness as a means of storytelling. You have said that you don't consider yourself a "regionalist," which makes sense to me because these crucial details in the poems point to a vision that is much greater than setting. In your prose memoir *Local Wonders*, however, place seems to preserve the past, but at the same time, it is fluid and reflective of subtle changes in the people who are practically or emotionally dependent on place. What does place mean to you? In your poetry, do you find yourself creating new places or renewing the old ones, or both?

Ted Kooser: When I listen to everyday conversations, I've noticed that nearly every anecdote opens by establishing a setting: "I was in Houston last week. . . ." If place is left out of a story, you can count on the listener to ask, "Where did that happen?" Thus, place is inseparable from how we talk about experience, and we probably have been doing this since long before language was written down. As to whether I create new places or revisit and refresh the old ones . . . if I have ever "created" a setting, I've merely assembled it from places I've been familiar with.

Harris: Is *Local Wonders* compiled from an existing journal? Have you always kept a journal? Is it portable like the painting easel you built to fit on your steering wheel, or do you write at home?

Kooser: *Local Wonders: Seasons in the Bohemian Alps* is a compilation of short pieces written over a twenty-year period. Since I always include settings in my writing, and since settings include seasons, the individual pieces fell into four relatively equal piles. At that point, it seemed I'd been assembling a book of the seasons without knowing it. All of those pieces arose from journal writing. I customarily do my daily writing at home, very early in the morning, a practice I began when I had a full-time job at the insurance company.

Harris: Talking about journals and notebooks, you have a poem called "Spiral Notebook," which ends with these lines: "you weigh in your hands, passing / your fingers over its surfaces / as if it were some kind of wonder." I've been thinking about how your poetry depends a lot on wonderment, especially in *Braided Creek: A Conversation in Poetry with Jim Harrison.* It is as if the poet renews the wonderment the first person would have felt at creation. What do you recollect of your first wonderments growing up?

Kooser: I fear I use the words *wonderful* and *marvelous* all too much when I'm talking to people, but both wonders and marvels are very important to me and help keep me delighted with life, and I look for marvels under every stone in the road. To show my readers something remarkable about an ordinary, ubiquitous thing is part of my calling as a writer. The most meaningful compliment I've ever received came from a reader, years ago, who told me that after reading a poem I published about mice moving their nests out of a freshly plowed field, she would never look at a plowed field in the spring in quite the same way. Yes! I said to myself, that is what I want to do with my life; to serve others in that way, to be of service.

As to early wonderment, I remember something that happened when I was a little boy. My family was visiting relatives on a farm, and after supper I went out on the back stoop and sat by myself looking at the starry sky and listening to the crickets. Behind me, I could hear the family talking in the kitchen. I glanced down and, right beside me, as if to keep me company, was a big brown toad. We sat there looking into the night without a word between us, like a couple who had been married so long that words were no longer necessary. I have been blessed with delights like that all my life.

My poems are accessible to a broad general audience, and that helps immensely. Poets are always complaining that nobody buys books of poetry, but if we want to sell books, we have to write books that people want to buy.

Harris: About the plowed field. There is one place in *Local Wonders* where you write about seeing the tree branches as antlers and how that vehicle changes how we view things, as if a good metaphor is so natural that it seems to the reader as if it's always been that way. Metaphor certainly vitalizes language; otherwise, it would exhaust into cliches. Do you think that Williams succeeded in writing antipoetic "metaphorless" poems? What about Karl Shapiro's "The Fly"? Was there a metaphor in there? He was your teacher; did you ever hear him read the poem out loud? What was the audience's response?

Kooser: There are some Williams poems that don't use metaphor as we know it, and others in which metaphor is central, as in that one in which old age is a flight of small cheeping birds skimming bare trees above a snow glaze. In "The Fly," Karl begins by saying the fly is a hideous little bat as small as "snot," and that's enough of a figure to capture what we detest about house flies. I did hear him read that poem once or twice and seem to remember him enjoying making us squirm, but that was forty-five years ago, and memory fades.

Harris: "To Waken an Old Lady," the Williams poem you just referred to, is the poem that launches off with "Old age is a flight of cheeping birds," and then the vehicle takes over as if it were the tenor circling back to old age by inference. You talk about this process of diversion in making a poem. I think you attributed an idea to John Berger.

Kooser: I haven't read Berger in a long time, but he was writing there about how artists draw. They begin with their concentration mostly on the subject beyond them, but at some point, the drawing itself becomes of more interest, and the subject falls back. There are points at which the vehicle of a metaphor becomes of more interest than the tenor and takes over.

Harris: In his essay "What Is Not Poetry?" Karl Shapiro defines his conception of the poet: "The poet does not see the world differently, and everything in it . . . what the poet sees with his always new vision is not what is 'imaginary'; he sees what others have forgotten how to see. The poet is always stripping away the veils and showing us his reality." I can't think of a better description of your process. For you, what is the relationship between the imagination and reality? Doesn't Shapiro sound a bit like Stevens here?

Kooser: I like that Karl said "his reality"; recognizing that reality for each of us is unique. For me, the imaginary can seem every bit as real as is "reality," which is why it is possible in a poem like Frost's "The Silken Tent" to completely lose track of the tenor, the woman about whom he's writing, and accept the vehicle, the silken tent, as the reality. I have a very vivid imagination, and sometimes when I am completely awake but daydreaming, I'll imagine something so frightening that I scare the hell out of myself and jump right out of the chair. So I am often on the reverse side of the mirror looking back at the world.

Harris: You've written about this in an essay entitled "Metaphor and Faith," which uses the Frost poem in comparing world religions and their relationship to divinity to poetic vehicle and tenor. I found it to be very affirmative. Could you describe the gist of it?

Kooser: In that essay, I suggest that all religions can be seen to be metaphorical vehicles, all of them referring back to a common tenor, which is a belief in some kind of a great mystery or unifying order beyond us. For example, when I participate in the Episcopal liturgy, I am immersing myself in the Episcopal vehicle. All of the warring between religions is the warring of competitive metaphors, but the tenor is the same for all, no matter what we call it, or call Him.

Harris: What was your graduate experience like? Who were you reading then? What was the trend in poetry as you began to write?

Kooser: There was no creative-writing program at Nebraska when I went there, and I was enrolled in a regular scholarly MA program. I have never been equipped for serious scholarship, and all I cared about was writing poetry. I spent much of my time following Karl around, learning what it was to be a poet. I watched him at work on his prose poems in *The Bourgeois Poet*, which he was finishing then. As to the rest of my program, I didn't do anything I was supposed to, and the department took away my assistantship after one year of bad grades and misbehavior. It was my inability to fit into an academic program that killed off my potential to be a professor. In those days I was reading Karl's poems, and those of Williams, Randall Jarrell, Elizabeth Bishop, May Swenson, and others. Whatever was at hand, I read. May Swenson was an important early influence. She seemed to be able to write in every form and to write well about anything. I wish more young poets were familiar with her work.

After I was tossed out of grad school, I went to work in the life insurance business, not as a salesman, but as a clerk at a desk, and I did that for thirty-five years. I occasionally taught a night class in beginning poetry writing as an adjunct, but that was the extent of my involvement with the academic world. I was good enough at holding down a desk job to be a vice president when I retired. I did eventually finish my MA degree by taking night classes, but it took me six years. I finished in part because my father told me he was tired of writing, in his annual Christmas letters, "Ted is working on his master's degree."

Harris: Your friend Leonard Nathan had interesting things to say about American poetry in that essay entitled "The Private I in Contemporary Poetry." He said that the main aim of poetry is pathos, and pathos seems to demand the convention of a personal voice and loosened form and structure, and yet he had an awareness of tradition? What was your friendship with him like? You said he read and edited your poems? Actually, you called it a "touch." He touched them.

Kooser: Leonard was a professor of rhetoric and not of creative writing. I say that to point out that he was a professional scholar, with a PhD in Yeats's drama, as well as being a fine poet. If he said that the main aim of poetry is pathos, he had good reason to say it, and we should all be thinking about that.

When I was about thirty, I saw a poem of Leonard's in the *New Republic* and wrote him to say how much I liked it. Whence ensued a correspondence of thirty-five years in which we exchanged poems by mail and frequently talked on the phone. When he died, I wrote a piece for the funeral that was later published in *Prairie Schooner* in which I said that I doubted that I had a poem in print that Leonard hadn't had his hands on at some point. His friendship was one of the greatest gifts of my life. And he affected the lives of many other writers younger than he, such as Naomi Shihab Nye. Both Naomi and I were devastated when Leonard developed Alzheimer's disease. There was a heartbreaking moment when Carol, his wife, told me, "Leonard will never write again, Ted, but he walks around with a pencil in his hand." Carol has since died, too. They were fine people.

Leonard's poetry never got the attention it deserved, and perhaps a few people reading this interview will take a look at his books. *The Potato Eaters*, a late book from Orchises Press, would be a good introduction.

Harris: One digression here—Orchises Press was started by Roger Lathbury, who teaches right here at George Mason University where AWP is based. Orchises was a labor of love for Roger, who started it on a single idea about enriching the lives of others with poetry. Tell us about your long relationship with your publishers at Copper Canyon and University of Nebraska. What is the state of small-press publishing of poetry these days?

Kooser: I've been very fortunate in securing publishers for my work, beginning when I was thirty, and the University of Nebraska Press published my first book of poems, *Official Entry Blank*. They had a poetry series in those days but discontinued it in the early seventies. Then, about ten years later, Ed Ochester wrote to me saying that he had read a lot of my work in chapbooks and journals and thought I might want to consider doing a selected poems with Pittsburgh. That led to three books with them. Much later, Pitt combined my first two books with them into one volume, *Flying at Night*. Ed didn't want the fourth manuscript I sent him back in 1999, but Jerry Costanzo at Carnegie Mellon did, and *Winter Morning Walks* was published by Jerry the following year. Then Jim Harrison and I did our *Braided Creek* book with Copper Canyon, where Jim was already publishing, and when I had my next book of poems ready, *Delights & Shadows*, Copper Canyon accepted that one. I am very happy to have Copper Canyon as the publisher of my poems. The University of Nebraska Press has published my prose, two books of what we might classify as memoir, and two books on writing. They also published my book of Valentine poems and reprinted my poems about the blizzard of 1888, but I intend to keep my regular poetry collections with Copper Canyon. As to the state of small-press publishing, it seems to me to be very healthy. *The International Directory of Little Magazines and Small Presses*, published by Dustbooks, is as fat as a metropolitan phone book, and that testifies to the many presses in operation. I've done some small-press editing and publishing. It's not the kind of thing anyone should choose as a career because very few presses are ever in the black, but it's a worthy activity.

Harris: I read that *Delights & Shadows* has sold around one hundred thousand copies. To what do you attribute that success?

Kooser: The Pulitzer Prize, of course, and the publicity that goes with it. But I've been told that the book is selling well six years later because of what publishers call "word-of-mouth"—people just telling each other about the book. My poems are accessible to a broad general audience, and that helps immensely. Poets are always complaining that nobody buys books of poetry, but if we want to sell books, we have to write books that people want to buy. Just because so many of us work at universities doesn't mean that our poems must read like research.

Harris: You always have such a succinct way of putting things, getting right to the heart of the matter. You have a relationship with the spiritual side of things without making liturgical or scriptural references. What role does religion or the spiritual play in your life and your writing? Were you raised as an Episcopalian?

Kooser: The Koosers were Methodists, and my mother's family, the Mosers, were German Lutherans, but for years I stayed away from formal religion altogether. Then I spent about ten years attending Unitarian services in Lincoln because the minister was such a fine speaker. My wife and I became Episcopalians only about two years ago, and we belong to a tiny congregation in an almost exclusively Lutheran town. I am not a traditional believer, but instead someone who likes to sit for an hour on Sunday morning with a group of people who are trying, one hopes, to think in the right direction. For me, church is mostly about community.

Harris: This question is in two parts: Let's turn to *Delights and Shadows*, for which you won the Pulitzer Prize. Looking at your earlier books, such as *Sure Signs* and *Flying at Night*, it seems to me that this book is about absence as much as presence—things and people seen in their solitariness and illuminated against a background of darkness. The play of light and shadow is alive in these poems. Do you believe, as the impressionists did, that light saturates all objects, light being more important than line? Do you prefer the sense of a sketch as opposed to the finished picture, a spontaneous work, rather than a calculated one?

Kooser: It's true that the poems in *Delights & Shadows* are such that the delights play in front of a field of darkness, but don't you think that that's true of everything we do? Every activity in life is undertaken with death observing from a distance. Joyce's great story "The Dead" is all about this, with death as the backdrop for the feasts we enjoy. At so many feasts, we find ourselves setting a place for the dead—"Oh, don't you wish Aunt Mabel were here?"—and the nearness of death lends the food savor.

As to drawing and painting, line is used to suggest mass by defining it, and that would seem to make mass more important than line, but it would take somebody like Gombrich to speak of this with any authority. When it comes to looking at works of art, I do like sketches far better than finished paintings, in part because with a sketch we are always aware of the effort of drawing or painting, whereas finished works often bury that activity behind the polished surface. John Marin's apparently dashed-off watercolor seascapes are far more engaging to me than any number of perfectly finished marine paintings.

Harris: "Every activity in life is undertaken with death observing from a distance." You also write in a poem: "There are days when the fear of death / is as ubiquitous as light. It illuminates / everything." In your memoir, *Lights on a Ground of Darkness* (which I will ask about later), your grandfather had something to say at the cemetery.

Kooser: I think the passage you are referring to is the one in which my grandfather says to the groundskeeper at the cemetery, "Keep your shovel sharp." Granddad was then in his nineties and had lost his wife, his brothers and sisters, a son, a son-in-law, and most of his friends. It's my impression that by the time we get that old, we may be at ease with death.

Harris: What did you learn from Frost about encounters with the natural world?

Kooser: Though the setting of many of Frost's poems is the rural outdoors, I feel that for him nature is just that, a setting within which humans are the real interest. But, of course, there is a lot of Frost to think about, and I'd have to give that question more thought. There are those poems like the one about the moth and the heal-all plant in which he very closely observes nature.

Harris: Do you believe that some poems written and read for solace truly provide comfort to us when we are most tested? Poetry, as Don Hall has said, can give us an education in emotions by providing the words for what we all experience in grief or joy.

Kooser: Tens of thousands of people have read and are reading the psalms, and I'd guess many of them do it to find some solace. For me, the solace in reading comes not so much from any inspiring message the poem offers, but from the beauty of the writing. Beauty offers solace, or so it does for me. For example, I find a lot of solace in reading, from time to time, Robert Bly's *Silence in the Snowy Fields*.

Harris: How did you meet your wife, Kathleen?

Kooser: We met in Lincoln in 1976. We had mutual acquaintances and would run into each other from time to time. On our first evening together, we took a long walk and discovered that not only had she lived in my hometown, Ames, Iowa, as a little girl, but that their house was on my paper route. Her father was in the air force, and he was stationed in Ames for several years, at the ROTC unit at Iowa State.

Harris: What are your discussions like when she comes home from the newspaper office? Do you talk more about politics than literature?

Kooser: Kathy is now retired from her editorship of the Lincoln daily paper, but when she was working, we did talk about politics and current affairs a great deal, rarely literature. I save the shop talk for my writer friends, like you. It can be dangerous to bore a spouse.

Harris: How have your children reacted to your success that has drawn such national and international attention?

Kooser: I have just one son, Jeff, who has children of his own, and I think he's proud of my achievements. His interests are very different from mine.

Harris: You have said that you have taken traits from one branch of the family; I believe Grandmother Kooser. What kind of a woman was she?

Kooser: She was a stern, sober, judgmental woman, and there are times when I am stern. And I have been sober for many years. And I am trying hard not to be judgmental. I more closely identify with my Moser ancestors. Grandfather Kooser died when I was two, and Grandmother Kooser, when I was about ten. The Mosers lived many years longer, and I knew them much better. My grandfather Moser lived to be ninety-eight, and he and I were on the planet together for thirty-five years.

Harris: You like the Ashcan painters, their truth and honesty and desire for democracy. Is there one painter in particular? I always think of Williams's "Proletarian Portrait" as a poetic ancestor of your portraits of people caught unsentimentally in their unique and specific environment.

Kooser: Robert Henri was a Nebraskan, and his paintings mean a lot to me and to other Nebraskans. But I also like the urban paintings of John Sloan. I've read Sloan's journals and would love to have met him. There is a painting by Sloan in the Brooklyn Museum, of the excavation for Grand Central, that looks so much like the photographs of what was left of the World Trade Center towers that it's chilling.

Harris: Ecological writing and ecopoetry have gained prominence as genres committed to studying the landscape in art. You've said you're interested in this movement. Can you tell us about it?

Kooser: At the university where I teach, there is a lot of interest in what they're calling ecocriticism, and I have sat in on some discussions, which I've found to be interesting. But it seems to me to be one of those fields in academia, like creative nonfiction, that has come up with a new moniker for something we've always had, in an effort to inaugurate yet another field of professional inquiry.

Harris: Your mother taught you to use your observing powers to regard everything in creation and added that this capacity for being surprised by things will never leave you lonely. Rilke said something of the same thing as he was giving advice to Mr. Kappus in *Letters to a Young Poet*: "If your everyday life seems poor, don't blame it, blame yourself; because there is no poor, indifferent place." You must receive many letters asking your advice.

Kooser: I do get a lot of mail from people who aspire to be writers, and my advice to them is simple: "Read, read, read." I tell them that reading is how we learn to write and that they can learn from any and all kinds of writing, good and bad.

Harris: Critics have been consistent in praising your work. One critic wrote that your poetry rings particularly true, allowing the human sound of being to exist on the page. Others talk about your clarity, mastery of subjective description, and perfect self-containment. The effects may appear simple, but I find your work full of paradox, where nothing is ever so simple. Observation takes discipline. Have you always been a disciplined person? Are you often surprised by your own epiphanies in poetry as well as prose?

Kooser: Not every critic has liked my work, and a few have disliked it intensely, but I have learned not to read anything that's published about my writing, good or bad. The bad reviews hurt, and the good ones all too often feel overblown. As to disciplines, I have grown to be ever more disciplined as I've grown older, which I suppose has to do with a need for control. The older I've become, the more there is that begs to be controlled, and I have developed disciplines to address that. As to surprises, I am often surprised, astonished even, by interesting associations that surface while I'm working. The most fascinating metaphors seem to arrive through some door that can only be opened during the contemplative act of writing. They never arrive through the doors of intellect or reason.

Harris: How do you view elegy? You have written some of the finest elegies of ordinary people, and people who were only acquaintances. Talking about simplicity and understatement, I would imagine you appreciated [Edwin Arlington] Robinson's "Richard Cory" when you were a student?

Kooser: Robinson was one of the poets I read with great interest when I was young. Robinson and [Edgar Lee] Masters and Sherwood Anderson seemed to be showing me ways I could write about the rural and small-town people among whom I lived. As to elegy, it seems to me that almost all of my poems are elegiac, but I suppose there are exceptions.

Harris: You referred to Eliot and Pound as writing "difficult, challenging poetry," and postmodernism is equally challenging with its linguistic turn. The splitting of signifier and signified denies language its unifying function, making it more difficult to articulate what the deep image poets articulated—a relationship between the secular and ultimate. How do you feel about the current trends in poetry?

Kooser: A poem either interests and moves me, or it doesn't, and I'm not at all interested in categories or theory. I respond to poems as a reader, with my heart, not as a scholar, with my intellect.

Harris: Do you think graduate schools should be educations in form and meter or theories of poetics? Or both?

Kooser: Far be it from me to make pronouncements as to what graduate schools should be doing. Remember that I was thrown out of graduate school. When I teach, I do two things. I encourage my students, and I try to help them make their poems more effective. None of that involves theory, but it might involve form.

Harris: Could we have an example of one of your favorite poems—to be reprinted here—at this juncture as we near the close of our interview?

Kooser: I am very fond of my little poem "Screech Owl," from *Delights & Shadows*. I believe that it's my writing at its surest and truest.

"Screech Owl"

All night each reedy whinny
from a bird no bigger than a heart
flies out of a tall black pine
and, in a breath, is taken away
by the stars. Yet, with small hope
from the center of darkness
it calls out again and again.

Harris: There it is: the mystery of where things go, along with a faith in their continued presence. Coleridge said fusing oppositions such as light and dark, birth and death, sleep and waking, was the task of the poet.

Kooser: I was much blessed to have that little owl spend time on our farm.

Harris: I just read *Lights on a Ground of Darkness*. It took my breath away—this crisp, revivification of place and time, Guttenberg, Iowa, in which memory comes alive in the people remembered. You wrote it for your mother?

Kooser: Mother was very ill and not expected to live more than a few months, and for years, I had wanted to write something about her family. Her severely disabled brother seemed to be an armature about which the family's love was wound, and I wanted to write about that as well as about others in the family. I determined to get it written before she was gone, as a gift to her, and I was able to show her the manuscript a couple of months before she died. I was worried that it might make her sad since nearly everyone I talk about was dead, but she liked it. You mentioned elegy earlier. This little book is elegy through and through.

Harris: Tell us about Uncle Elvy.

Kooser: He was my mother's one surviving brother. Another little boy had died at birth. His given name was Alvah, and he had cerebral palsy and was terribly disabled. In ways, his frailty held the whole family together, and that was his gift to us. He was never institutionalized and was able to live his whole life with his family. The way his parents loved and cared for him was the soul of goodness. When my grandmother died in her late eighties, and my grandfather, then in his midnineties, moved into a nursing home, Elvy moved into the room with him. He survived my grandfather by a couple of years, and I'm sure they were the only lonely years he ever experienced.

Harris: His death is described with remarkable pathos. And there appears a sign. Your father looks in the mirror in your uncle's room and sees a full handprint, intervening between your father and his own reflection, a sign of death. Again, the light is ubiquitous with death, but perseveres.

Kooser: That happens in that nursing home I mentioned just now.

Harris: Finally, the poem in memory of your mother, written on your birthday, is a unique poem for you. It has a perfect symmetrical form, and the caesuras fall equidistant to one another in each stanza respectively.

Kooser: I hadn't noticed that, but if that happens, I'll take credit for it. If you make a three-cushion bank shot in a game of Eight Ball, you want to pretend you planned it that way.

Harris: The end of the poem refers to your own axiom, rekindled through hers: "Were it not for the way you taught me to look / at the world, to see the life at play in everything, I would have to be lonely forever." But the reader feels that you will be lonely for her—or that loneliness will be a way to remember her by seeing the life in her death. Delight in shadows, right?

Kooser: Yes.

Harris: Finally, how did you envision your role as US poet laureate; were you intent on making poetry more accessible to a wider audience?

Kooser: Because I was the first poet laureate picked from the Great Plains, I wanted to prove that somebody from out here could do it, and I threw myself into it, seven days a week. I wanted to show everyday readers that poetry needn't be feared and shunned, that it had something to offer. I made two hundred appearances in the twenty months of my two terms and did around one hundred interviews. I talked to librarians, book clubs, students, Kiwanians, Rotarians. I started my newspaper column, "American Life in Poetry," which is now five years old and still up and running. We have around four million weekly readers in a couple of hundred papers. I publish short poems that I think average readers can appreciate. Bob Hass also started a column, "Poet's Choice," when he was the laureate. It was a longer and much more explicative column, very well done.

Starving for Order:
A Conversation with Ted Kooser

Daniel Simon / 2017

The following interview was conducted at the 2017 Nebraska Book Festival by Daniel Simon, editor in chief of *World Literature Today* and editor of the award-winning *Nebraska Poetry: A Sesquicentennial Anthology, 1867–2017* (Stephen F. Austin State University Press, 2017). It first appeared in *World Literature Today* in November 2017. It is reprinted with the permission of Daniel Simon.

Daniel Simon: "On every topographic map, / the fingerprints of God." That couplet appears in *Braided Creek* (2003), your "conversation in poetry" with Jim Harrison. Is there a sacred geography in your poetry?

Ted Kooser: I described the place most sacred to me in my prose memoir *Lights on a Ground of Darkness* (2005), Daniel, and looked at it again in my children's book *The Bell in the Bridge* (2016). It's my maternal grandparents' house and roadside Standard Oil station at the edge of Guttenberg, Iowa, a magical place when I was a boy. I think my true center is there.

Simon: You write so sweetly about John and Elizabeth Moser, your maternal grandparents, especially in your memoir. And you've written at least a couple of poems about Elizabeth's funeral in January 1962, when it was twenty-two below. The striking visual in those poems for me is the thawing barrels in the cemetery, which the two men stoked all night in order to soften the ground for the burial.

Kooser: And you could see that from the house. The dining room on that house had windows facing west, and it overlooked a patch of corn that was about a hundred yards across. A creek ran through there, and then the land sloped up to the cemetery. It was a wooded hillside, but in the winter the trees were all bare. And you could see that smoke up there—the graves are just over the top of that hill.

Simon: You write about your grandfather sitting there on the morning of the funeral, already dressed, looking up the hill toward the cemetery. That night, you slept in your uncle Elvy's bed, and the wind just howled through the cracks in the windows and through the cemetery.

Kooser: I'll never forget Elvy walking along behind the coffin. His mother was so dear to him; she had protected him all those years but was a little too softhearted and let him eat things he wanted but shouldn't eat. Although he was diabetic, she always had cookies and cakes for him. At the funeral, they had to carry her coffin slightly downhill in the snow and ice, and Elvy stumbled along behind, wanting to put his hand on the coffin.

Simon: You would have been in your early twenties then? Obviously, when you speak of sacred geography, you invoke childhood memories but also returning to Guttenberg later in life.

Kooser: Yes, I was twenty-three when Grandma Moser died. You know, I think part of the attachment to my mother's family, Daniel, is that my Kooser grandparents didn't live very long. My grandfather Kooser died when I was two, and my grandmother when I was ten. I have memories of her, but the Mosers lived on and on and on. Granddad died in 1972, so I would have been thirty-three, something like that.

Simon: There's a scene in the memoir where you write about Uncle Elmer and Uncle Elvy driving down the road in this '49 Chevy with a fishing pole sticking out the back window. As a reader, I thought that was a striking visual detail.

Kooser: Elmer Morarend had been one of those very, very shy German farm kids. As an older man, he hardly would say a word and had a real squeaky little voice. . . . That world of the Mosers and Morarends is really at the center of everything: my emotional heart is always that family. And to this day, when I see parents raising disabled children like Elvy, and I see them out in public, boy, that really hits me hard. The other day, there was a television show about a girl who had some kind of palsy; she was elected homecoming queen, and I found myself weeping uncontrollably. Everybody gathered around her . . .

Simon: In your essay on "Metaphor and Faith," which uses the extended metaphor of Robert Frost's "The Silken Tent" as an analogy for faith, you write: "Every religion, and each person's private faith, leans like a ladder against this presence that stands beyond the reach of our intelligence" (*Seminary Ridge Review*, Spring 2011). Is poetry one of those ladders for you?

Kooser: Writing poetry does feel to me like prayer. When I'm writing, early in the morning, I'm oblivious to everything around me and to time. I guess for those moments, I'm on a ladder magically leaning on air.

Simon: In that same essay, you write about being "swept up and away" into the "enormous compelling mystery" of belief. Yet isn't Frost's sonnet as much about our "bondage" to "everything on earth" as the "pinnacle to heavenward"?

Kooser: When I wrote that about the Frost sonnet, I wasn't thinking about what might be his meaning, but instead simply stealing his metaphor. It's a poem I'm very fond of, but like many of my favorite poems, it's what I make of it that's important, not what the poet might have meant. I think once a poet gives a poem to the world, he, say Frost, gives up all control, and the reader can use it as he or she wishes to. That may be to find meaning, or it may be to enjoy the play of the language.

Simon: When it comes to Frost's language, I like to think that the play itself is the meaning. (He has a poem called "To Earthward" that begins: "Love at the lips / Was touch as sweet as I could bear.") Would you like to say a little bit more about the play of language in Frost's poetry or your own?

Kooser: Part of that comes from my own experience as a writer and how those poems come together. And the way I work is that I'm sitting there in the morning, just randomly jotting down things in my notebook, and a particular metaphor will occur to me. And then what I do is I dress the metaphor. I add to it, as much as I can add without it exploding—or imploding. So the metaphor is at the center of the poem, and I suspect that the silken-tent metaphor in that Frost poem is the point from which the poem pulls out and away from.

You can't plug a metaphor in a poem. It has to be organic. For me, that's really where the magic is. The space between the tenor and the vehicle is like looking into something beyond us, the magnificent thing which happens in that association.

I have grad students who will be working on a draft of a poem, and they will say, "Don't you think I ought to put a metaphor in here?" And well, you can't plug a metaphor in a poem. It has to be organic. You know, there are pretty successful poets who really can't do metaphor. But for me, that's really where the magic is. The space between the tenor and the vehicle is like looking into something beyond us, the magnificent thing which happens in that association.

Simon: Which Aristotle recognized, way back in the *Poetics*: the genius of metaphor, the space where that kind of synapse happens.

Kooser: You bet. Robert Bly wrote some things about that years ago, how the farther apart the tenor and the vehicle are, the more powerful the metaphor is. If the Big Bang is true, and everything originated at that point and emanated out from it, then all these things are related. These are moments of recognition: that this thing is like that . . .

Simon: Gerald Stern has said, "I suspect that the actual writing, the continuous writing, the writing over and over again, the commitment, is a kind of devotion. Maybe it's not the devotion of a priest; it is certainly the devotion of a mourner. I'm in complete agreement with Simone Weil's statement that 'absolute unmixed attention is prayer.'"[1] Is your writing, as a form of paying attention, such a devotion? The title of *Lights on a Ground of Darkness* comes to mind: perceiving light against the pattern of darkness. Or "the puff of yellow pollen" that appears in "A Glimpse of the Eternal" (*Delights & Shadows*), that kind of momentary perception. And in *Winter Morning Walks* (2000), I see observation in those poems as a type of reverence.

Kooser: Dan Gerber, who is a friend of mine and a very good poet, thinks that *Winter Morning Walks* may be my best book. Those poems are really good examples of what we're talking about. I would go out and come back and sit down, early in the morning, and some association would have come to me, and they spin out from that, one after another after another, driven by anxiety . . .

Simon: You were recovering from surgery and radiation therapy for cancer at the time, right?

Kooser: Yes. I always avoid thinking of writing as therapeutic, but that's exactly what those poems were. I've given a lot of copies of that book to medical students, and I've given presentations talking about the fact that if you can make some kind of order when you're dealing with cancer, which is chaos, if you can find a small piece of order in that, there can be a great deal of comfort in it. During the course of all this, I had asked my doctor, "If this tumor comes back, what will happen?" And he said it will follow a predictable course: it will go down your neck and into your thorax and from there on. As horrible and as frightening as that was, there was some assurance in the fact that there is a pattern to cancer. I was so starved for order that I could see order in that.

Simon: Walking out into the darkness, walking back, putting one foot in front of the other, and then the lines on the page just have that sense of security.

Kooser: The composer Maria Schneider has had a lot of success with that "man with the moon on a leash" poem [the November 18 poem from *Winter Morning Walks*, which Schneider set to music for soprano Dawn Upshaw and won three Grammys for]. She's coming out here next spring to see the sandhill cranes.

Simon: I had hoped to make it back this spring to see them. When Don Welch and I were emailing back and forth about the *Nebraska Poetry* anthology last year, before he passed, I told him that my idea of the Elysian Fields was to go out to Kearney and see the cranes with him.[2]

Kooser: When Don was in his last days, I heard from the family that he had gotten somebody to adopt all his pigeons. And one day, Kathy and I went down to Branched Oak Lake for an early morning walk. Nobody was around, and out on the point, we came upon a white pigeon, sitting in the parking lot, with scarlet underwings. Obviously not a wild pigeon. And I thought, "*This is it . . .*"

Simon: You've told me that Don's poem called "Funeral at Ansley" (*Dead Horse Table*, 1975), with its autumnal wind coming through the cemetery during the funeral, always makes you think of Harvey Dunn's painting *I Am the Resurrection and the Life* (1926). Do you think about poetry and painting a lot, as an analogy for your own work?

Kooser: Yeah, I suppose it's because I have this love of painting. That's probably the reason my work is so visual. But it's frequent for me to think of paintings while I'm writing. That Harvey Dunn painting and many of his other marvelous paintings are in the permanent collection of the art museum at South Dakota State in Brookings, and would be worth a side trip sometime when you're back in our area.

Simon: You do have these great visual moments that jump out in your prose and poetry which reveal your painterly eye. I'm thinking of the county courthouse in *Lights on a Ground of Darkness*, where you notice the red scarf of a woman leaning out the window. And in "A Winter Morning," you write:

A farmhouse window far back from the highway
speaks to the darkness in a small, sure voice.
Against this stillness, only a kettle's whisper,
and against the starry cold, one small blue ring of flame. (*Delights & Shadows*)

To me, this poem embodies the prophecy of the everyday in your work, in which God is not in the wind, the earthquake, or the fire (1 Kings 19:11–12) but in the "still small voice" of a kettle on the stove. What accounts for such an aesthetic in your work?

Kooser: You're correct, Daniel, in seeing what I'm up to in that poem. I really do believe that God is in the details and, in this instance, in the ring of flame under the kettle. Also, as a writing strategy, a reader can "see" a kettle on a stove but can't see an idea.

Simon: In terms of a writing strategy, do you feel a kinship with other writers in this regard?

Kooser: I have noticed a lot of poems that are like that, from time to time. I was really taken with a poem in *The Writer's Almanac* this week by Anya Krugovoy Silver. It's a poem about a woman who has a hole in the end of her sock and has pulled her sock and then tucked it under so that no one can see the hole. It seems to me that that is such a powerful thing, just to be able to see that tiny detail. I love that kind of simplicity in poetry.

I was so proud of myself when I wrote the poem called "Two" in *Splitting an Order* (2014) about running into the two men on the staircase in the parking lot. Because it has that: it has nothing in it other than that moment where we pass.

Simon: Where the conjoined hands of the two men—the son in his sixties and his father in his eighties coming down the steps—separate to let you pass, like a river flowing around a sandbar . . .

On another note, I'm struck by the "little system[s] of . . . care" that pervade your poetry ("Flying at Night"). Yet the human presence in your verse is often marked by loss. Is language (art) enough to compensate?

Kooser: I wish that a poem could compensate for a loss, but it can't, at least completely. But it can help by clarifying feelings. When a person wakes at two in the morning, obsessing about something, perhaps something he should have said and didn't say, going over it again and again and again, if he will get up and write down what he's been thinking, the obsession will almost always go away, and he can get back to sleep. For me, poetry is a way of clarifying and specifying feelings.

Simon: Talking about feelings, I'm reminded of your poem "The Screech Owl," with the line about that "small hope / from the center of darkness / [calling] out again and again" (*Delights & Shadows*).

Kooser: That's probably my favorite poem. There again, no extraneous material is in there, just that little thing.

Simon: You often ascribe these anthropomorphic qualities to nature. The feelings that come through these poems, to me, are always very grounded in that quality of observation. Especially in your poems about birds: I see them as a metaphor for the poet's imagination, the spirit wanting to escape mortality or something that's a weight in our lives.

Kooser: You're too young to remember this period, but part of the awful influence of Eliot and his people was that they were so opposed to the pathetic fallacy, the notion of assigning qualities to inanimate things. And

I rebelled against that from day one. I figured screw it; this is where the fun is: the real delight in finding life in a stone. What can be wrong with that? I often wonder if after they had set down their rules, they didn't regret it a little bit because it was so limiting.

Simon: So often in your poems there's an image, like the tractor in the doorway of the church ("The Red Wing Church") or in "Abandoned Farmhouse" (both in *Sure Signs*), famously, where you set a scene that evokes a former human presence which has become an absence. The feelings that come through in the absence of what was once there are especially powerful in your work.

Kooser: I can't remember whether I told you about this book that Connie Wanek and I put together, which Candlewick Press has accepted, called *Making Mischief: Two Poets at Play among Figures of Speech* [Published as *Marshmallow Clouds: Two Poets at Play among Figures of Speech* in 2022. See Mary K. Stillwell's 2023 interview for an explanation of the title change.] In the collection, it doesn't indicate who is the author. We didn't collaborate on any of the individual poems, but the whole book is a collaboration. There are about twenty-five poems, maybe thirty, in there, and they're all that way—they're all at play in that way, and it was really a lot of fun. We sent it to Candlewick not feeling confident whether they'd really be interested in it or not, and they liked it a lot. That'll be out in about eighteen months.

Simon: You did that with Jim Harrison in *Braided Creek*, where you were exchanging postcard poems, and in the final gathering of the book, you didn't attribute specific poems to one writer or the other.

Kooser: It would have really made that book very stiff if those poems couldn't flow together like that. What happened was, we'd been exchanging this stuff for years with no idea of a book whatsoever, and Jim, who was always ready to have another book because he was making his living with books, said let's do a book of these, but you put it together. So it was up to me. I had all the poems on three-by-five index cards, and I stretched them out through the length of our house and kept moving them around until I arrived at something that felt like it had some sort of overall sweep to it. But I didn't want a poem by Jim and a poem by Ted and a poem by Jim and a poem by Ted, so in some cases there are two by him and one by me or one by him and two by me.

It's funny, in one of the first reviews that came out of that book in a literary magazine, the reviewer said, "Those of us who are familiar with the work of Ted Kooser and Jim Harrison can easily identify who wrote which poem." And then he quoted a poem and said this is clearly a Harrison poem, and it wasn't.

Simon: Well, I'd like to think that the poem about the topographic map being the fingerprint of God was one of your poems.

Kooser: Yeah, that was one of mine.

Simon: Now I can't look at a topographic map and not see that fingerprint on it.

Kooser: Well good, I'm glad it works that way. I've probably told you that years ago I published this little "Spring Plowing" poem about the mice moving out of the field into the fencerow (*Sure Signs*). And a woman from Omaha saw that poem in a literary magazine and wrote to me, telling me that she'd never pass a field in the spring without thinking of those mice, and immediately I thought, "Boy, this is what I want to do."

Simon: In your poems, God often appears as a benevolent watchman: he can be glimpsed walking the bean rows, cupping the heart of a turtle, or bemusedly watching us "make our way across" the road like a family of wild turkeys. Yet your poems often touch on "the center of darkness." What consolation does an avuncular God provide against that darkness?

Kooser: First, it's very hard for me to imagine a God who has taken a personal interest in what one old man in rural Nebraska is doing or thinking, but it's fun to imagine him being that kind of a spirit, walking among us, amused by our foibles, shaking his head at our stupidity. I like your use of "avuncular" in that an uncle isn't quite as invested in us as is a father or mother. I liked my uncles and great-uncles, who weren't going to discipline me, or restrain me, but were just interested in me for who I was.

Simon: In "On the Road," the pilgrim-poet kicks a quartz pebble, picks it up, and "almost see[s] through it / into the grand explanation" (*Delights & Shadows*). He quickly puts it down, however, and keeps walking. Do the "grand explanations" frighten you?

Kooser: Once in a while, I get a rare glimpse into something beyond our world, often through the window of a coincidence. If in fact everything in the universe originated in a speck of dense matter, exploding outward and still in motion, then everything has to be related, no matter how far afield the two elements are. Coincidences seem to me to be glimpses into those relationships. In the poem you're referring to, it was as if I had glimpsed something so enormous that it was frightening, and I turned away.

Simon: How so? Could you say more about that?

Kooser: A parallel example would be when I took a philosophy course as an undergraduate, and it scared me. I don't know who we were reading at the time, but I began thinking about what I was thinking about what I was thinking . . . and I got caught up in this sort of vortex of stuff that I couldn't quite break out of. And it just scared the hell out of me. It's that same kind of fear: I'm not sure I want to look beyond that point or look beyond what I can see. I can sense things out there, but I don't want to be out there with them.

Simon: Pulling back from the abyss?

Kooser: I don't know. I don't think I can articulate it very well. There's a huge empty void out there, and I don't want to get there. I want all these things in front of it.

Simon: The theme for our November issue is Belief in an Age of Intolerance.[3] What can poetry teach us about tolerance?

Kooser: Tolerance in physics, as I understand it, sets acceptable or understood limits for deviations, and civil behavior also exists between agreed-upon limits. I think poetry can illustrate or display examples of those tolerances. My poem "Two," which we talked about earlier, is about how we accept and accommodate each other. It's a favorite poem of mine because of its apparent simplicity. But it isn't simple at all. I was pleased that David Barber at *The Atlantic* seemed to see in it that complexity in the presence of the simple.

Simon: Is there anything else you'd like to add in that regard?

Kooser: What I might say is that I see writing poems and painting pictures as being affirmations of life. And I don't like art, poetry in particular, in which judgments are being made about others. So much topical poetry is that way. From time to time somebody might say, "You don't write political poems. You don't write about what's going on in the world. You really ought to do more of that." Well, I can't remember who it was, Stanley Kunitz perhaps, who said that poetry in itself is its own form of subversion. In its subversion, poetry stands apart. I haven't worked that out very well . . .

Simon: In terms of poetry as affirmation, so often we read poems that are too much about the darkness, or all about political disorder, that it's refreshing to read poems about accommodation, poems that represent, as you said, the more fundamental human relationships that tie us to one another.

Kooser: I did recently write a poem about the president. I emailed it to some people, and it went on beyond where I thought it would go. I'm glad that people fastened upon it and liked it, but I'm still not terribly comfortable with such a topical poem.

Simon: I'm reminded of the great pinochle gathering in *Lights on a Ground of Darkness*, where you write about all the relatives, the uncles and aunts, coming together. That in itself is an affirmation of community: gathering around the card table, and the elaborate ritual of your grandfather getting out the two decks of cards and shuffling them, while your grandmother prepared refreshments for the company. It reminded me a lot of my own grandparents, our card games and gatherings . . .

Kooser: I wondered at the time when I was a kid what the fascination was with card playing, and when I got to be a grown man, I realized that part of it was that it didn't cost any money. They didn't have to spend anything to do that—they could have a really nice evening and didn't have to spend a dime.

Simon: And the game itself can be just an excuse to get together and visit, to enjoy each other's company.

Kooser: And personalities would come out and differentiate themselves. When they would let me play, if I was a little bit slow getting my cards in order, Ella Borcherding, who was a cousin of my mother's, would whack me on the knuckles. Daniel, let's let your readers know that Ella was like that, somebody who'd rap a kid on the knuckles if he was too slow!

Simon: We never played pinochle. It was always ten-point pitch or skat, a game of thirty-one, which was always fun for the younger kids as well as our parents and grandparents, aunts and uncles. I have lots of great memories of those kinds of get-togethers as well.

Kooser: A few weeks ago, I drove up to Red Wing, Minnesota, to do a reading there. Robert Hedin at the Anderson Center had a book coming out, so I went up there to help him launch the book. And I drove through Guttenberg and stopped at the house, which is now the office for a nursery. My granddad's station has been gone for years—they tore it down. The nursery itself is a separate building, and I suppose they use the house to keep the books and do that kind of thing. I stopped and talked to the owner, and God, the change is so incredible. You know, when I was describing that strip of corn between the house and the cemetery, that was low ground, and Miners Creek ran through it. When the Mississippi flooded, the water would back way up into that creek and fill the basement of my grandparents' house. They had a drive-down driveway with a garage underneath the back, and there would be standing water there, sometimes for weeks. I said to the woman, "You've filled it in back there," and she said they had put in ten feet of fill dirt all the way back. So they brought in tons and tons of earth to cover that area up. So that back porch my grandmother used to throw the dishwater off of, down into the ditch, which I describe in my poem "Dishwater," now that back stoop looks straight out. To think of somebody going to all that effort and expense!

Simon: When the river could wash it out on a whim. How far was their house from the actual banks of the Mississippi?

Kooser: A quarter of a mile. It was typical river bottom, pretty heavily wooded. So you couldn't actually see the river from the house, even in the winter. But it was right out there, and you could hear the boat traffic going up and down. There was a railroad track that came up on the other side of the highway from my granddad's station too, and when the trains would come in, going north along the river, the engineers would blow the whistle and wave at my granddad, who would be sitting in his gas station behind the window and would wave back. And I remember thinking, "Wow! My grandfather is really important!"

Simon: So the county seat was actually in Elkader, right?

Kooser: That's right. Elkader is the town in "Pearl," the poem about my mother's cousin (*Delights & Shadows*). I had a very nice compliment from B. H. Fairchild about "Pearl." I had read it somewhere in public, maybe at the Dodge Festival, and Fairchild came up to me afterward and said, "If you had written only one poem, that one would be enough." I felt really good about that. [An adaptation of the poem, directed by Dan Butler and starring Butler and Frances Sternhagen, can be seen on YouTube.]

Notes

1. Gerald Stern, "The Devotion of a Mourner," in *A God in the House: Poets Talk about Faith*, ed. Ilya Kaminsky and Katherine Towler (North Adams, MA: Tupelo Press, 2012), 24–25.

2. Welch wrote,

I have been having some health issues, but if I can help with the launch of the book in Kearney, I certainly will. Lord knows, I have scheduled enough of these over my teaching and writing lifetime at the university here, and the Museum of Nebraska Art would be a great place, especially its main gallery, to welcome a book like this and to present it to people in central Nebraska. I would love to get my former students in the book to come back to Kearney for a joint appearance and reading. Now that would be something. I could then go off to the Elysian Fields where the wind through the tall grasses produces a dulcet pentameter. (email to Daniel Simon, May 30, 2016)

3. In 1828 Goethe remarked: "These journals, as they reach a wider public, will contribute most effectively to the universal world literature for which we are hoping. There can be no question, however, of nations thinking alike. The aim is simply that they shall grow aware of one another, understand one another, and, even where they may not be able to love, may at least tolerate one another." For years this quote appeared on the masthead of *World Literature Today*.

Interview with a Poet: Ted Kooser

Tyler Robert Sheldon / 2020

Tyler Robert Sheldon is editor in chief of *MockingHeart Review*, where this interview appeared in October 2020. It is reprinted with the permission of Tyler Robert Sheldon.

Tyler Robert Sheldon: Hi, Ted. Good to talk with you! When we last spoke, your new book *Red Stilts* was just coming into the world. I've enjoyed so many of the poems therein, and as in other collections, here you shed light on the potency of "small" moments, showing them to be larger than one might first think. Could you speak a bit about the genesis of this new collection?

Ted Kooser: I try to write every morning, and I have no greater plan. It's enough work for me to have one poem to concentrate on, and concentrating on that poem excludes everything but itself. I write a few promising poems each month, and many not so good, and many, many bad ones, laughably bad. Given time I can see which stand out as stronger than the others. Those I submit to literary magazines, where some get accepted for publication. If by the end of a year's writing I have eight or ten poems that have found publication, that's a good year for me. And eight or ten years of that, and I'll have what may be a book of poems. I never plan, but since my life and personality are reflected in my writing, the overall direction of my life is an organizing influence.

Sheldon: This new book emerges into a year stricken by vast social upheaval, the ongoing COVID-19 pandemic, and other concerns. How has 2020 been for you so far?

Kooser: On New Year's Eve this year, many if not most of us will be happy to put 2020 behind us forever, don't you think? That's probably enough said. . . . But I will say that I pray that I will live long enough that our country will be reunited under wise leadership.

Sheldon: *Red Stilts* chronicles memorable moments, only some of which are overtly happy—I think first of the poem "Mother and Child," where the two characters engage with "one / of those red, blue, and yellow / plastic play sets"—and we see that in many instances, color is of vast importance. In "Raspberry Patch," a "black-and-yellow spider" and "white and blue butterflies" tend to their busy lives, and "the old garage lifts a yellow cuff." What role does color play in your writing and in your life around that work?

Kooser: I have enjoyed drawing and painting since I was a little boy. I love looking at the world and trying to catch things I see with a sketch, and I sketch both in words and in line and color. My notebooks are full of both kinds of those sketches. At times when I'm not either drawing or writing, I feel awful, as if I'm throwing my life away.

Sheldon: Family is a very important thread through the poems in *Stilts*. "An Overnight Snow" resonates strongly, wherein you hear "a word or two, muffled, back and forth between / my father and our next-door neighbor, Elmo Mallo, / who was out shoveling [snow], too." When writing about family (and people in general, if you like), what do you find yourself focused on most? And in your estimation, what people-centered moments lend themselves best to a poem?

Kooser: Readers seem to prefer poems in which there are people. I don't think that's a considered preference, but I feel it there. I write a lot of poems about inanimate things, and though I delight in writing them, they're never as warmly accepted. As to writing about people, over the past twenty-five years or so, the poems I've been happiest with are those in which I stand aside, invisible, and observe one or two people who are oblivious to me looking on. The poem you mention is an example of the type; others are the one about the man at the bulletin board in the grocery store entryway, the one about the man coming out of the bakery, the woman standing in the rain talking to the two men in a truck, and so on. Take the most ordinary moment, say a man flicking an ash from a cigarette, and describe it carefully, and everything out and around it will drop away, and it will seem bathed in a remarkable light. I try to focus on things to the exclusion of everything else. If you look at some part of the world through a cardboard toilet paper tube, what you see gains in interest and even importance.

Sheldon: Because the book is so full of compelling snapshots, I shouldn't be this definitive, but "The Dead Vole" contains the moment that hits me hardest, even now. Holding this creature, this "dab of thunderhead gray," the narrator muses: "even such a miniscule being, I thought, / ought to weigh something in death, / a little more than itself." Leaning into that metaphor, what do you suppose death signifies? And importantly, what does (or should) it signify in our current moment?

Kooser: I am the narrator, Tyler. I never speak in a voice other than my own. Years ago, I wrote some dramatic-monologue-type poems, but I haven't written one for years. But to your question: I don't think I have a good answer for you. In poems like the one about the vole, I am myself trying to work out what death means. I've been working on that all my life, it seems. A few years ago, the honors group at our university asked me to give a "last lecture," what I would say if I were about to die. I told my wife I didn't know what I was going to say, and she said, "Ted, it ought to be easy. You've been giving your last lecture all your life!"

Sheldon: Nature is always close by in your work, and in *Stilts*, even poems that aren't about the natural world still keep it in the periphery. I think of "Applause," the closing poem, wherein a girl finishes a performance: "At the close of her piano recital . . . the clapping keeps leafing down." As in this poem, we often invoke nature to describe our lives. Why do you think this is so? What are we humans trying to say?

Kooser: I don't know that I'm making a statement. I don't intend to be. But I'm happy to be a small part of the grand natural order, and I suppose that shows.

Sheldon: Surely a lot of folks would like the world to go back to the pre-COVID world, but we've all made adjustments under the assumption that it'll be a while. To that point, you mentioned in a recent letter that your writing practice has shifted somewhat. Now that things in the world are so different, what are your plans? And what should your readers keep an eye out for next?

Kooser: Earlier, I suggested that I didn't plan beyond the poem right under my nose. I really don't know what's to come, and I have no plan other than to keep writing. I do have more time at home now, and I like that. It's a blessing to me when there are no invitations to go somewhere and do something. I've written a handful of poems about the pandemic, but I don't like them much. They have a topic, and having a topic is to have an agenda. Agendas are poisonous. If tomorrow morning I find myself writing about an acorn, that's what will concern me.

Sheldon: Lots of writers have rituals around their work—William Stafford's presunrise couch writing with toast, the music so many of us put on when we compose a poem or an essay, and so on. Do you have a writing ritual of sorts?

Kooser: As I said earlier, my routine is to get up early, four or four-thirty, and to sit with my notebook and coffee, hoping that something good will happen. Often, what I write is silly or goofy or cheesy or stupid, but unless I'm sitting there ready, I'll miss the good one when it flies past. Kate DiCamillo, the wonderful writer of books for young people, was asked at a conference I attended why she wrote so early in the morning, and she said that she wanted to get her writing done before the critical part of her brain woke up. I thought that was a fine way to explain it.

Sheldon: And before we adjourn, I should ask—what advice would you share with writers who are just starting out in their craft?

Kooser: Read, read, read! Reading is how writers learn to write. When I was still teaching, I told my grad students that they ought to read a hundred poems for every one they try to write. I have never seen a poorly written poem that couldn't have been made better had the author read more poetry.

Renowned Poet and Nebraska Resident Ted Kooser Is Still Hitting His Stride

Chris Christen / 2021

This interview first appeared in the *Omaha World-Herald* on January 3, 2021. Permission to reprint it was granted by the *Omaha World-Herald*.

Ted Kooser's byline is disappearing from a popular weekly poetry column, but fans need not worry. The Pulitzer Prize winner and former US poet laureate, now an octogenarian, is as prolific as ever—maybe even more so in a pandemic.

As Kooser's final installment of "American Life in Poetry" hits some 250 newspapers—including the *World-Herald*—his latest book is taking flight. In early January, *Red Stilts* had a growing wait list at the Bookworm in Omaha, where a new shipment of the hardback was due any day.

We caught up with Kooser in an online interview from his home in rural Garland, in the heart of Nebraska's Bohemian Alps—his longtime muse.

Chris Christen: Your fifteenth book of new poetry, *Red Stilts*, was released last September. Your publisher, Copper Canyon Press, describes you as being at the top of your imaginative and storytelling powers. What sets *Red Stilts* apart from your other published collections? Is it, perhaps, more personal and reflective of your life?

Ted Kooser: I'd like to think that all of my books have reflected the life I was living when the poems were written. The poems in *Red Stilts* are those of a man entering his eighties, a much different man than I was at thirty, publishing my first collection, *Official Entry Blank*. Those early poems are embarrassing to me now, but they represented who I was back then.

Christen: People are reading more because of the pandemic. Was the release of *Red Stilts* planned for 2020, or was the timing a happy accident?

Kooser: Neither I nor Copper Canyon had any idea that this pandemic was on its way. The poems were collected mid-2019, from work I'd done since *Kindest Regards: New and Selected Poems*, which came out in 2018.

Christen: What are you currently reading?

Kooser: I'm always reading a number of books at the same time. Just now I'm reading two books of essays by Clive James, Julius Lester's wonderful retelling of the Uncle Remus Tales, a new novel, *Snow*, by John Banville, and Richard Chase's 1943 book of *Jack Tales*.

Christen: You have said that your favorite poem is the one you've just completed. Is that still the case?

Kooser: Yes, I'm always thrilled with what I've just written, and that may last for about a half day before it begins to smell, sometimes a really awful smell.

Christen: You founded "American Life in Poetry" as US poet laureate in 2005 in partnership with the Poetry Foundation and began offering a free weekly poem to roughly 150 newspapers across the United States. Your last installment—no. 823—reached some 4.5 million readers worldwide in early January. What brought you to that decision?

Kooser: The funding for the column was inextricably bound to my (University of Nebraska–Lincoln) teaching position, and I wanted to retire from teaching. Had there been a means of continuing the column from home I probably would have kept it up, but there was no way of putting that together.

Christen: You established "American Life in Poetry" to raise the visibility of poetry. Will the mission continue under another author?

Kooser: I asked my colleague at the university, Kwame Dawes, to take over the column, and he did so on January 1. Kwame is a great asset to Nebraska. He's the current editor of *Prairie Schooner* and the author of many books of his own poems. He also edits a series of poetry collections by African poets for the university press.

Christen: Each year, you donate bound volumes of personal correspondence and journal entries to the UNL libraries. What will we find in your random thoughts and observations on the pandemic, quarantine, and isolation?

Kooser: In my lighter moments you'll find an introvert relishing social isolation; in my darker moments, you'd see me feeling very sorry for the hundreds of thousands of people affected. Just this morning, I received news from a friend of the death of someone quite close to him. The virus keeps closing the circle, like one of those wire snares in the grass. Step into it, and it snatches you into the sky.

Christen: You're a twenty-year cancer survivor and have lectured on "Healing through Poetry." Did you find yourself drawing on your own advice to get through the trials of 2020?

Kooser: Jon Hassler, the great Minnesota novelist, had a Parkinson's-like disease, and he told me once that were it not for his writing, he would have fallen into a pit of despair. I know what he meant.

Christen: I last saw you at your neighboring studio in Dwight. Do you still hang out there?

Kooser: I sold my building in Dwight this past April. I enjoyed it for a dozen years but didn't want the responsibility of taking care of the property any longer.

Christen: Is your collection of vintage LPs intact?

Kooser: Yes, I have maybe fifteen or twenty feet of LPs.

Christen: You've had a lot of fun as Dwight's artificial florist.

Kooser: I've retired from the artificial florist distinction and returned all the flowers to the thrift shop where I bought them. Finis!

Christen: Do you continue to be an early riser, starting your day at four thirty or five a.m., drinking freshly brewed coffee while answering mail and writing in your journal?

Kooser: Yes, the coffee first, the journal with the coffee, and then the mail.

Christen: What was your journal entry for December 29, 2020, the day I requested this interview?

Kooser: "Snow blowing from the roof in feathery gusts." There's an Andrew Wyeth painting I've always loved called *Tenant Farmer*, a picture of winter stillness, a cold-looking old brick farmhouse with a deer carcass hanging from a bare tree in the yard, and from the roof of the house a little plume of snow is lifting.

A Conversation with Ted Kooser: In Dialogue with Judith Harris

Judith Harris / 2023

This interview first appeared in the *North American Review*'s online publication, *Open Space*, in September 2023. It is reprinted with permission of poet/scholar Judith Harris and *North American Review*.

For two decades, Ted and I have conversed through email, so it was the natural medium for us to discuss his work and his background growing up in the Midwest. We conducted this interview in a period of a week. I would send one or two questions at a time, and Ted would write back promptly with his replies. One thing I've learned is that in its spare, simple, but elegant diction, a Kooser poem works like a well-oiled machine: each word is carefully chosen, each inference accounted for, and each stanza carefully honed. His poetry reveals a complicated man who would probably refer to himself as simple. His reminiscences and comments in the following conversation will surprise and delight readers listening in.

Judith Harris: As I think of the arc of your work and what readers might want to ask about, one of them has to do with your mentorship of so many who have studied with you or corresponded with you and benefited from your writings on writing. The University of Nebraska published *More in Time* (2021), a volume made up of a wide spectrum of writers reflecting on the significance of your work and friendship. "More in Time" is often the way you close an email or letter, an ending that suggests leaving the door open to further exchanges. And to turn this around a bit, could you talk about the importance of reading poets as a young man and throughout your career?

Ted Kooser: I have always emphasized to my students how important it is to read the poetry of others and to read a lot of it. I made my grad students read ten poems a day, week in and week out. We learn to be poets from other poets. Every poem that fails shows that not quite enough poetry has been read.

Harris: Did you have mentors?

Kooser: Though I didn't have the word *mentor* in my vocabulary until I was well into middle age, I did have people to whom I've looked up. Will Jumper, who taught writing at Iowa State, was my first real literary mentor, to be followed by Karl Shapiro when I got to Nebraska, Karl to be followed by Leonard Nathan, with whom I connected by mail after seeing a poem of his in the *New Republic*. I sent him a fan letter, and he wrote back, whence ensued twenty-five years of weekly correspondence. Leonard was teaching at Berkeley, and we didn't meet in person until we were deep into our letter exchange. Our correspondence was worth more than any other help that I've ever had. Leonard ("Uncle Leonard") was about fifteen years older than I, and in his early eighties he lapsed into senile dementia. I remember so very clearly a letter from his wife, Carol, explaining his long silence, saying that "Leonard will never write again, Ted, but he walks around with a pencil in his hand."

Harris: Yes, I was familiar with Nathan, but it wasn't until we discussed him earlier that I went to a poetry book I owned by him and was astonished by his singular style—he was an original. And like Shapiro, perhaps, one of your most powerful influences. Your work doesn't resemble either one of them, and yet there is a zeitgeist around all three of you, just as it should be. When you were starting out as a young poet, what were you like?

Kooser: I was a nasty, rebellious teenager, and I certainly didn't look up to my parents, my uncles and aunts, during those years. I thought they were stupid conformists. If I had somebody to look up to in those days, it would have been someone like Don Garlits, who held the world's record in burning up a drag strip. One hundred forty-eight miles per hour in a quarter mile, as I remember it. Cars and girls were what I cared most about. I wore a leather jacket with the name of our hot rod club on the back, the Nightcrawlers. I was doing everything I could to be unlike my parents. There were long, dark silences in our house, weeks and months long. I was terribly hard on my mother and father, who loved me unstintingly through it all.

Harris: That is very interesting since the takeaway from most of your poems about your parents are tender reflections on their goodness, their strength, in elegies like "Mother" and "Father." And I've read elsewhere that you regard your childhood as a happy one. But a family wouldn't be a family without some discord. I've always suspected that there was another side to it. What other things come to mind?

Kooser: My friends were from a notch or two lower than my own upper middle class, sons and daughters from working-class blue-collar families. We were staying out to all hours, souping up our old cars, drag racing, and so on. We boys tried to look like James Dean and had James Dean haircuts. We sometimes hung out with hotrodders from nearby towns, and I remember a car club from Marshalltown, in which there was a boy, Kai or Sky, something like that, who dated Jean Seberg, whom I remember as being just another cute girl.

My interest in writing in those early years was part of my hot-rod persona, and I wrote Robert Service–like ballads about drag races, one of which was my first published poem, appearing in a teenage magazine called *Dig*. One of my friends submitted it without telling me. I was also writing poems for my girlfriend, things I'd be mortally embarrassed by were they to turn up today. I was greatly relieved, after we'd finally broken up during our freshman year in college, to learn that she'd burned all those poems. Then I was told many years later that she still had some of them, God forbid.

In the fall of 1957, I started college at Iowa State, as an architecture major, and lived at home. My high school advisor had looked over my grades and noticed I had all A's in art classes, so he had steered me toward architecture. High school counseling was that rudimentary then. But I was more interested in writing and took my first creative-writing class as a freshman, from Will Jumper, who I mentioned earlier. Will had a PhD from Stanford and had studied poetry with Yvor Winters. He was a stickler for traditional prosody. For example, in the iambic pentameter line he'd let us substitute a trochee or spondee in the first and third foot, but never in both in the same line, and never in the second or fourth foot. That kind of stickler. The first formal poem I wrote pleased him so much that he sent it to *Poetry*, and I got a nice letter of rejection, on thin, blue airmail stationery, from John Frederick Nims, then the acting editor. That was my first interaction with the greater poetry world.

I also belonged to Writers' Round Table, sixteen students who met weekly, under Will Jumper's supervision, and critiqued each other's work. It was invaluable. One of the other members would go on to Congress as Senator Tom Harkin, where he served many years. He was a better senator than he was a poet, as I recall.

Harris: Other than for those early mentors like Will Jumper, who has influenced your work?

Kooser: I've had many friends with whom I've exchanged poems, including you, Judith, but none whom I think of as mentors, us being all from about the same generation, just helping each other. There were always, though, notable poets in the generation just ahead of me to whom I looked up, like Donald Hall, Maxine Kumin, Robert Bly, Elizabeth Bishop, May Swenson, Galway Kinnell, Tom McGrath, Denise Levertov, James Wright, and others, some of whom are now almost forgotten, like Brewster Ghiselin.

Harris: Place holds the past even when we lose our sense of connection to what has gone before. Place outlasts much that has vanished. What is remarkable about your poetry is its wonder of place—whether it is a remote, abandoned farmhouse in the plains or in a Goodwill store or on a long winter walk. In a few master strokes, place opens up in your poems. Could you please talk about "the place of place" in your poems?

Kooser: One notices how an anecdote often begins, "I was on my way to the grocery . . ." or "It was raining cats and dogs. . . ." There's a convention for helping the listener to immediately situate himself or herself on the ground of a story. I have no doubt that this goes back to the earliest experiences we humans related to each other. I don't know that I ever consciously thought to do this in a poem, but it happened naturally, just as it would in conversation. And, working toward economy and compression, in revising poems I've tried to make those settings as vivid as possible. Wasn't it Eudora Welty who said that place is "the racing heart of fiction"? I think it's the racing heart of poetry, too.

Harris: The intimacy of your poetry has led to its enormous popularity in part due to your keen ability to discern poetic language in everyday speech that is also marvelously sonorous and imagistic. Your careful selection of words often speak for the ineffable—human emotions of love, grief, heartbreak, joy, poems that others can model their own emotions on. This is why people use poetry on occasions to articulate a significant event: weddings, funerals, inaugurations, when people feel too deeply for words. It is well known that you write every day before sunrise; do you have moments in which you recognize an early draft is especially good, or vice versa?

Kooser: One of the reasons I write, perhaps the primary one, is to please myself, and on a good day, I really delight myself. Many poems always look brilliant for a few hours, then start to fade, then start to smell. It's best to let them rest until they're old enough that it seems I am reading the poems of somebody else.

Harris: What is your daily practice like?

Kooser: While working, I try not to think too much about where the poems are coming from because that questioning or critical part of my mind is a sure killer of associational play. I most often start out my writing time by reading a few poems by somebody else, and something might nudge me to write a few words, or I sit looking out of the window into the predawn darkness and just wait for a few words to come to me. This accounts for the dozens of poems I've written about what it's like before dawn, sometimes in moonlight, sometimes in utter darkness with the lamp by my chair being the only light in the world.

Harris: Another well-known feature of Kooser folklore is your dislike of academic posturing or pretentiousness in poetry and life, and your poetry has become synonymous with integrity. As an autobiographical poet, could you comment on your use of the autobiographical *I* and why you never caught the fever of mid-twentieth-century dramatic personas?

Kooser: When I was a young man, I tried to write like the contemporary masters. I remember a poem in the manner of Pound, for example, and metrical narratives like Browning. Once, for a final paper in an undergraduate class in literary criticism, I wrote 550 lines of heroic couplets in response to Pope's "Essay on Criticism." Fortunately, it got lost years ago! It was part of my growing up, emulating the great. As a mature man, though, what I'd tell my students is that the most important goal is to write like yourself, to be completely yourself. It's a difficult task, but if you write long enough, you'll slowly drift in that direction. It takes confidence, lots of it, but that eventually builds on its own. The "myself" who I write like is loath to talk too much about himself, though I do seem to be going on and on here!

Harris: You possess a rare quality that readers trust—it is something that can't be captured or described, but it is there. A reader just senses it so that when one reads a book of your poems, the speaker is continuous from poem to poem. This is pure artistry, and I'm reminded of something that Denise Levertov told me about her preference for poems that are composed extemporaneously, and therefore become transformative. Although she herself wrote dramatic monologues, they were not as existential in process. Do you think that poetic ventriloquism is tantamount to truth or fiction?

Kooser: Again, I'm not sure. . . . I do at times make up things, but I've found that no matter how convincing they may sound, there's something missing. This morning, I saw a newspaper photograph of a group of people doing this and that at a political rally. One of the men was bent down as if to reach for a hat lying on the ground. I might have made up what he was doing: His hat blew off, and he was picking it back up. Or perhaps it was somebody else's hat, and he was picking it up to give it back to the owner. Or perhaps he wasn't reaching for it at all and instead had just set it on the ground to cover up something. Those all would be possibilities for fabricated or fictionalized poems, but the true poem is in not knowing what he was doing, and "fessing up" to that ignorance. For me, a true poem presents what we actually see. I may not understand what I see, but that ignorance is essential to the poem. I want my readers to do what they want to with just what I've given them. Does that make any sense?

Harris: Indeed, it does; it was the in-betweenness of knowing and not knowing that became interesting, and there is power in confiding in a reader one's uncertainty. It isn't wishy-washiness; it is genuine. Valuing honesty is something you make quite clear in your essay "Lying for the Sake of Making Poems."

Kooser: I published that essay in *Prairie Schooner* years ago, and it's been reprinted in the Graywolf anthology *After Confession: Poetry as Autobiography*. In that article, I talked about poets who've manipulated their readers by making up things. One woman wrote a series of poems about her father sexually abusing her, and they were accepted and published. But I learned that her father hadn't abused her and was living. What kind of a person writes something like that just to get a publication credit for their CV?

Harris: Something that not all readers know about you is that you are a gifted painter. When I think of your paintings, I think of impressionists painting in the "open" air in order to paint the presence of natural light and forms that they couldn't get quite right in the studio. Could you say something about what most critics have noted about your poetry: a striking visual world on the page?

Kooser: I'm a competent painter, Judith, a "Sunday painter," a sketcher, but I'm not an artist in the best sense of that word. I have good friends who are artists, and I wouldn't presume to elevate myself into their ranks. I don't exhibit my work; I don't sell it. Sometimes I give it away. If I were to try to show my work for sale, it would ruin the pleasure of painting. I once sold a painting for a good price, and I've regretted it every day since. Selling it made me into somebody I didn't want to be. When money gets into anything it makes it rot from the core. But how much fun it is to have a visitor compliment something I've painted and then to be able to just give it to them, to say, "Here, it's yours."

Harris: Those two words, "It's yours," say so much about your sensibility beginning with the first poem in *Sure Signs*, "Selecting a Reader," in which you very subtly turn the egotistical tables on poets who disregard the reader's needs and immerse themselves in the self-dialectic of the poem as an immediate reflector of the self. But as we've been discussing the relationships between poet and reader in the context of the human world, let's segue into talking about your vast body of nature and animal poems. Do you sense a difference in how you approach the nonhuman world? Are there writers who you like to read who write about the landscape?

Kooser: Because my wife and I live in the country, we have experiences with wildlife every day. Within a few yards of the house, we have deer, rabbits, raccoons, woodchucks, opossums, and a pond with snakes, frogs, and so on. Wild turkeys, too. Owls, hawks, dozens of species of songbirds. Nearly all of my poems about animals portray them as sympathetic fellow travelers, just doing their best to get through their lives. Most often there's a little humor in those poems because the animals and I are attuned to our foibles. As to other writers who write about landscape, many do, but in the poetry of most of those people, the landscape is just a backdrop. I prefer to think of it as having its own life.

Harris: One of the more noteworthy aspects of the *Selected* is the inclusion of poems from *Winter Morning Walks: One Hundred Postcards to Jim Harrison* (2000), a book that is as unassuming as it is poignant. Something unspoken is adrift here: the speaker is increasingly aware of life's vicissitudes, "Just so I awoke this morning, / wrapped in fear." Watching a plastic flag—the kind that the people who maintain roads use to warn of hazards— propped up again and again, the speaker muses, "Give me your courage." Could you talk a bit about the affirmative qualities of poetry and also your focus on individuals on the borderlines of the social world, and who elicit in your speakers an understanding of collective experience?

Kooser: I think all works of art are affirmations of life, and we can see affirmation in the poems leading up to the terrible moment when all of that affirmation reverses, and a suicide follows. I find it very difficult to read the poems of people like Sylvia Plath because I know what is coming. In van Gogh's work, the affirmation is so vibrant and colorful that it is still burning bright more than a hundred years later. As to the second part of your question, I do write about people set apart from what's fashionable because their lives are of interest to me. In my next book I have a poem about watching some moving men take an upright piano down a flight of stairs, a magical feat, far more impressive than anything the Kardashians have ever done, and I dedicated it to a moving man who was a neighbor of mine.

Harris: In an essay, "Metaphor and Faith" you write: "Of the possible existence of a supreme order, Robert Frost once said, 'With so many ladders going up everywhere, there must be something for them to lean against.' And there are lots and lots of ladders, in every corner of the earth, each leaning up against The One Big Thing." You then discuss "The Silken Tent" to make a point of your own about the varieties of religious belief.

Prominent in all categories of your work is the importance of metaphor. Could you say a bit about it?

Kooser: If I have a gift as a writer, it's a gift for association, or metaphor making. While I'm writing, the metaphors come unsummoned out of somewhere inside me. I have never invented one, that is, consciously set out to construct one from scratch. They are revealed to me in that trance-like state of concentration I fall into while there is nothing else in the world but the tip of my pen on the paper. Pop! There's a metaphor. I've had students show me a draft of a poem and say, "Do you think I should put in a metaphor here?" Well, metaphors aren't like that. You can't take one out of its plastic wrapper and plug it in. They aren't ready-made, on display at the Metaphor Counter in Walmart. They come up from within us, miraculously.

Harris: Could you tell us more about your children's books? Recently you collaborated with Connie Wanek on a book from Candlewick Press, *Marshmallow Clouds: Two Poets at Play among Figures of Speech*, but you have written others as well. What are the similarities and differences between writing for an adult or children's audience?

Kooser: I find that if I let myself play in my writing, a playfulness comes through, and the more playful the poems, the more appropriate for children they seem. So when I've finished a poem, I let it sit for a few days until it begins to look like someone else's poem, and I ask, "Just who is the reader for this?" Most of my poems in *Marshmallow Clouds* weren't written for children but seemed as if children might like them. I've never set out to write a poem for a child.

Harris: In writing my book about elegy, I found that your elegies were consolatory in ways that others are not, as you find the perfect image that needs no more explanation for feeling than itself. Also, what is striking about your poems that often reflect loss and time passing is the way that your love for the deceased comes through as in this beautiful elegy, "Father" that closes with these lines on the anniversary of your late father's birth:

> On this day each year you loved to relate
> that the moment of your birth
> your mother glanced out the window
> and saw lilacs in bloom. Well, today
> lilacs are blooming in side yards
> all over Iowa, still welcoming you.

In the end is always a beginning, and your poems are often cyclical, and numinous, but is there a poem or series of poems that were particularly transformative for you, both as a poet and a human being? One poem I recall your pointing out as especially meaningful for you is "Screech Owl":

All night each reedy whinny
from a bird no bigger than a heart
flies out of a tall black pine
and, in a breath, is taken away
by the stars. Yet, with small hope
from the center of darkness
it calls out again and again.

Kooser: I do like that poem, largely for its compression. If it were possible, all of my poems would be of about that length, or even shorter. But sometimes they have to be bigger to accommodate what I want to fit in. For me, a poem's size depends on letting it fill its own skin, almost to popping, and stopping there. Many of our contemporaries write poems that go on for a couple of pages, and nearly all of them seem to me to be too long, too "talky." Like a long clothesline hung with wet laundry, they sag in the middle.

It's interesting to me that the sonnet seems to me to be of about the perfect length and organization, and perhaps that's why it has lasted so long. Maybe we're hardwired for poems of about that length. This is not to disparage the longer poem, which when executed by a word-artist can be breathtaking. But in the hands of lesser artists those long poems look like stacks.

Harris: Many of your poems conclude with a sound in nature that is as eternal as it is hopeful, even from "the center of darkness." Would you say that hope is limitless?

Kooser: I hope that it is. Without it, our species just wouldn't be "human." When I've said that every poem, every work of art is affirmative, I mean that it not only honors life but celebrates it. The hopeless among us shrivel and blow away.

Harris: In the prominent book *Can Poetry Matter*, Dana Gioia writes this about you and your work: "It has been Kooser's particular genius to develop a genuine poetic style that accommodates the average reader and portrays a vision that provides unexpected moments of illumination from the seemingly threadbare details of everyday life." Could you comment on the direction you see today's poetry currently heading?

Kooser: I don't know how anybody could make a good assessment of the state of American poetry today. I read not too long ago that there are about ten thousand books of poems published each year. I might read thirty or forty. I can say, with confidence, that poetry publishing seems to be overwhelmingly healthy! I'm no different from any other reader: there are poems I like better than others, of course. I prefer work that has charm, in the better, older sense of that word, that is, magic. Today I was rereading Nancy Willard's *Swimming Lessons*, a masterwork of that kind of poetry. There are tens of thousands of poems short on charm, but they have other objectives and have my respect. I've said this elsewhere, but what could be wrong with a world in which everyone was writing poems? We'd be doing no harm.

July 2023:
A Conversation with Ted Kooser

Mary K. Stillwell / 2023

This interview, conducted by poet and scholar Mary K. Stillwell, author of *The Life and Poetry of Ted Kooser* (University of Nebraska Press, 2013), appears in print for the first time. Permission to print the interview was granted by Mary K. Stillwell.

Mary K. Stillwell: "Life is a long walk forward through the crowded cars of a passenger train," you wrote in *Local Wonders*, and as I've prepared for our email conversation, I've realized what a lot of the "bright world" has raced past since our first exchange twenty-six years ago. The train has picked up considerable speed since then; the view from the windows has been filled with so many colorful, flying leaves.

Maybe a good place to start, Ted, is with congratulations on your most recent award. Your fifth children's book, *Marshmallow Clouds*, cowritten with poet Connie Wanek and illustrated by Richard Jones, has just been presented with the CLiPPA (the Centre for Literacy in Primary Poetry Award) in the UK. The award, established in 2003, celebrates outstanding poetry published for children. Quite an honor!

Although collaboration is not new to you, the poems in *Marshmallow Clouds* have one seamless voice. How did the idea for the book emerge? How did you and Connie Wanek come about writing it? Did you come up with a trajectory before working on specific poems or vice versa? Do you both contribute to each poem? As in the case of *Braided Creek*, the poem's author goes unnamed. How did you go about maintaining a single voice as you worked on the poems?

Ted Kooser: Hello, Mary K.! Connie and I tried out several ideas on each other, having a number of poems we thought of as possibilities for a collaborative children's book. It was she who came up with the idea of organizing a group based on the four elements. As to who wrote what, we may have made small suggestions to each other, but the poems were written by one or another of us, never by both. The manuscript was originally called "Making Mischief: Two Poets at Play among Figures of Speech," but "Making Mischief" had been previously used, and our editor at Candlewick wanted a different title.

Stillwell: It's July in Nebraska, where we are frequently "boiled and salted / like a peanut" and "the meat / in a heat sandwich, the dog in a hot," to quote *Marshmallow Clouds.* How are you spending your days? What—and where—are you writing? What's on your mind?

Kooser: I had nine hours of jaw cancer surgery in January of 2022, and a great deal of my waking time since has been spent in recovery, though a better word might be *acceptance.* I've had to accept a liquid diet and slurry, less than articulate speech, as well as the recognition that I'm starting my eighty-fifth year on a song and a prayer.

I do my writing, as I always have, from about four or four thirty in the morning, till eight or nine, though sometimes I'm at it till noon. I work best very early. I attended a conference at which Kate DiCamillo spoke and then took questions. Someone asked why she wrote so very early in the day, and she said that she wanted to get her writing done before the critic inside her woke up.

I'm able to write something each day, and something that I think is worthwhile about once every ten days. I just checked my records, and I have, as of today, 930 unpublished poems, most of them probably *justly* unpublished, many that have never been sent out.

Stillwell: When we last spoke at length, you were working at your home in Garland or in your studio in Dwight, painting and making and repairing poetry there. Life had slowed down a bit since your travels as the US poet laureate, but you were still very busy, publishing *Valentines, House Held Up by Trees, Bell in the Bridge, A Wheeling Year: A Poet's Field Book*, and tending to your weekly "American Life in Poetry" newspaper column. Your long poem "Pearl" was made into a short film. Kooser Elementary School had opened to students. *Splitting an Order* was due out. You were lunching at Cy's Café or traveling to Lincoln to see friends.

Kooser: I sold my building in Dwight and moved all my books and art supplies back to our acreage, though I donated twenty-five hundred poetry volumes to Kwame and Lorna Dawes for an initiative of theirs, to set up libraries of American poetry in African countries. I've been able to cram all my art supplies (I'm less an artist than I am a collector of art supplies) into my corn crib art studio here at home, and I do some sketching, some watercolors, and so on. Lately, I've been painting postcard-sized watercolor landscapes and sending them out as postcards to friends. The postal sorting and canceling machines add their own little touches.

For the past couple of years, I've been posting new poems on Facebook, which has been both pleasurable and informing. As you know, with traditional-print journal publishing, we poets submit five or six poems to one journal or another and wait six or eight months before getting a rejection. If a poem gets accepted, there's another six- or eight-months' wait before we get our two free contributor's copies. At my age and with my medical history, I don't have the time to do a whole lot of waiting.

Then with pride we open the journal and look at our poem and think, "Will anyone find this and READ it?"

But with Facebook, there's an immediate response and a lot to be learned from the number of "likes" and what's said in the "comments." I've learned, for example, that readers prefer poems with people in them to poems of pure description, which I often write. But if there's an opportunity in a poem of description to personify something, people will more readily warm to it. I've also learned how much people like poems that remind them of something in their own lives, something with which they identify. Their comments are like little encores to what I am doing. I don't post my more "literary" work on Facebook, and save that for the SERIOUS poetry community, that of the small literary quarterlies, which I still respect.

Stillwell: You quote E. B. White in the epigraph to *Cotton Candy* (2022): "As a writing man, or secretary, I have always felt charged with the safekeeping of all unexpected items of worldly or unworldly enchantment, as though I might be held personally responsible if even a small one were to be lost." On Facebook, you can keep safe items of enchantment with (at least) five thousand others who go on to share them even more widely!

Kooser: I see myself as a community poet, someone who feels he is part of a community. In our little village, Garland, for years, there was a woman who was the community artist. She was self-taught, and any professional critic would have looked at her work with disdain. If you wanted a favorite pony painted on your mailbox or a picture of your farmstead painted on the blade of your grandfather's old crosscut saw, she was the person who could do that for you. The community supported her artwork by making use of it. It was useful. She was their artist. A community poet might be like her, providing a service. On Facebook, I feel I'm doing just that. I've always wanted to be a popular poet, in the best sense of that word. I'd like to earn a broad audience of everyday readers, and I seem to have found one. This doesn't mean that I write *down* to my audience but that I try to respect who they are.

Stillwell: I'm reminded of Seamus Heaney, whom you quote in *Local Wonders*, "The aim of poetry and the poet is finally to be of service, to ply the effort of the individual into the larger work of the community as a whole." That's one of the things that "American Life in Poetry" did nationally. No matter where we lived, we shared this poem, this experience. Facebook does this to some extent as more and more poems appear there.

Two of the "services" provided by the poems and commentary on your Facebook page seem more intimate: they allow for—and prompt acceptance of—our frailties ("when you attain Medicare age") while at the same time they celebrate what it is to be human ("Spill," for example), and they stimulate readers' memories ("Rafter Square"). The comment section reflects a community engaging common experiences together, perhaps noticing them for the first time, and remembering a rich moment of their own past greeting them because of your posted poem. How did you arrive at Facebook? Did you anticipate the response—quality and quantity—that you and your work have received?

Kooser: Years before I ventured into Facebook, one of the publicists at the University of Nebraska Press had encouraged me to build a social media presence, but I was wary and put it off. I didn't really know what Facebook was and how it worked. After my retirement from teaching, though, I missed the tutorials with my students, the back and forth, and thought I'd give Facebook a try, thinking that perhaps I could do some conversing there. So I began posting poems that I thought might engage Facebook friends, as if striking up a conversation. It's been great fun for me to read the responses, and to respond to those. It's a community that's quite easy to be a part of on one's own schedule.

Stillwell: You mention the months it takes to hear back from publications, but more often than not, there is a fee to submit poems—and often a substantial fee, discouraging to young poets especially. Would you advise students to publish on Facebook?

Kooser: Years ago, before the internet, I got the idea of publishing by "chain letter." If a poet had a poem he or she wanted to try out on the world, he or she would send copies to friends and ask them to send the poem on to other friends if they liked it and to have those people do the same. I figured that most poems wouldn't survive the first cut, and it would take a very good poem to move on and on out into and over the world.

Well, publishing on Facebook is a little like that, and it doesn't require making copies and buying stamps and envelopes. And a poet can see how successful he is by the responses (likes and comments) he receives.

It could be a very good lesson to a poet to post a poem that almost no one responds to. Dead silence is not a response we'd hope to receive. So I do think a young poet might learn from doing some Facebook posting. However, posting on Facebook is "publishing," and a poem appearing there is thus ineligible for publishing elsewhere. Most young poets don't have a whole lot of poems to spare, and if they're hoping to enhance their resume, they're going to want to publish in the traditional print quarterlies that have a reputation for publishing quality.

Stillwell: You've written about E. B. White that when it comes to making you "feel good about being alive," no writer approaches him. In your own work, the pleasure of an unforgettable morning unfolds in "A Morning in Early Spring" from *Splitting an Order*: "No other day like this one." Relishing existence and being aware of even the smallest creatures in our world have been present to a greater or lesser degree in your poems, especially from *Sure Signs* on. Delight and shadow still appear side by side. Your collections seem to have become more tightly thematic over the years, carefully "paced" and the sections deftly tailored. Which leads me to another craft question, one that might be of assistance to other poets, especially those coming up: How do you go about putting together your collections? How do you order sections? What advice might you offer?

Kooser: In the manuscript for my forthcoming collection, I have three sections of about the same length. The first section has poems in which my point of view is at a distance, observing people, what I used to tell my students was the "spy-in-the-lobby" point of view, as in those old films where the spy sits peering over the top of an open newspaper. The second section has poems about things, not so much about people, and the third section has poems of family, in which I appear, just a little more visibly than in the others. I've used that kind of loose thematic organization in other books as well.

Stillwell: From your Facebook postings, commentary, and poems, you are very busy with the upkeep of your home and acreage. Happily busy. You've taught poetry part time off and on since 1970—fifty years! Do you have time to miss teaching?

Kooser: I loved teaching, and I might have kept at it for a number of years, but I was having serious health problems and thought it would be better to devote my time to "putting my things in order," as they say, while I was still healthy enough to do that. That meant emptying and selling my building in Dwight, clearing my university office, seeing to the disposition of my "American Life in Poetry," and so on.

Stillwell: You are starting your "eighty-fifth year on a song and a prayer." *Raft*, your collection out next year, is filled with song and prayer. Life is celebrated deeply, without reservation, even as you acknowledge human mortality. As "The Red Wing Church" suggested years ago, the sacred lies all about us. In "Hospital Parking Ramp, 6:00 a.m.," the ark is "floating at anchor" as patients with their loved ones arrive in pairs, an allusion to the biblical story of Noah. A sense of ordering resides in your poems and your paintings. I'm thinking of E. B. White again, feeling "charged with the safekeeping of all unexpected items of worldly or unworldly enchantment." Where did that sense of safekeeping, of ordering, come from?

Kooser: I think the safekeeping and ordering come from being a little on the obsessive-compulsive side, wanting control. It's why I'm so drawn to miniature things, doll houses, etcetera, everything in its place. When I finish a poem, I want every element in its perfect place, every punctuation mark, every line ending, and so on.

Stillwell: Thanks, Ted, for bringing us up to date on your rich life of poetry and relationship in the Bohemian Alps of Nebraska. Here's to you, your poetry, and—to return to the final pages of *Local Wonders* again—to the "many cars ahead."

A Poem Is "A Hand-Drawn Treasure Map": Ted Kooser in Conversation with John Cusatis

John Cusatis / 2024

This interview was conducted from December 8, 2023, through January 8, 2024, via email. It appears in print for the first time.

John Cusatis: Let's start off with a fundamental question, Ted. What is a poem?

Ted Kooser: Surprisingly, I haven't been asked that question very often, but I've thought a good deal about a possible answer. To me, a poem is the record of a discovery, be it the discovery of something in the outer world, or within oneself, or perhaps in the haphazard juxtaposition of sounds and sense within language. It is also a map, a hand-drawn treasure map that a reader can follow to a reward otherwise unattainable.

I make a distinction between *poem* and *poetry*: a poem is the document you hold in your hand and read from, while poetry is something that magically happens in the indefinable space between a poem and its reader.

Cusatis: Your work has developed considerably in the fifty-five years that separate *Official Entry Blank* and *Raft*. If an interviewer had asked you this same question in the spring of 1961, when you published "Cold Pastoral" in *Sketch*, the literary journal of Iowa State, or even 1969, when that poem appeared in your first book, how might your answer have differed? That is, how has your view of a poem evolved?

Kooser: Oh, John, that's so long ago. . . . But I do remember being much more taken up with form, as if that was what made a poem a poem. Once, to fulfill an assignment for a class in literary criticism at Iowa State, I wrote 550 lines of closed iambic pentameter couplets about Pope's "Essay on

Criticism." That's how nuts I was about form. Thank God that show-offy poem vanished long ago.

Cusatis: Along the same lines, composing poetry has been a constant in your life since at least young adulthood, an abiding and defining vocation. You've joked about your desire to attract girls and need to distinguish yourself in a way that athletic or musical ability had not. But clearly these early motives are not at the foundation of the poet you became. Do you recall your very early poetic impulses? What prompted them and what nurtured them?

Kooser: I had a wonderful fourth-grade teacher, Miss Kirby, who was able to show us the fun of making poems and reciting them, and it was that fun that I think kept me at it and still keeps me at it. If teachers could show students that poetry is pleasurable, we'd have a lot more poets and readers of poetry.

Cusatis: The poet B. H. Fairchild, who has praised your work emphatically, discusses the challenges, to put it mildly, of growing up in the rural Midwest while harboring a proclivity for beauty and its expression. He recalls in his poem "Beauty" that for males, the use of this word *beauty* was basically forbidden in the ironically named Liberal, Kansas, where he grew up, except "in reference, perhaps, to a new pickup or a dead deer." Fairchild attributes "the local library and jazz" to his survival, until he was liberated from Liberal when he enrolled at the University of Kansas. I've never heard you comment on feeling alienated or self-conscious about your early affinity for painting and literature. You write fondly of your native, Ames, Iowa, and Guttenberg, where you spent parts of your summers. Were these towns conducive environments for an aspiring artist to grow up—both privately and publicly—or did you look forward to eventually moving to a big city as a young man?

Kooser: I remember thinking, as a teenager, that Ames was provincial, and I was disdainful of it, as were all my friends. I thought my father's job running a department store was stupid and conforming, that people in Ames weren't really with it, and so on. I wasted a lot of time trying to be unconventional, and I must have been very hard on my parents during those years, yet, somehow, they put up with me. I was a typical nasty, arrogant teenager who really knew nothing. As you can see from the poems, I now look upon Ames and Guttenberg with affection, though there were things about Ames that I'm not proud of, the kept-under-cover racism and other whispered prejudices, against Catholics, against Jews. And the classism in small towns, whew! If you belong to the country club in a town of four thousand, you're really someone! I know of a couple who had considered moving to the Ozarks in their retirement but decided not to because in the Ozarks they'd be nobodies, but at home in Iowa, members of the town's country club, they were somebodies.

Cusatis: So you were a rebellious teenager in the postwar years, when teen rebellion in America had famously blossomed. This is the time of James Dean and Marlon Brando. What movies were you tuned into during the fifties?

Kooser: I remember only *Rebel Without a Cause*, from those years. We had two movie theaters in Ames, and they no doubt made most of their money by showing Bing Crosby and Bob Hope.

Cusatis: In one of the scores of unforgettable passages in *Local Wonders*, you express affection for the care, kindness, and reverence of the Mennonite women running the Et-Cetera Thrift and Gift Shop in Seward, Nebraska. The passage reminds me of Holden Caufield's description of the nuns he meets in a diner in *The Catcher in the Rye*, a landmark novel of teenage rebellion that would have been newly popular during your teenage years. Did you read Salinger's novel as a young man? And you were about eighteen when Kerouac's *On the Road* appeared? Did these books and others help fuel your desire "to be unconventional"?

Kooser: I'm embarrassed to say I've never read *Catcher in the Rye*, but when I was in Washington, I was introduced to a woman who had been courted by Salinger, who had told her that if she'd be his lover, he would give her the original manuscript. She turned him down.

I did read *On the Road* and loved it. It's one of those books that if I went back to it now, I probably wouldn't like it at all.

Cusatis: In 1963, you left your Iowa high school teaching job to move to Lincoln, Nebraska. To what degree was this a liberating move? In addition, Nebraska clearly had a large impact on your writing, as many of the poems in *Official Entry Blank* illustrate. But aside from the region, what impact did the era have on you, being a poet and also a graduate student in the culturally and socially dynamic 1960s?

Kooser: As you know, John, I only went to graduate school in Nebraska for one year and performed so miserably as a scholar that my assistantship was revoked, and I had to find work. So I lived in the suit-and-tie business world through the sixties and on, and it was hard to be hip when you had to keep your shoes shined. I did finish an MA degree by taking night classes, but I was hip deep in my eight-to-five insurance job by then. I had friends who were hippies and knew a couple of young men who were in the Weather Underground. On weekends I tried hard to get with it, but on Mondays, there I was in my proper white dress shirt, dark suit, and dark tie, walking to work with my briefcase, working my way up in the business world. I remember when Allen Ginsberg and retinue came to Lincoln, not at the invitation of the university but by a young man, Steve Abbott, and there were parties that I attended. Ginsberg had no interest in me, a clean-shaven young man with short hair, but he did like my wife and spent quite a long time sitting on the floor knee to knee with her, talking about whatever they talked about. That was the trip during which that conglomeration of poets and rebels misplaced Peter Orlovsky's brother and didn't find him again for a few years, or so I recall it. Too much smoke in the air.

Ginsberg came back to Lincoln once, a number of years later, at the invitation of the local Buddhist group, and while he was signing books after his reading, he said to a man I knew, "Imagine it. I'm now worth $1 million."

Cusatis: In 1984, you and your second wife, Kathleen Rutledge, moved to the home and wooded acreage just outside of rural Garland, Nebraska, which you have shared ever since. Many poets have attached deep significance to settling into what became their ultimate home. "We had found our place," Robinson Jeffers commented after he and Una moved to the still unspoiled Carmel, California. And W. S. Merwin claimed he "never lived anywhere that was more true" than the sixteen acres on Maui where he and his wife, Paula, moved in 1983. In what ways has moving to your home of nearly forty years affected you personally and artistically?

Kooser: I love being able to pee in the yard, John. While our house was being rebuilt in the early nineties, we rented an apartment in Lincoln for six months, and I had to learn to control the urge to relieve myself outside. But, seriously, living out here in the country, where we have sixty-two acres of hills and trees and an abundance of wildlife has been wonderful for me. So much of my poetry has as its subjects things within a hundred yards of our door. My chapbook *At Home* is made up of poems like that. This morning, I wrote, and posted on Facebook, just such a poem:

"In the Stars"

There are times when a person likes to switch off
every lamp in the house and let all the dark
come in through the windows, and then to sit
for a good long while among the stars, which aren't
really all that far away at all, no farther apart
than we are from them, the huge blackness between
holding us all from falling, like the silvery drops

of overnight dew held in place by a spider's web
spread on the dark grass not far from your door.

Cusatis: We began by talking about how your idea of "what made a poem a poem" has developed. I'd like to ask you how your thoughts may have evolved regarding the *usefulness* of poetry. You told Mark Sanders in 1983, "I do believe that poetry has little practical value." More than four decades later, you spoke to Judith Harris about the "useful" service of a Garland artist who would paint "a favorite pony" on a neighbor's mailbox "or a picture of your farmstead . . . on the blade of your grandfather's old crosscut saw." Certainly, words like *useful, practical,* and *worthless* can be understood in a variety of ways. But, what about all the testimonials that you have lifted readers' spirits, heightened their attention, and altered their perception of the world? "In the Stars" received abundant and effusive positive response on Facebook within hours. How have your views on the usefulness of art, particularly poetry, changed?

Kooser: I do think a poem can to some extent change readers who come upon it, can be useful and helpful. But to do that, it has to be someplace where it can be found. The traditional literary journals in print editions may reach a few hundred paid subscribers, and some of those will undoubtedly read the poems. How many? Even in a magazine like the *New Yorker*, there's a good chance that the poems get passed over in favor of the cartoons.

As much as I love poems printed in ink on good paper, online publication seems to be the direction in which we're moving, and a poem on line is likely to have more readers than it would in one of the quarterlies. But there are other possible venues. I found while I was editing "American Life in Poetry" that I could reach tens of thousands of readers via newspapers and newsletters. Plus, we had a sizeable email distribution as well. When I turned it over to my successor, we had 4.3 million readers worldwide. The usefulness of those poems can be measured, it seems to me, by the wide circulation. That is, if the poems weren't found to be helpful or useful, those readers would have dropped aside.

Cusatis: A great many poems are written in response to national or worldly events, wars, natural catastrophes, the COVID pandemic, and so on. Do you think a poem can be of any help in those situations?

Kooser: I don't think poems are a good way of bringing about big social change, though we see lots of writers trying to do that. A poem about breast cancer, and there are many, can be of help to families who are dealing with that frightening disease, but no poem is going to cure cancer, nor is it likely to bring about big grants for research. If its ambitions are to do that, well, good luck, but. . . . But a fine poem about one person's breast-cancer experience and survival may find a grateful audience. Never, though, are we going to be able to stop a war with a poem.

Pablo Neruda, in his memoirs, tells a story about being a combatant in the Spanish Civil War. His company was bivouacked somewhere, waiting for the action to come to them, and while there, he and his men located an old printing press and some paper and printed up a small collection of Neruda's poems. Then, after a while, they were attacked by some of Franco's army, and they had to retreat, and in a hurry. Neruda followed his men as they ran from Franco's foot soldiers, and, here and there, he came upon one of his soldiers lying dead by the road, his backpack burst open, and those books of poems spilling out. That's a good example of how a poem can find great meaning to someone at war, but it can't solve a war.

Cusatis: In the same interview in 1983, Mark Sanders referred to your "success," to which you responded, "It could be said that I am a moderately successful businessman—I make a good salary at my job at the insurance company—but I am not a successful poet," prefacing this statement with the fact that you were "brought up by people who equated success with money." One would be hard pressed to dispute, four decades later, that you are a success by any measure. How do you think about success today?

Kooser: I think success may now come to me through the appreciation of someone who lets me know that what I've written has been meaningful. I get a lot of wonderful letters from readers whose lives I've brightened in my small way. These aren't professional literary people but part of a community of everyday people who have found in poetry, mine and that of others, something they love.

Cusatis: Moving to a related subject—fame—I'll return to Jeffers, who referred to fame as "the smoke that chokes the flame." In his poem "Let Them Alone," his description of a poet fits you when he says, "A poet is one who listens / To nature and his own heart." He goes on to caution that "prizes" and "ceremony" are "what withered Wordsworth and muffled Tennyson, and would have / killed Keats." Fame, he concludes, is what "makes / Hemingway play the fool and Faulkner forget his art." In his essay "Poetry, Gongorism, and 1000 Years," Jeffers further states that "Posthumous reputation could do you no harm at all, and is really the only kind worth considering." You've commented on this subject and wrote about it humorously in the poem "Success," which appeared in the *Kenyon Review* [see David Baker's interview], but while fame expanded your audience, it has not seemed to alter you or your art in any visible way. What are your observations and experiences about fame and the artist?

Kooser: As you know, I was a close friend of the late poet and novelist Jim Harrison. Jim was deservedly famous, and he developed a public persona to present to the world, which eventually caught him up, and as he aged, that persona became harder and harder to maintain and sustain. He was no longer physically capable of doing all the drinking, smoking, eating, and so on. No longer was he up to the image he had presented to the world. After his death, there were articles here and there in which people reminisced about having high times with Jim, and who they had been with was that persona. Another of Jim's friends and I were talking not long after his death and he said, "We loved Jim, but we didn't like The Jim Show." I don't want there ever to be a Ted Show, though I suppose even an interview for a book puts a mask over the Ted that I really am. I'd like to be appreciated and even loved, but I don't want to spend any more of my time listening to long, glowing introductions, my bowels growling, before getting up to read my poems. I did enough of that as poet laureate for two lives. I'm done with that public stuff and am happy to just slide my poems out under the door, hoping that someone passing by will like them.

Cusatis: In addition to your poetry, your prose has been highly praised. Naomi Shihab Nye called *Lights on a Ground of Darkness* "one of the most exquisite slim memoirs ever written on this earth," and Jim Harrison called, *Local Wonders* "the quietest magnificent book I've ever read." These, as well as your other nonfiction book, *The Wheeling Year*, are as poetically rendered as your verse. What for you distinguishes poetry from prose?

Kooser: The way I see it: in a finished poem, it shouldn't be possible to change a word for its synonym, to change a line ending, to change a period for a semicolon, to change anything about it without at least slightly diminishing the poem's effect on the reader. In prose you can make some of those changes, and a reader won't feel anything. To illustrate this, let's use Williams's "The Red Wheelbarrow," which is a poem that's been kicked around in one way or another for years but survives:

so much depends

upon

a red wheel
barrow

glazed with rain
water

beside the white
chickens

Let's make one little change:

so much depends upon

a red wheel
barrow

glazed with rain
water

beside the white
chickens

See the diminishment? By changing that one line break, we lose the tiny, momentary suspense that follows *depends*. Take any poem you feel to be a masterwork and try moving something. I think you'll see what I mean. There are, of course, finely written passages of prose that are also that precisely made; "poetic prose," we might call them.

Cusatis: How does the prose poem figure into this?

Kooser: The prose poem has the same perfection as the lined-out poem, but it sets aside one tool, that of the line ending.

Cusatis: How important is the line ending for you?

Kooser: As in the Williams example, line endings are useful tools like rhyme and meter. There's a difference in effect between

She ran to the edge of the precipice and leapt
into the void.

and

She ran to the edge of the precipice
and leapt into the void

In the first example there's an instant of dramatic suspense (between verb and adverb phrase) at the end of the line. And coupled with a driving iambic measure you can get something like this:

At thirty-five, he squeals to see the ball
Bounce in the air and roll away

Where the reversed foot, that trochee, "Bounce in," actually gives us a little bounce. Those lines are from Karl Shapiro's poem "The Mongolian Idiot," which today has probably been edged out of the standard anthologies because of its title.

Cusatis: You've credited these two poets, William Carlos Williams and your friend and teacher Karl Shapiro—both Pulitzer Prize winners—with having a significant early influence on you. What abiding influence would you say remains from these poets, even today?

Kooser: The influence of those two poets on my work has been quite different. What I learned from Karl was how a poet goes about his life. We were friends, and I was frequently at his side as he did this or that. I read and studied his poems of course, which are quite different from mine, though his ability to write about subjects not thought "poetic" continues to appeal to me. I may have learned more about poetry from watching Karl live than I did from his poems. I didn't know Williams of course, but I loved his poems for their clarity, economy, and humility.

Cusatis: As you mention, Williams's "The Red Wheelbarrow" has been "kicked around in one way or another for years." In an interview with the *Cream City Review* in 1999, you described this poem as "perfect in every way." I think it's natural for many readers, especially students, to be a little perplexed by the poem and also its unshakable place among the American canon. In addition to the precise placement of words and line breaks, what makes this a perfect poem for you?

Kooser: That poem completely captures a moment, to the exclusion of everything else out and around it, much in the way the great Tang masters, and later, the Japanese haiku poets, wrote their poems, with the Whole present in one of its parts. Here's a little homage I wrote a while back:

"With Li Bai"

The water followed Li Bai down the river,
sometimes running ahead, then waiting for him,
at other times falling behind to roll in an eddy
or paw at the roots of a tree. From time to time
the master would reach up, pick a willow leaf,
and bending, propped on his stick, slip the leaf
in the water's lips, then lick his fingers to taste
what the water had tasted. The water was happy
to be with Li Bai, his blanket and stone bottle,
as the two of them made their way downstream
through centuries, past crude dooryard gates
and fine temples, and at times, when the water
had fallen behind it would, late in the evening,
come running up with a moon for Li Bai.

Cusatis: What a beautiful tribute to Li Bai [701–62 AD]. I've never seen this poem. Is it previously unpublished, or is it in a chapbook or journal?

Kooser: Unpublished, and it's never been out on trial. But I like it.

Cusatis: I do, too. Thanks for sharing it. How about metaphor? The playwright Edward Albee visited the University of South Carolina in 2005, and the moment I remember best from his lecture is his saying that our opposable thumbs are not what most definitively distinguish us from the other animals: it's our ability to create metaphor. Your originality and agility with metaphors is a hallmark of your poetry and your prose. Can you comment on your attraction to metaphor?

Kooser: Do you remember Emerson's "Over-soul" idea? In my interpretation, he envisioned what I see as a great stellar disk of everlasting power and unity and beauty, everything in it related, even when far separated. His Oversoul is an all-encompassing unity.

If we think of the result of the Big Bang, that can help us understand Emerson. If everything in the universe originated from one speck of dust, then everything must share common features, common makeup, common spirits. Metaphor displays those relationships by isolating two elements and showing us, in an instant, how they have something in common. [Thomas] Tranströmer, in "The Couple," my favorite of his poems, says that the fading glow as a light bulb goes out is like a tablet dissolving in a glass of darkness. Wow! That metaphor shows us, in a flash, the commonality of two very dissimilar things. I'm thrilled to come upon that sort of magical writing and just as thrilled, if not more so, to have a metaphor appear before me while *I'm* writing. A big part of my love of writing is those surprise appearances of associations, surprises I can't plan or predict or expect but that do happen on a lucky day.

When I was teaching, I would occasionally have a student point to his or her manuscript and say something like, "Do you think I need to put some kind of metaphor there?" Well, we need to keep in mind that you can't select a metaphor off the shelf or from a revolving display. You don't choose them; they choose you. They come to you on their own if you happen to be receptive to them, as I am, and as are many other poets. I don't think you can teach a person to come up with effective metaphors, but you can show them how best to fit them into a poem, to fine-tune them.

There are fine poets, too, who never or rarely use metaphor. It's possible to write a strong, moving poem without them, but I happen to much prefer poems with metaphors, the bigger the better, and by that, I mean, the farther apart are the two halves, the greater the effect on me. And that effect, even in a poem of grief or loss, is for me, well, delight.

Cusatis: Emerson wrote in his essay "The Poet" that "all poetry was written before time was," and it is the job of "the finely organized" poet with "a delicate ear" to catch the "primal warblings" and "attempt to write them down." The poet who tries to "substitute something" of his own threatens to "miswrite the poem." He is describing what you called at the outset, the "discovery" that a poem documents. To what degree is the documenting of this discovery an organic process rather than a mechanical one for you?

Kooser: The only "primal warblings" I've ever heard were coming from a thirty-eight Chevy coup in the back row at the Starlite Drive-In in Ames, Iowa, in the midfifties. As to the process, for me, the discoveries are almost always from a time remembered and are thus "organic" if I'm understanding this correctly. Something that I witnessed in nature five minutes before is already in memory, already being altered and shaped. In Emerson's sense, I am always miswriting the poem.

Cusatis: While we're speaking of Emerson, the notion of the oversoul that you mention is at the heart of his pantheism. He writes in his essay "Nature": "What is a farm but a mute gospel? The chaff and the wheat, weeds and plants, blight, rain, insects, sun—it is a sacred emblem from the first furrow of spring to the last stack which the snow overtakes in the fields." You've spoken in these interviews of your belief in an order underlying creation, and you expressed to Daniel Simon that writing poetry feels like prayer to you. It seems as if you would relate to this quote from Emerson. Is a farm a mute gospel? If so, how and what is it tacitly preaching to you throughout the year?

Kooser: Was Emerson hard of hearing? There's nothing "mute" about farms. There are noises wherever you stand. But as to a gospel, if he means that there is something sacred about the natural world, I'd agree about that. I sense a great unity of which I am a small part.

Cusatis: Emerson seems to be describing you—probably when you *weren't* enjoying your back row seat at the Starlite Drive-In—when he refers to "the finely organized poet." Thoreau "went to the woods to live deliberately," and so, it seems, did you. I can't imagine you are ever bored. Whether you are fixing something, building or planting, writing or painting, there is an order that underlies your own acts of creation. To what do you attribute your gift of order, energy, and discipline?

Kooser: My mother, my model in shaping so much of my life, was as organized a person as I've ever known. For example, she wrote down in five-and-dime spiral-bound school notebooks every penny she spent from the day of her marriage in 1937 to the day of her death in 1998. Every penny, in cursive handwriting that meandered over the page in her last couple of years.

Cusatis: Revisiting Emerson led me to reach for my old Willa Cather novels. There must be something transcendent about the prairie: her novels are deeply Emersonian. Like you, both these writers relished the early morning hours. Emerson distinguished between *vespertina cognitio* and *matutina cognitio*, evening and morning knowledge. He called the former "the knowledge of man" and the latter "the knowledge of God." Cather writes in *The Professor's House*, "Every morning, when the sun's rays first hit the mesa top, while the rest of the world was in shadow, I wakened with the feeling that I had found everything, instead of having lost everything." How important has arising early been to the quality and quantity of your poetic output over the decades? And to what degree did giving up alcohol in the mideighties help?

Kooser: I probably have said this in print somewhere else, but it's worth repeating: I attended a talk given by the fine children's writer Kate DiCamillo, and after her remarks, someone in the audience asked why she got up and wrote at such an early hour. She said that she wanted to get her writing done before the critic inside her woke up. I think that's brilliant, don't you? I was, of course, sort of forced into writing at those early hours because for thirty-five years I had a job I had to report to at eight or so, and if I wanted to write, I had to do it before getting ready for work. Lots of writers get their work done in the evenings and on into the night, but my mind is too cluttered by the end of the day.

As to alcohol, I used to say that I quit drinking because it was like holding down a second, part-time job. It took up an enormous amount of time. If you're a drinker, everything you do is organized around the next drink. You're hung over in the morning, spend the day feeling half alive; you go to the bar after work, are late for dinner, drink through the evening, and go to bed loaded. Where can you fit writing a poem into that?

Cusatis: You have not commented much in these interviews on your reading of Cather. I suspect you read her early on. Do any of the novels still resonate?

Kooser: I'm glad you asked. The only really memorable class I took as a graduate student was a seminar in Willa Cather, led by the late Bernice Slote, a Cather scholar, and her long-time companion, the late Virginia Faulkner, then an editor at University of Nebraska Press, who offered her own expertise about Cather. At that time, those two held the reins of all Cather scholarship and had access to all sorts of memorabilia. I remember them bringing one of Cather's childhood scrapbooks to class, and so on. We read ALL of Cather, all the stories, all the novels.

When I was poet laureate, the National Endowment had a project in which they were asking for the opinions of writers about Cather's influence, and I was asked, too. I hadn't read Cather for years but took my copy of *My Ántonia* on a plane on my way to do something somewhere. I was seated between two overlarge men, reading my book in their heat, and when I got to the end, I began weeping. They looked at me as if I were a leper. That novel, with its theme, always so attractive to me, of the missed opportunity, is so wonderfully written. That's the theme, of course, of many works, including the films, *The Remains of the Day* and *A Month in the Country*. I'm a sucker for sad endings like those.

Cusatis: Is there a fable, legend, biblical or mythological story that is particularly meaningful to you that serves as a lens through which to view the world or some aspect of it?

Kooser: The children's book *Lentil* by Robert McCloskey was very important to me. Given to me when I was quite young, it's the story of an awkward kid who finds himself and his talent for playing the harmonica. A good story for all children who feel as if they don't fit in. Lentil winds up riding in a parade, and I wound up riding around in Governor Bob Kerrey's official car, he and I having a fine time driving the country roads with the siren turned on.

Cusatis: You said in your 2023 interview with Judith Harris that you spent a decade attending the Unitarian church, and currently you and your wife attend Episcopal services, but you are "not a traditional believer." You've frequently mentioned an "order" you feel exists in the universe. Can you comment a little more on that?

Kooser: If the Big Bang was the origin of the universe, or *our* universe, then everything in the universe has to be related. I've had the idea for a number of years that metaphors, or what happens in the space between tenor and vehicle, are glimpses into a grand universal order. Coincidences, too. I keep records of coincidences, big and small, and the more you become aware of them, the more seem to be happening. Here is the greatest coincidence of my life:

On December 30, 1979, Kathy and I were living in Lincoln and having an early New Year's Eve party, and the house was full of people. I was still drinking in those days. At about nine in the evening, I answered the phone, and it was Mother, calling from Cedar Rapids, Iowa, where they were living in those years. She said that Dad had collapsed in the bathroom, and they'd taken him by ambulance to the hospital, and that it looked bad. She felt I ought to come over right away.

I waited till morning, though, because I'd been drinking and didn't want to risk driving. By morning, it had started to snow, one of those Great Plains snowstorms with the snow blowing sidewise out of the north. I set out in my car, hung over and feeling terribly sad about Dad and fighting bad roads all the way.

When I got to Des Moines, I decided to turn on the car radio to WOI in Ames, my hometown. WOI, at Iowa State College, was one of the country's first public radio stations, and my dad's brother, Uncle Tubby, had had a show for a time. Sometimes when I was on one of the hills near Lincoln, I could pull it in, but not often, and I loved that station, for which I always felt a lot of nostalgia.

A man named Doug Brown had a book show, on which he read from books he liked, and that show was on when I tuned in. He was that day reading Christmas and holiday poems, and within five minutes of my tuning in, he read a poem of mine, set at Christmas, about my father. Dad was a hypochondriac, and the poem was one that I had never shown him because it has an image about him carrying his heart "in its cage of ribs like an injured bird," ["Christmas Eve" which originally appeared in *Not Coming to Be Barked At* (1976) and, later, *Sure Signs* (1980)] and I thought he'd think I knew something about the condition of his heart that he didn't.

I was overcome with sadness and pulled off the highway and sat on the shoulder while snow piled up on the hood and windshield. After a while, I got myself together and continued on to Cedar Rapids. I went straight to the hospital, where I learned that Dad had died while I was on the road.

Sometime later, I wrote a letter to Doug Brown inquiring about that moment, asking why and where he'd found that poem. He wrote back saying that it was one he'd found that morning in a file of poems he'd saved.

Cusatis: Wow, what a heart-breaking, yet magical, story. Surely synchronicity. While we're speaking of your father, the opening poem of *Winter Morning Walks* closes with his reassuring words, as he "lovingly" smooths the wrinkles from a literal and metaphorical roll of "softly glowing fabric," smiling: "You can make something special with this?" Most recently, in "By Heart" from your latest book, *Raft*, you fondly recall his recitations of a short bit from Longfellow's "The Children's Hour." How did your father affect your view of the world and your artistic connection to it?

Kooser: Dad was a terrifically entertaining storyteller, a model of that. I remember one of his friends saying that they'd rather hear Dad describe someone than to see that person themselves. I remember his once remarking that a "large" woman we knew moved "like a piano on casters."

Cusatis: Thoreau recalls in *Walden*, "I once had a sparrow alight upon my shoulder for a moment, while I was hoeing in a village garden, and I felt that I was more distinguished by that circumstance than I should have been by any epaulet I could have worn." Reverence for the other animals characterizes so much of *your* work. *Raft*, for example, includes such poems as "A Fox," "Magpie," "Rabbit," "Vulture," and "Anniversary," which pays homage to "a sleek, handsomely patterned" bullsnake, "about the size of a pencil," crushed on your driveway. Most would find a dead snake a small matter, and many would call animal control if they spotted a red fox trespassing in a cemetery. You've mentioned a connection among all things. Can you comment on your affinity for the nonhuman world?

Kooser: Harkening back to my mention of Mother, she taught my sister and me to respect the lives of all living creatures, including we humans. I remember once, as a young man, making a joke about somebody wearing "polyester," and Mother saying, "Ted, she's wearing polyester because that's what she can afford." I don't know that she knew that old saw, "Whomever you meet may be fighting a great battle," but she would have agreed.

Cusatis: You've mentioned your early fixation with poetic form, which you outgrew, but in addition to the precise imagery in your poems, the sounds of the words and the meter contribute seamlessly to their aesthetic allure. Theodore Roethke called free verse "a denial in terms," suggesting its existence as verse reigns it in, in ways that paragraphs cannot confine or *re*fine prose. You've talked a little about the difference between poetry and prose, but can you comment on your careful handling of sound devices— assonance, consonance, alliteration, internal rhyme—as well as metrical variation in your poetry?

Kooser: I am fortunate to have a "good ear," and the effects that you mention come to me quite naturally. I don't notice that I've internally rhymed or used alliteration, etcetera, until I later stand apart from a poem and look at it coolly. Some of my revision is in taking out more of that than I think the poem needs. Though I don't often write in fixed forms, I do count syllables and accents and use those counts loosely. Just lately, I've written a few poems in roughly a fourteen-syllable line, and they felt quite natural and conversational.

Cusatis: In addition to *The Poetry Home Repair Manual*, you've written literary critical essays espousing your views on the art, such as "Lying for the Sake of Making Poems" and "Metaphor and Faith," among others. Are there any critical essays from other poets that you have learned from or consider valuable to a student learning to better read or write poems?

Kooser: I used to recommend to my students Dick Hugo's books on writing and [William] Stafford's several books in the Michigan series [Poets on Poetry, University of Michigan Press, founded by the poet Donald Hall in 1978]. Actually, all the Michigan books could be helpful.

Cusatis: Many of your books draw their title from a central poem in the collection; however, a few do not. For example, your second major book, *A Local Habitation & a Name*, borrows its title from Theseus's opening mono-logue in the final act of *A Midsummer Night's Dream*. What has Shakespeare meant to you? And while we are on the subject of legendary English bards, what about Chaucer?

Kooser: I'm not a close student of Shakespeare, John, I'm embarrassed to say. The language of his plays and poems was always too much work for me. I know four people, all poets, who meet to read Shakespeare aloud, each taking various parts, and I envy all the fun they have, but I'd much rather hear about it than do it. Chaucer I'm a little more comfortable with because *The Canterbury Tales* breaks down into clearly defined, manageable units. If you were to ask me about Dante or Milton, or Spenser, or Keats, or any of the great writers in English, you'd find that I'm really quite poorly read. The poems I most enjoy reading are those of *my* period, those who were writing when I was a boy and young man and who are writing today, in a comfortable, familiar idiom: Randall Jarrell, Karl Shapiro, May Swenson, Elizabeth Bishop, and so on. I'd much rather read a contemporary "nature poet" like David Wagoner than anything Wordsworth wrote. This shouldn't be interpreted as if I'm disdainful of the masters but rather about what I most prefer to read. I can see my writing as being one side of a conversation with other poets. I start my daily writing by reading in, say, a contemporary anthology, a poem or two, and then I am spurred to write as if in answer. Something in a Maxine Kumin poem, say, sparks an answering poem in me. This fruitful "conversation" is among my close contemporaries. I can't converse with Blake or Keats or Elizabeth Barrett Browning because we don't speak the same language. There's nothing in Shakespeare that initiates that sort of answer from me.

Cusatis: That makes sense, Ted, especially since you approach the poems as a fellow poet. I like the idea of a conversation between you and the modern poets you've been reading for so long. Can you think of one of your poems that bears the influence of another contemporary poet?

Kooser: Yes, I can see Robert Bly's general influence in my little poem "A Winter Morning":

A farmhouse window far back from the highway
speaks to the darkness in a small, sure voice.
Against this stillness, only a kettle's whisper,
and against the starry cold, one small blue ring of flame.

Cusatis: The Ted Kooser Contemporary Poetry series, published by the University of Nebraska Press, which is about to print its eighth volume, is a wonderful collection of books featuring poets who were surely less widely read before these editions of their selected poems appeared. In a very big way, it carries on the spirit of your weekly poetry column. Can you comment on the genesis of this series and the success it has enjoyed?

Kooser: I started the series solely because I wanted to do a collection of Jared Carter's poems, having great admiration for Jeb and his work, and the press did a beautiful job, so I did another and another. But it was the Carter book, *Darkened Rooms of Summer*, that got it started. Because of my age and the fact that I've done these books a couple of years apart, I may be at the end of the run with the next book, by Bob McEwen, a terrific narrative poet whom few readers know of. As to my newspaper column, I just saw a Facebook post in which Sam Gwynn [publishes as R. S. Gwynn] named Louis Untermeyer, Garrison Keillor, and me as "popularizers" of poetry. I'm happy to accept that distinction.

Cusatis: Congratulations! Sam's a first-rate critic and poet. Speaking of which, when Garrison Keillor published his anthology *Good Poems* in 2002, it caused a literary uproar in the pages of *Poetry* magazine, with a dual review in which Dana Gioia praised the collection, while August Kleinzahler ridiculed it for making "no demands on its reader" and proving that "American poetry is now an international joke." Keillor's book did well, as did its sequels, the second of which included your poem "A Spiral Notebook." Unquestionably, your project as poet laureate, "American Life in Poetry" (Americanlifeinpoetry.org), started in 2005, immeasurably impacted the popularity of poetry in America. Yet, when you initially launched what eventually reached approximately 4 million readers, you had a few naysayers who questioned placing poetry in newspapers, as if this were demeaning its status as an elite artform. How do you feel about elitism and pretentiousness in regard to poetry, and as United States poet laureate, did you find yourself having to defend the notion that the enjoyment of poetry is for everyone?

Kooser: I don't recall ever being directly challenged, face to face, about my column or my work as poet laureate, and if the literary professionals were snapping at my heels, I didn't notice. It's easy to ignore criticism. Must painting make demands on its viewers? Must music make demands on its listeners? I've mentioned this elsewhere, but it's worth repeating: I attended a panel discussion at the Dodge Poetry Festival at which a prominent poet said that it was the obligation of the reader to educate himself or herself to a level at which they could understand "our" poetry. Fat chance of that! That sort of arrogance and exclusivity (and stupidity) just discourages readers. Fortunately, there are poems for everyone, both easy and difficult. Readers who want difficult, challenging poems know where they can find them. I like showing the many *other* readers that there are poems they can enjoy without taking a three-hundred-level course in Paul Celan's importance. My late friend Jim Harrison used to say that you can't democratize the arts, yet his own writing had tens of thousands of "popular" readers. I have, and regularly read, all three of Garrison Keillor's anthologies, and those Billy Collins has done, and they haven't poisoned me. Another fine popular anthology, by the way, is *The Rattle Bag*, which Ted Hughes and Seamus Heaney edited.

Cusatis: In addition to student readers, student writers often become disenchanted. Flannery O'Connor was asked whether she thought beginning writers were often discouraged by their creative-writing courses and workshops, to which she replied, "Not enough of them." As someone who has taught poetry writing at the University of Nebraska for many years, what do you think about that?

Kooser: Pretty witty, but wrong. Teaching should be about encourage-ment, not discouragement. When I was just starting out, I wrote lots of really awful poems and was so lucky that no one discouraged me, though anyone in his right mind would have recognized I didn't show much prom-ise. I've said this before, but what could be wrong with a world full of people writing poems? No one would be harmed.

Cusatis: Finally, Ted, it's now 2024, and you have been at this a long time. Let's close with this question: What is the most important lesson you've learned in your six and a half decades as a writer?

Kooser: I once tried writing a novel, a satiric novel about the insurance company where I worked for many years and in which I made fun of a lot of people with whose foibles I was more than familiar. At that time, I went to lunch each Thursday with a small group of university faculty, with a lawyer and a couple of others thrown in. One of the faculty members, a distin-guished professor of English, whom I admired, happened to be there one day when I had my manuscript in tow, and I asked him if he could read over one brief section I thought was particularly funny. He did that for me, and chuckled, then turned to me and said, "Ted, don't be too hard on those people. Nearly everyone is doing as best they can."

I was then in my forties, and I thought, "Why has no one ever before told me that?" It seemed so kind, so tolerant and wise. I eventually destroyed my funny novel, and I've tried to live by his words ever since. Tolstoy said somewhere: "Nothing can make our life, or the lives of other people, more beautiful than perpetual *kindness*." I'll never achieve perpetual kindness but may be a better man by the effort.

Index

Abbott, Steve, 213

Abrams, M. H., xiv–xv; *The Mirror and the Lamp*, xv

After Confession, 199

Albee, Edward, 219

American Library Association, 147

"American Life in Poetry," xx, 81, 105, 119, 133, 139, 146, 174, 191, 192, 205, 207, 208, 214, 226, 227

American Poetry Review, 5, 31

Ames, IA, xvi, xix, 52, 75, 77, 141, 170, 211–12, 220, 223

Anderson, Sherwood, 172

Anderson Center at Tower View, 184

Anyone for Tennyson? (television program), 106

Aristotle, 177; *Poetics*, 177

Ashcan School (painters), 122, 171

Atlantic, The, 183

Auden, W. H., 26

Ault, George, 43; *August Night at Russell's Corners*, 43

Bacon, Francis, 55

Baker, David, xx, 215

Balzac, Honoré de, 52, 100

Bankers Like Nebraska, xvi, 65

Banville, John, 192; *Snow*, 192

Barber, David, 183

Barillas, William, xv, xvii; *The Midwestern Pastoral*, xv

Barnes & Noble (Discover Great New Writers program), 62

Baxter, Charles, 65, 87

Beat movement, 141

Beecham, Thomas, 139

Bellow, Saul, 7

Bennett Martin Public Library (Lincoln, NE), 63

Berger, John, 122–23, 165

Berryman, John, 37, 78

Big Bang Theory, 177–78, 219, 223

Billington, James H., 140

Bishop, Elizabeth, 21, 166, 196–97, 225–26

Blake, William, 82, 226

Bly, Robert, 20–21, 31, 44, 101, 170, 177, 196–97, 226; *Silence in the Snowy Fields*, 170

Bohemian Alps, 89, 191, 209

Book of Ecclesiastes, xx, 51

Book of Kings, 179

Book of Psalms, 170

Borcherding, Ella (cousin), 184

Borland, Hal, 61; *Sundial of the Seasons*, 61

Bracker, Jon, 105

Bradford, William, 131

Brando, Marlon, 212

Brautigan, Richard, 162

British poet laureate, 128

Brooklyn Museum, 171

Brooks, Gwendolyn, 8

Brown, Doug, 223–24

Browning, Elizabeth Barrett, 226
Browning, Robert, 198
Brummels, J. V., xvi; *On Common Ground*, xvi, xvii, xxi, 15, 25
Burke, Edmund, 130
Burke, James Lee, 161–62
Butler, Dan, 185

Candlewick Press, 181, 201, 205
Capote, Truman, 13
Carnegie Mellon University Press, 40, 167
Carter, Jared, 226; *Darkened Rooms of Summer*, 226
Carter, John, 143
Casari, Laura, 61
Cather, Willa, 27, 58, 140, 221, 222; *My Ántonia*, 222; *The Professor's House*, 221
Cavalieri, Grace, xiv
Cedar Rapids, IA, 76, 223–24
Celan, Paul, 227
Chaplin, Charlie, 34, 82
Chappell, Fred, 37; *A Way of Happening*, 37
Chase, Richard, 192; *Jack Tales*, 192
Chaucer, Geoffrey, 225; *The Canterbury Tales*, 225
Cheney, Dick, 127
Ciardi, John, 26
Cicotello, David, xiv
City Lights Booksellers and Publishers, 35
Coleridge, Samuel Taylor, 173
Collins, Billy, 117, 227
Copper Canyon Press, 62, 103, 112, 167–68, 191–92
Costanzo, Jerry, 11, 167
COVID-19 pandemic, 187, 189, 191–92, 214
Coward, Noel, 52
Crazy Horse, 147
Cream City Review, 33, 218
cowboy poetry, 106, 128–29

Crosby, Bing, 212
Cy's Cafe (Dwight, NE), 205

Dante, xix, 225; *Inferno*, xix
Dawes, Kwame, 192, 205
Dawes, Lorna, 205
Dean, James, 196, 212
Death of Marat, The (painting), 55
de la Mare, Walter, 142; "The Listeners," 142
Des Moines, IA, 75–76, 223
DiCamillo, Kate, 190, 205, 221
Dickinson, Emily, 44
Dig, 196
Dinge Dichter ("thing poet"), 57
Directory of American Poets and Fiction Writers, A, 119
Dodge Poetry Festival, 185, 227
duende (spirit, passion, aura), 114–15
Dull Knife, 147
Dumas, Alexandre, 100
Dunn, Harvey, 179; *I Am the Resurrection and the Life*, 179

Earl Carter Lumber, 45
ecocriticism, 124, 171
Eisenhower, Mamie, 76
Eisenhower era, 141
Eliot, T. S., xvii, 21, 121, 145, 172, 180–81; *The Waste Land*, xvii
Elkader, IA, 185
Emerson, Ralph Waldo, xv, 48, 219, 220–21; "Nature," 220–21; "The Over-Soul," 219; "The Poet," xv, 220
Episcopal church, 166, 168, 223

Fairchild, B. H., 185, 211; "Beauty," 211; reaction to "Pearl," 185
Faulkner, Virginia, 222
Faulkner, William, 25, 52, 215
Fine, Warren, 38

Fox, John, Jr., 52, 100
Franco, Francisco, 215
Frost, Robert, 21, 23, 33, 46, 48, 86, 100, 116, 165, 169–70, 176–77, 200; "Design," 170; "The Figure a Poem Makes," 23, 46; "To Earthward," 177; "The Silken Tent," 33, 48, 165, 176–77, 200
Furst, Alan, 162

García Lorca, Federico, 17, 114
Garlits, Don, 195
Gerber, Dan, 178
Ghiselin, Brewster, 29, 197
Gifford, Prosser, 110
Ginsberg, Allen, 213; *Howl*, 35
Gioia, Dana, xvi–xvii, 31, 121, 140, 161, 202, 227; *Can Poetry Matter?*, xvi–xvii, 140, 202; "Explaining Ted Kooser" ("The Anonymity of the Regional Poet"), xvi–xvii, 202
Glück, Louise, 8, 30, 31
Goethe, Johann Wolfgang von, 186n3
Goldberg, Rube, 46
Golden Bough, The, xvii, 146
Gombrich, Ernst H., 169
Goya, Francisco de, 55
Grammy Awards, 178
Gray, Thomas, 16–17; "Elegy Written in a Country Churchyard," 16–17
Great River Review, 44–45, 91
Gregg, Linda, 84
Gregory, Hilda, 11
Griffith, E. V., 11
Grossman, Allan, 129; "Two Waters," 129
Guthrie, Woody, 118, 127
Guttenberg, IA, 44–45, 173, 175–76, 184–85, 211
Gwynn, R. S., 226

Hall, Donald, 21, 61, 170, 197, 225; *Kicking the Leaves*, 21; *String Too Short to Be Saved*, 61

Harkin, Tom, 196
Harnack, Adolph, 102; *Outlines of the History of Dogma*, 102
Harper's Magazine, 57
Harris, Judith, xiv, 214, 223
Harrison, Jim, xviii, xix, 40, 41, 62, 65, 69, 95–96, 103, 143, 145, 147, 149, 161, 162, 164, 167, 175, 182, 200, 216, 227; *Dalva*, 143; *The Summer He Didn't Die*, 149
Harte, Bret, 5–6
Hass, Robert, 174; "Poet's Choice" (newspaper column), 174
Hassler, Jon, 193
Hatcher, Arnold, 26
Hayden, Robert, 116; "Those Winter Sundays," 116
Heaney, Seamus, 207, 227
Hedin, Robert, 184
Hemingway, Ernest, 215
Henri, Robert, 171
Hillard, Steve, 62
hip-hop, 128
Homer, Winslow, 111
Hope, Bob, 212
Hopper, Edward, 20, 111
Hubbell, Sue, 61
Hudson Review, xvi, 6, 101, 150, 154
Hughes, Ted, 227
Hugo, Richard, 8, 34, 225
Huntsville, TX, 132, 149

Ibsen, Henrik, 100
International Directory of Little Magazines and Small Presses, The, 168
Iowa State College of Agriculture and Mechanical Arts (now Iowa State University), xvi, 52, 57, 141, 170, 195, 196, 210–11, 223

Jacobsen, Rolf, 101
Jacobshagen, Keith, 91–92, 97
James, Clive, 192
Jarrell, Randall, 8, 21, 102, 166, 225–26
Jeffers, Robinson, xiii, 21, 213, 215; "Consciousness," xiii; "Let Them Alone," 215; "Poetry, Gongorism, and 1000 Years," 215
Jeffers, Una, 213
Jerome, Judson, 24
Johnson, Samuel, 40
Jones, Richard, xx, 204
Joslyn Art Museum (Omaha, NE), 43
Joyce, James, 169; "The Dead," 169
Jumper, Will, xvi, 195, 196
Jung, Carl, xiii–xiv; *Memories, Dreams, Reflections*, xiii–xiv

Kane, Paul, 129
Kansas Quarterly, 22
Kardashian family, 200
Kearney, NE, 179, 185n2
Keats, John, 215, 225–26
Kees, Weldon, 27
Keillor, Garrison, 226–27; *Good Poems*, 227
Kenyon Review, 125, 136, 139, 215–16
Kerouac, Jack, 212; *On the Road*, 212
Ketner, Carla, xxii; *Ted Kooser: More Than a Local Wonder*, xxii
Kierkegaard, Søren, 102; *Fear and Trembling*, 102
Kinnell, Galway, 121, 197
Kinzie, Mary, 31
Kleinzahler, August, 227
Kloefkorn, William, xvi, 25–26, 27, 28, 58, 59, 105; *Alvin Turner as Farmer*, 105; *Uncertain the Final Run to Winter*, 105
Kooser, Grace (paternal grandmother), 90, 170, 176
Kooser, Herold Lang (Uncle Tubby), 223

Kooser, Jeffrey (son), 3, 170
Kooser, Judith (sister), 90, 224
Kooser, Ted: adolescent rebellion, 37, 78, 102, 141, 195, 211–21; advice to beginning writers, 22–23, 35, 45, 62, 108, 171, 190, 194–95, 208; affinity for all living things, 71, 85, 94, 113, 164, 199–200, 213, 224; aims as a poet, 5, 14, 15–16, 19, 33–34; alcohol use, 114, 170, 221–22, 223; arranging a book, 103, 117, 143, 181, 187, 204, 208; art as affirmation, 30, 61, 86, 162, 193, 200, 202, 208; art studio in Dwight, NE, 193, 205, 208; autobiographical poetry, 18–19, 30, 115, 198–99; aversion to money as a motive for writing, 7, 12–13, 23–24, 87; aversion to poems of self-absorption or self-pity, 5, 30, 111; aversion to political poems, 8, 183; aversion to pretentious poetry, 198, 227; aversion to writing occasional poems, 127; balancing clarity with poetic substance, 105, 122, 131–32, 136–37, 162, 183; beginnings and development as a writer, 57, 78–79, 102, 160, 198, 211, 228; belief that everyone should try writing poems, 63–64, 104, 203, 228; benefits of working outside the academy, 4–5, 29, 36–37, 133; bringing one's own experience to a poem, 129–30; cancer diagnosis, treatment, and recovery, xvii, 33, 39, 40, 41, 42, 51, 56, 65, 69, 71–72, 73, 76, 89, 95, 107, 111, 113–14, 116, 134, 141, 144, 148–49, 178, 193, 205, 208; childhood, xix, 97, 141, 156, 164, 175, 184, 195, 211; children's books, xiv, xx, xxii, 160, 175, 201, 204, 222; chronicler of the world's wonders, xv–xvi, 51, 54, 86, 164; clarity in

poetry, xvii, 5, 19, 36–37, 38, 42, 65, 81, 101, 121–22, 130–31, 133, 137, 140, 146, 155, 162, 164, 168, 171, 174, 218; CLiPPa Award winner, xx, 204; coincidences, 223–24; concision in poetry, xvi, 33, 35, 38, 42, 113, 146, 154, 161, 174, 202; concrete visual imagery and subjects, 20, 28, 30, 35, 42, 54, 57, 87–88, 103, 111–12, 131–32, 141–42, 154–55, 188, 189, 199, 201; consciousness, xiii, 49; considering the reader, 5, 19, 138, 146, 162, 199; counterculture, 212–13; creative writing programs, 38, 104, 121; critical reception, xvi–xvii, xviii, xx, 171, 216; culture of Nebraska, the Great Plains, and the Midwest, 121, 144–46, 161; definition of poetry and poem, 210; difficult and obscure poetry, 14, 17, 34, 106, 121–22, 128, 130, 131, 155, 172, 227; dismissal of Midwestern writers, 6, 7, 109, 144; dreams, 91; early riser, xvi, xviii, xxi, 39, 41, 49, 60, 66, 69, 70, 85, 95, 104, 107, 114, 134, 156, 163–64, 176, 178, 189–90, 193, 197–98, 205, 221–22; elitism in literature, 63, 128, 227; emotional power of his work, 82, 197; enduring poems, 115, 142; failed poems, 10–11, 27, 30, 42, 56, 107, 138, 144, 195, 197; fame and celebrity, 139, 215–16; fearing vs. enjoying poetry, 133, 174; female poets, 8; fiction preferences, 162; garage sales, yard sales, and thrift shops, 89, 160–61; generosity to other writers, 105; giving away his paintings, 112, 199; goodness in humanity, 132–33, 148–49; government leadership, 133, 187; government support of artists,

29–30, 106; graduate student, xvi, 3–5, 38, 57–58, 67, 104, 141, 166, 172, 195, 222; habitual reading and writing, 45, 62–63, 108, 123–24, 135, 160, 171, 190, 194; haiku, 41, 71, 143, 218; hopeful tone in his poems, 161, 202; hotrods and drag racing, 109, 141, 195–96; human connection in his work, xix, 86, 158, 159, 183; impression of effortlessness in poetry, 33–34; indifference to literary theory, 122, 129, 172; influence of insurance career and colleagues on his writing, 4–5, 29, 65–67, 68, 103–4, 133, 157, 160, 162, 228; influential poets, 20–21, 35, 57, 86, 100–101, 103, 116, 141, 162, 195, 197, 218; insurance industry career and retirement, xvi, xviii, xx, 3, 4–5, 29, 58, 60, 63, 65–68, 73, 85, 103–4, 120, 133–34, 157, 159–60, 163–64, 166, 212–13, 221, 228; judging poetry contests, 123; keeping a journal or notebook, 17, 44, 47, 76, 91, 135, 163, 188, 189–90, 193; kindness and tolerance, 132, 212, 228; knowing a poem is finished, 155; line breaks, 216–18; literary boosterism, 27–28, 59; literary community, 29, 36–37, 133, 160, 215; literary reputation, xvi–xvii, 27; local surroundings as subject matter, xvii, xviii–xix, xx, xxi, 15, 28, 35, 43, 50, 59, 74, 100, 114, 141, 146, 156, 157, 161, 163, 179, 213; loneliness in his work, 20, 161; loss in his work, 83, 172–74, 180, 181, 201; magical effect of poems, 84, 139, 203, 210, 219–20; mailing paintings and/or poems on postcards, 40, 41, 42, 69–70, 95, 143–44, 181, 205, 206; making sacrifices to find writing time, 38–39; metaphors and other figurative language, xiv, xv, xvii, xix, 19, 22, 29, 33, 47–48, 50, 51, 52, 91, 103, 107, 116–17, 123, 126, 135–37, 138–39, 140, 142, 144, 154–55, 162, 164, 165–66, 172, 177, 180, 188–89, 200–201, 206, 219–20, 223, 224; mortality, xiii, 17, 49, 61, 62, 65–67, 68–69, 71, 84, 106, 114, 116, 157, 169, 174, 180, 188–89, 209; motivation to be a poet, 37, 78–79, 102, 141, 159, 196, 197, 211; moving to and living in Lincoln, NE, xvi, 3–4, 57, 67, 141, 212–13, 223; moving to and remaining in Garland, NE, xvii, xxi, 74, 145–46, 205–6, 213, 214; narrative poems, 91–92, 101; order and unity in creation, xix, 48, 71, 101, 114, 132, 166, 177–78, 182, 189, 219, 221, 223, 224; organic development of poems, 15–16, 136, 177, 197, 201, 220; originality of his work, xvii, xviii, 158–59; painters and paintings, 55, 97, 122, 169, 170, 227; painting and drawing, xvi, 3, 20, 39, 45, 50, 74, 78, 103, 108, 111, 122, 130, 134, 142, 159, 163, 169, 179, 188, 199, 205, 211, 221; paying attention, xiv, xxi, 35, 43–44, 84–85, 94–95, 113–14, 122, 138, 158, 171, 178, 208; perfect poems, 17, 34, 84, 154, 161, 217, 218–19; personal favorites among his poems, 161, 173, 180, 192; perspective-changing tendency of his work, xxii, 164; pleasure derived from reading poems, 21, 48, 130, 133, 174, 227; pleasure derived from writing poems, 5, 16, 130, 138, 180–81, 211, 220; poem as a means to discovery, 210, 220; poet as entertainer, 9, 26; poet as observer rather than participant, 20, 68–69, 75, 83, 111, 115, 148, 156, 158, 188, 208;

poetry and healing, 116, 147, 193; poetry and painting, 33–34, 35, 55–56, 111–12, 115, 122–23, 124, 129, 130, 169, 179, 183, 188, 205, 209; poetry as "a piece of order," xix, 23, 69, 107, 113, 117, 130, 144, 178, 180, 209; poetry as a service to others, xiv, xxii, 97, 142, 143, 148, 164, 206; poetry as celebration, 30, 68, 69, 209; poetry as play, 16–17, 20, 112, 117, 126, 130, 139, 177, 180–81, 201, 211; poetry as prayer, 176, 178, 220–21; poetry contrasted to prose, 216–17; poetry readings, 9–10, 23–24, 26, 33, 72, 75, 116, 128, 130, 148, 165; popular poetry, 226–27; postcard messages as poetry, 42, 44, 54–55, 70; preference for modern and contemporary poetry, 225–26; preferred audience, 36, 42, 101, 102, 128, 133, 140, 145, 206; pride in being a Nebraskan, 134, 174; proportion of his new poems he considers worthwhile, 10–11, 113, 135, 156, 187, 205; prose poems, 39, 54–55, 61, 166, 217–18; public vs. private poet, 24, 102, 216; publishing in literary journals and magazines, xvi, xxi, 7–8, 9, 11–12, 22–23, 42, 150, 154, 156, 187, 205, 206, 208; publishing on Facebook, xxi, 206, 207–8, 213–14; Pulitzer Prize winner, xix, xx–xxi, 133, 140, 141, 168, 191; reaching a wide audience, 87, 105–6, 133, 139, 142, 206, 216; reading reviews of his work, 31, 101, 147, 172; recognizing a good poem, 135, 138; record album collection, 193; regional poetry and writing of the Great Plains, xvi–xvii, xx, 5–6, 14, 25–26, 27–28, 31, 58–60, 74, 97–98, 100, 109, 126,

140, 141–42, 144, 161, 212; religion and spirituality, 101, 132, 155–56, 168, 176, 200, 223; restraint in poetry, 19, 30, 44; revision process, 22, 38, 42, 88, 101, 112–13, 154–55, 225; role of the reader, 14, 15, 177, 199; rural life as a subject, 116, 172; rural living, 145–46, 200, 213; sacredness of poetic composition, 9–10; schools ruining poetry for students, 128, 129, 130; schoolteachers, 119, 128, 130, 146–47, 160; seasons and weather in his work, 17–18, 50, 115, 163; seeing the extraordinary in the ordinary, xiv, xv, xxi, 40, 43, 44, 47, 49, 51, 100, 113, 188, 202; selecting a Nebraska State Poet, 25–26; self-effacement, 126, 145; sentimentality in poetry, 34, 131; sign painting, 4; signature "Kooser poem," 108, 161, 173; simplicity in poetry, 130–31, 137, 155, 180, 183; situating a reader, 197; solace in beauty and poetry, xxii, 170, 180; soliciting editing suggestions from others, 37–38, 41–42, 166–67, 196; solitude, 9–10, 114; song lyrics, 142–43; sonnets, 202; sound devices and rhythm, xix, 34, 36, 93–94, 225; stylistic and thematic unity in his work, xix, 131, 135, 144, 161; subject and style as an extension of personality, 131, 154, 187, 191; suicide among artists, 162, 200; taking risks as a poet, 34, 82, 115, 131; teaching graduate school, 3–4, 29, 35, 60, 64, 67, 85, 104, 112, 120–21, 134, 137, 159–60, 166, 170, 172, 177, 190, 192, 194–95, 198, 207, 208, 212, 220, 227–28; teaching high school, xvi, 57, 212; textbook appearances, 28; thoughts on success, 24–25, 28, 97, 123, 139, 164, 215; tinkering culture, 144–45; topical poetry, 183, 189; undergraduate student, xvi, 142, 196; universality of his work, xvii, xix, 74, 140, 158, 163; US poet laureate, xix, xx–xxi, 65, 69, 73–74, 81, 89, 96, 106, 109–10, 117–18, 119, 121, 123, 125–27, 129, 133, 134, 140, 141, 145, 146, 160, 174, 192, 205, 222, 227; utility of poetry, 7, 26, 29, 214–15; waiting for a poem to arrive, 10, 11, 135, 155; writer's lifestyle, 38, 102, 218; writing as communication, 16, 19, 91; writing book reviews, 30–31; writing durable poems, 9; writing fiction, 19, 22, 31, 228; writing for everyday people, 5, 35, 102, 128, 131, 133, 142, 145, 174, 206, 215, 227; writing founded on a sense of place, 59, 61, 74, 163, 197; writing habits, xvi, xviii, xxi, 10, 38, 39, 41, 60, 66, 85, 104, 107, 134–35, 163–64, 187, 189–90, 205; writing honestly, 6–8, 20, 23–24, 115, 198–99; writing instinctively, 15–16, 154, 172; writing letters, 43, 97; writing poetry as an antidote to depression and/or despair, 17, 41, 56, 69, 107, 144, 178, 193; writing process, 15–16, 34, 38, 39, 47, 51, 88–89, 123, 154–56, 177, 179, 197–98

Books: *At Home*, 213; *Bag in the Wind*, 160–61; *The Bell in the Bridge*, 175, 205; *Blizzard Voices*, 31, 103, 168; *A Book of Things*, 53; *Braided Creek*, xix, 62, 95, 103, 111, 143, 147, 164, 167, 175, 181, 204; *Cotton Candy*, xv–xvi, xx, 206; *Delights and Shadows*, 62, 65, 69, 74–75, 76–77, 80, 87, 101, 103, 107, 113, 117, 139, 140, 149, 161, 167, 168, 169, 172, 178, 179, 180, 182, 185;

Flying at Night, 167, 168; *Hatcher*, 31; *House Held Up by Trees*, 205; *Kindest Regards*, 192, 200; *Lights on a Ground of Darkness*, 91, 155–56, 169, 173, 175, 178, 179, 183, 216; *A Local Habitation & a Name*, 42, 44, 225; *Local Wonders*, 49, 61, 80, 85, 89, 94, 132, 137, 161, 163, 204, 207, 209, 212, 216; *A Man with a Rake*, xx; *Marshmallow Clouds*, xx, 181, 201, 204–5; *Mr. Posey's New Glasses*, xxii; *Not Coming to Be Barked At*, 223; *Official Entry Blank*, xvi, 103, 141, 142, 167, 191, 210, 212; *One World at a Time*, xvii; *The Poetry Home Repair Manual*, 62, 63, 64, 65, 66, 79, 91, 102, 104, 142, 145, 225; *Raft*, xvi, xix, xxi, 209, 210, 224; *Red Stilts*, 187–88, 191; *Splitting an Order*, 180, 205, 208; *Sure Signs*, xvi, 31, 142, 168, 181, 182, 199, 208, 223; *Valentines*, 157, 168, 205; *Voyages to the Inland Sea*, 26; *Weather Central*, xvii, 104, 108, 117, 144, 157; *The Wheeling Year*, xvi, 205, 216; *Winter Morning Walks*, xviii–xx, 40, 41–42, 44, 47–48, 50–51, 52, 53–54, 56, 61, 65, 69, 70–71, 103, 112, 113–14, 115–16, 143–44, 167, 178, 200, 224

Books (as publisher): *As Far as I Can See*, 58, 105; *The Windflower Home Almanac of Poetry*, 105

Essays: "Lights on a Ground of Darkness," 44–45, 49, 91; "Lying for the Sake of Making Poems," 199, 225; "Metaphor and Faith," 165, 176, 200–201, 225; "Nonsense of Place," 59; "Riding with Colonel Carter," 103; "The Two Poets," 24

Journals (as editor and publisher): *Blue Hotel*, 29, 58, 105; *New Salt Creek Reader*, 11, 29, 58, 105; *Salt Creek Reader*, 105

Poems: "Abandoned Farmhouse," 35, 116, 142, 181; "After Years," 86–87; "Anniversary," 224; "Applause," 189; "As the President Spoke," 85; "At the Cancer Clinic," 85–86, 148–49; "The Beaded Purse," 91–94, 97, 101; "Cold Pastoral," 210; "The Dead Vole," 188–89; "A Death at the Office," 65–67; "december 12," 50; "december 24," 47; "december 25," 72–73; "Depression Glass," 89–90; "Dishwater," 184; "Etude," xvii–xviii, 108, 116–17, 135–36, 137, 144; "Father," 76–77, 201; "february 19," 70–71; "A Fencerow in Early March," 15–16; "First Snow," 18; "Flying at Night," xxii, 180; "Fort Robinson," 147–48; "Four Secretaries," 104, 157; "A Fox," 224; "A Glimpse of the Eternal," 178; "A Happy Birthday," 80–81; "Hospital Parking Ramp, 6:00 a.m.," 209; "In Passing," 115; "In the Stars," 213–14; "It Doesn't Take Much," xix; "Lobocraspis griseifusa," 88; "Magpie," 224; "A Man with a Rake," xxi; "Memory," 155, 161; "A Morning in Early Spring," 150–54, 208; "Mother," xxi, 96–97, 174; "Mother and Child," 188; "Mourners," 68–69; "november 14," 71; "november 18," 178; "november 29," 200; "Old Soldiers' Home," 5; "On every topographic map" 181–82; "On the Road," 182; "An Overnight Snow," 188; "Pearl," 115, 185, 205; "Praying Hands," 131; "The quarry road tumbles before me," xviii–xx, 50–51, 224; "Rabbit," 224; "A Rainy Morning," 83–84,

138; "Raspberry Patch," 188; "The Red Wing Church," 132, 181, 209; "Screech Owl," xiv, 161, 172–73, 180, 202; "Selecting a Reader," 36, 199; "Skater," xiv, 84; "Snake Skin," 94; "So This Is Nebraska," xv, 161; "A Spiral Notebook," 87–88, 164, 227; "Splitting an Order," 158; "Spring Plowing," 182; "Student," 98; "Success," 123, 125–26, 135, 136, 215–16; "Surviving," 107, 113; "Tattoo," 74–75, 82–83, 159; "Tectonics," 79–80; "That Was I," 98–99; "They Had Torn Off My Face at the Office," 103–4; "Two," 180, 183; "Two Men on an Errand," 136; "Vulture," 224; "A Washing of Hands," 138–39; "West Window," 20; "Wild Asparagus," 39; "A Winter Morning," 179, 226; "With Li Bai," 219

Movie Adaptation: *Pearl*, 185, 205
Musical Adaptation: *Winter Moring Walks*, 178
Short Stories: "A Drowning," 22
Kooser, Theodore Briggs (father), xix, 37, 50–52, 75–78, 80–81, 100, 115–16, 166, 195, 201, 211, 223–24
Kooser, Vera Deloras Moser (mother), xxi, 37, 42, 52, 75–76, 91, 95–96, 100, 115–16, 156, 171, 173, 184, 195, 211, 221, 223, 224
Kooser Elementary School, 205
Kristofferson, Kris, 143; "The Last Time," 143
Kumin, Maxine, 21, 196–97, 226
Kunitz, Stanley, 82, 183
Kuzma, Greg, xvi, 25, 27, 28; *Adirondacks*, 28

Lester, Julius, 192; *Uncle Remus*, 192
Levertov, Denise, 5, 8, 21, 197, 198

Li Bai, 218–19
Liberal, KS, 211
Library of Congress, xx, 81, 82, 109–10, 118, 126, 127, 142
Life (magazine), 37
Lincoln, NE, xvi, xvii, 45, 67, 74, 133, 157, 158, 161, 168, 170, 205, 212–13, 223
Lincoln Benefit Life, xviii, 68
Lincoln Journal Star, xvii
Longfellow, Henry Wadsworth, 224; "The Children's Hour," 224
Lowell, Robert, 18–19
Luschei, Glenna, 35
Lutheran church, 168
Lydiatt, William, xix, 72

Mallarmé, Stéphane, 54; *A Tomb for Anatole*, 54
Marin, John, 169
Marshalltown, IA, 196
Mason, David, 101; *Ludlow*, 101
Masters, Edgar Lee, 86, 172
McCloskey, Robert, 222; *Lentil*, 222
McEwen, R. F., 226
McGrath, Thomas, 58, 97, 197; *Letter to an Imaginary Friend*, 58, 97
McKuen, Rod, 5
Meek, Jay, xiii, xv, xx; *The Memphis Letters*, 40
Mennonites, 132–33, 212
Merwin, Paula, 213
Merwin, W. S., 213
Methodist church, 101, 168
Midwest Quarterly, 147
Milton, John, 225
Milwaukee, WI, 33
mimesis, xv
Minneapolis Star Tribune, 86
modernism, xvii, 128, 145, 146, 180–81
Month in the Country, A (movie), 222
Morarend, Elmer (uncle), 176
More in Time, xxii, 194

Morris, Wright, 27
Moser, Alvah "Elvy" (uncle), 45, 135,
    173–74, 176
Moser, Elizabeth (maternal grandmother),
    44–45, 90–91, 156, 174, 175–76,
    184–85
Moser, John (maternal grandfather),
    44–45, 156, 169, 170, 174, 175–76,
    184–85
Moss, Howard, 25
Munch, Edvard, 55; *The Scream*, 55

Nabokov, Vladimir, 129
NASCAR Nation, 133
Nasjonalgalleriet (The National Gallery
    in Oslo, Norway), 55
Nathan, Carol, 167, 195
Nathan, Leonard, 21, 37, 41–42, 166–67, 195;
    The Potato Eaters, 167; "The Private
    I in Contemporary Poetry," 166;
    Returning Your Call, 21
National Book Award, 21
National Council of Teachers of English,
    118, 119, 146–47
National Endowment for the Arts, xvii,
    222
National Poetry Series, 30
Nebraska Humanist, 24
Nebraska Poetry, 179
Nebraska State Historical Society, 143
Neihardt, John G., 27
Neruda, Pablo, 215
New Directions Publishing, 102
New Republic, 167, 195
New York Book Fair, 62
New Yorker, xvii, 25, 130, 214
New Yorker Nation, 133
New York Review of Books, 6, 7
New York Times, 120, 145
New York Times Book Review, 31, 111
Nims, John Frederick, 63, 196

Nye, Naomi Shihab, xxii, 167, 216; "Ted
    Kooser Is My President," xxii

Ochester, Ed, 167
O'Connor, Flannery, 227–28
Oliver, Mary, 63; *A Poetry Handbook*, 63
Omaha, NE, 43, 72, 144–45, 148, 182, 191
Omaha Public Library, 72
Omaha World-Herald, 191
Orchises Press, 167
Orlovsky, Peter, 213
Osterlund, Steven, 29, 105

Paris Review, 6
Partisan Review, 6
Pastan, Linda, 8, 21, 101
pathetic fallacy, 180–81
Peattie, Donald Culross, 61; *An Almanac
    for Moderns*, 61
Piercy, Marge, 8
Pittsburgh, PA, 119
Plath, Sylvia, 162, 200
Poetry, xvii, 86, 196, 227
Poetry Foundation, 81, 133, 192
Poetry NOW, 11
Pope, Alexander, 198, 210–11; "An Essay on
    Criticism," 198, 210–11
Porter, Katherine Anne, 53; "Flowering
    Judas," 53
postmodernism, 172
Pound, Ezra, 21, 121, 172, 198
Prairie Schooner, 11, 167, 192, 199
Princeton University Press, 21
Prine, John, 81, 118, 127, 142–43; "Big Old
    Goofy World," 142–43
Pushcart Prize, 85

Ransom, John Crowe, 8, 21, 100, 102;
    "Dead Boy," 21
rap poetry, 106, 128
Ratliff, V. K. (Faulkner character), 52

Rattle Bag, The (poetry anthology), 227
Rebel Without a Cause, 212
Red Wing, MN, 184
Rembrandt, 55
Remains of the Day, The (movie), 222
Reynolds, Burt, 12–13
Rich, Adrienne, 8
Rilke, Rainer Maria, 52, 171; *Letters to a
    Young Poet*, 171
Robinson, Edwin Arlington, 21, 100, 172;
    "Richard Cory," 172
Rockwell, Norman, 122, 141
Roethke, Theodore, 112, 225
Romantic movement, xiv–xv
Roth, Philip, 7
Rutledge, Kathleen (wife), xvii, 71, 73,
    110, 114, 115, 133, 138, 146, 168, 170,
    179, 189, 200, 223
Ryan, Michael, 30; *In Winter*, 30

Salinger, J. D., 212; *The Catcher in the Rye*,
    212
Sanders, Mark, xvi–xvii, xxi–xxii, 214, 215;
    On Common Ground, xvi, xxi, 25;
    The Weight of the Weather, xxi–xxii
Sandoz, Mari, 27, 58, 140
Sarton, May, 20
Scheele, Roy, 27
Schneider, Maria, 178
Scott, Winfield Townly, 27
Seberg, Jean, 196
Seminary Ridge Review, 176
Service, Robert, 196
Seuss, Dr., 130
Seward, NE, 110, 212
Sexton, Anne, 18–19
Shakers, 131; "'Tis a Gift to Be Simple," 131
Shakespeare, William, xv, 52, 225–26;
    Hamlet, xv; *A Midsummer Night's
    Dream*, 225

Shapiro, Karl, xvi, 3–4, 5, 20, 21, 35, 38,
    54–55, 57, 67, 103, 141, 164–65, 166,
    195, 218, 225–26; *The Bourgeois
    Poet*, 54–55, 166; "The Fly," 164–65;
    "The Mongolian Idiot," 218; "What
    Is Not Poetry," 165
Sheldon Museum of Art, 111
Silver, Anya Krugovoy, 180
Silverstein, Shel, 130
Simic, Charles, 31
Simon, Daniel, 185n2, 220–21
Sketch, xvi, 141, 210
slam poetry, 106
Sloan, John, 171
Slote, Bernice, 11, 222
Snodgrass, William, 18–19; "Heart's
    Needle," 19
South Africa, 30
South Dakota State University, 179
Spanish Civil War, 215
Spenser, Edmund, 225
Stafford, William, 21, 38–39, 64, 109, 189,
    225
Stern, Gerald, 178
Sternhagen, Frances, 185
Stevens, Jim, 141
Stevens, Wallace, 4, 85, 120, 156–57, 165
Stillwell, Mary K., xvii, xxi
Strunk, William, Jr., 131; *The Elements of
    Style*, 131
Sundiata, Sekou, 71–72
Swenson, May, 100, 102, 166, 196–97,
    225–26; *To Mix with Time*, 100

Ted Kooser Collection (University of
    Nebraska Lincoln Libraries), 192
Ted Kooser Contemporary Poetry (series),
    xx, 226
Tennyson, Alfred, 215
Thompson, Jerry, 129

Thoreau, Henry David, 44, 50, 113, 221, 224; *Walden*, 113, 221, 224
Three Rivers Poetry Journal, 11
Tilden Store, The, xviii–xix, 51, 75, 90
Tolstoy, Leo, 228
Tonight Show Starring Johnny Carson, The, 12–13, 24
Toynbee, Arnold J., 85
Tranströmer, Thomas, 21, 101, 219–20; "The Couple," 219–20
Tressler, Diana (first wife), xvi, xvii, 3, 4, 67, 213

Unitarian church, 223
University of Kansas, 211
University of Michigan Press, 225
University of Nebraska Lincoln, 3, 57, 61, 62, 85, 97, 111, 113, 166, 171, 192, 195, 227–28
University of Nebraska Medical Center, xix, 72, 86, 116
University of Nebraska Press, 62, 91, 103, 167, 168, 192, 194, 207, 222, 226
University of Pittsburgh Press, xvi, xvii, 21, 103, 167
University of South Carolina, 219
Untermeyer, Louis, 226
Updike, John, 7, 57
Upshaw, Dawn, 178

van Gogh, Vincent, 200
Vendler, Helen, 131
Virgil, xix

Wagoner, David, 226
Wanek, Connie, xx, 181, 201, 204–5
Washington, DC, xx–xxi, 73, 81, 89, 110, 146, 212
Weather Underground, 212
Weil, Simone, 178

Welch, Don, xvi, 25, 27, 28, 58, 105, 179, 185n2; *Dead Horse Table*, 179; "Funeral at Ansley," 179
Welty, Eudora, 46–47, 163, 197; *A Curtain of Green*, 46–47; "A Memory," 46–47
Western Folklife Association, 129
White, E. B., xv–xvi, 131, 206, 208, 209; *The Elements of Style*, 131
Whitman, Walt, xix, 97; "Song of Myself," xix
Willard, Nancy, 8, 101, 203; *Swimming Lessons*, 203
Williams, William Carlos, 3, 21, 34, 35, 36, 86, 102, 121, 141, 142, 156–57, 164–65, 166, 171, 216–17, 218; *Patterson*, 35; "Proletarian Portrait," 171; "The Red Wheelbarrow," 34, 216–17, 218; *Selected Poems*, 102; "This Is Just to Say," 35; "To Waken an Old Lady," 165
Windflower Press, 3, 22, 29, 58, 105
Winger, Debra, 112
Winkler, Jack, 141
Winters, Yvor, 196
Witter Bynner Fellowship, 127, 146
WOI (public radio station in Ames, IA), 223–24
Woodard, Charles, 58; *As Far as I Can See*, 58
Woodland Pattern Book Center (Milwaukee, WI), 33
Wordsworth, William, xv, 215, 226; "I Wandered Lonely as a Cloud," xv
World Literature Today, 186n3
World Trade Center attacks, 144, 171
Wright, James, 197
Wrigley, Robert, 98, 119
Writer, The, 12
Writer's Almanac, The, 180
Writer's Digest, 12

Wyeth, Andrew, 193; *Tenant Farmer*, 193

Yale Review, 129
Yeats, William Butler, 167
"Young Goodman Brown" (Hawthorne),
        49
YouTube, 185
Younker Brothers Department Store
        (Des Moines, IA), 75–76

About the Editor

Photo courtesy of Harold Senn

John Cusatis earned a PhD in English from the University of South Carolina in 2003. He is the author of *Understanding Colum McCann*, the first critical study of the Irish-born National Book Award winner, and the editor of *Postwar Literature, 1945–1970*, three volumes of the *Dictionary of Literary Biography*, coeditor of *Conversations with John Banville*, and, most recently, editor of *Conversations with Billy Collins*. He teaches at the School of the Arts in Charleston, SC.